Tom Smith's Cricket Umpiring and Scoring

D0300129

Tom Smith's Cricket Umpiring and Scoring

Introduction by
Richie Benaud

Weidenfeld & Nicolson
LONDON

Contents

Introduction by Richie Benaud   viii

The Author   ix

Preface to this Edition   x

Acknowledgements   xi

PART I

The Umpires and Scorers   2

1 Training of umpires and scorers   4

2 Necessary qualifications   4

3 The role of the umpire   6

4 Dress and equipment   8

5 The umpire's duties   11

6 Positioning of umpires   15

7 Signals and signalling   18

PART II

The Laws of Cricket
with Interpretations   20

PART III

Scoring   238

PART IV

Appendices   276

APPENDIX A   278
Law 8 The Wickets

APPENDIX B   278
Law 7 The pitch and
Law 9 The bowling, popping
and return creases

APPENDIX C   279
Law 40.2 Gloves

APPENDIX D   280
Definitions and explanations of words
or phrases not defined in the text

APPENDIX E   284
Law 6 The bat

Index   286

First published in Great Britain in 2011
by Weidenfeld & Nicolson

3 5 7 9 10 8 6 4

A CIP catalogue record for this book
is available from the British Library.

ISBN-13 978 0 297 866441 1

Typeset by Bob Vickers

Printed in Italy

The Orion Publishing Group's policy is to use papers
that are natural, renewable and recyclable products and
made from wood grown in sustainable forests. The logging
and manufacturing processes are expected to conform to
the environmental regulations of the country of origin.

Weidenfeld & Nicolson

The Orion Publishing Group Ltd
Orion House
5 Upper Saint Martin's Lane
London, WC2H 9EA

www.orionbooks.co.uk

Since its formation in 1787, the Marylebone Cricket
Club (MCC) has been recognised as the sole authority
for drawing up the Code of Laws and for all subsequent
amendments. The Club also holds the World copyright.

The basic Laws of Cricket have stood remarkably well
the test of well over 250 years of playing the game.
It is thought the real reason for this is that cricketers have
traditionally been prepared to play in the Spirit of the
Game as well as in accordance with the Laws.

Although the International Cricket Council is the global
Governing Body for cricket, it still relies on MCC
to write and interpret the Laws of Cricket, which are
applicable from the village green to the Test arena.

Introduction

by Richie Benaud

A long time ago scoring in a cricket match was done by making a notch in a stick, or perhaps two sticks, and over the years we have moved from that classic piece of woodworking to scorers who have beautifully designed pages that allow those using them to recreate a day's play. Some, in these modern times, use computers, though I have a feeling you need to be of a younger vintage than some of us going around the grounds these days. A comforting presence, no matter if you are a 'notcher' or a computer whiz, is *Tom Smith's Cricket Umpiring and Scoring*, upgraded and updated to take into account MCC's changes to the Code of the Laws of Cricket in 2010.

MCC last made major changes in 2003 in relation to the 2000 Code of the Laws and a lot has happened to the game of cricket since then. It still remains a simple game between bat and ball, with cricketers in competition with one another and new forms of cricket coming on the scene in regular fashion. Tom Smith passed away in 1995 but it remains a fact that few people in the non-playing side of the game have done as brilliant a job. Tom didn't confine himself only to cricket as a player and administrator but he was a football referee as well as a cricket umpire, and cricket remains in his debt for the fact that almost 60 years ago he formed the Association of Cricket Umpires and Scorers. This was a very small organisation at first but it grew to almost 9,000 members and over 200 affiliated organisations before it merged with the parallel organisation at ECB to form the ECB ACO.

This updated version of Tom's book is a great read for anyone interested in any form of cricket. Watching at the ground, or on television, there are countless occasions where a question can be posed by a happening on the field and this book is so comprehensive, but easily readable, that the question is able quickly to be answered. It is a companion to the Laws of Cricket and still the focal point is The Preamble – The Spirit of Cricket which prefaces the Laws. The Preamble was devised by Ted Dexter and Colin Cowdrey in the 1990s and it sets out carefully and briefly what is needed to have cricket remain a much loved sport and the manner in which players should participate.

In this modern era, where machines have taken away some of the umpire's authority, MCC have produced Law changes involving a variety of matters, two of which I think are most important. The first relates to the umpires no longer offering the light to the batsmen and only taking the players off the field on grounds of safety or visibility. The second is a new definition relating to wonderfully athletic fielding near the boundary rope where, if the fielder is airborne, his final contact with the ground before touching the ball was within the boundary. Those and many other offerings make this a splendid cricket book.

The Author – Tom Smith

The late TOM SMITH, after many years as a player, football referee and cricket umpire, founded the Association of Cricket Umpires in 1953; he served continuously as General Secretary for twenty-five years and upon his retirement was appointed a Life Vice-President. Well known and respected in every cricket playing country of the world, Tom was recognised as an authority and umpire arbiter on the Laws of the game and the technique of cricket umpiring. For some years he wrote regularly for *The Cricketer* on field umpiring and problems of cricket Law.

During 1956–7 Tom Smith spent many long periods at Lord's assisting the late Colonel Rait Kerr with the preparation of the Association textbook; and in 1961, at the request of the late author, he took over the revising of the book until 1979. The 1980 Code of Laws brought the need for the production of a complete new up-to-date book.

For services to cricket, Tom Smith was awarded an MBE and honoured by the MCC with election to Honorary Life Membership – a distinction awarded to only a small group of people who have carried out special services for cricket – and in 1980, HRH the Duke of Edinburgh presented him with the National Playing Fields Association's Torch Trophy Award for outstanding services to cricket. He served a term as a member of the Test and County Cricket Board Cricket Committee, from its inception, as a member of the MCC Laws Committee, and at one time Chairman of the National Cricket Association Cricket Committee. He also served for several years on the National Association Management Committee and specialist Working Parties as well as the Surrey County Cricket Association Committee.

During 1974, Tom was appointed by the MCC to assist Mr S.C. Griffith, former MCC Secretary, in revising and redrafting the 1947 Code of Laws at the request of the International Cricket Conference.

During the years between the preparation of the new draft and final presentation to the International Cricket Conference, Cricket Council and other representative bodies, Tom Smith was appointed by the MCC to a special Redrafting Committee set up to produce the final draft of the new code, after giving careful consideration to all the suggestions and recommendations from the United Kingdom and overseas.

Tom Smith gave a lifetime of devoted service to umpires and umpiring and, under his leadership and inspiration, the Association of Cricket Umpires and Scorers has grown from a small beginning to become a recognised international association with over 8,000 members and 200 affiliated organisations.

He died on 14 December 1995. His legacy will long be remembered.

Preface to this Edition

Since Tom Smith assisted Colonel Rait Kerr in the 1950s in bringing this book to the light of day, it has subsequently been revised and rewritten by Tom in the 1960s and again for the 1980 Code. Another revision was published in 1989.

As changes were made to the Laws, further revisions were made in 1993 and 1996 by members of the Association of Cricket Umpires – later adding "and Scorers" to that title – taking Tom's original work forward and each following the ideals Tom established to make his book the most widely read publication on the subject throughout the world. When the millennium Code of the Laws 2000 was introduced, members of the Association of Cricket Umpires and Scorers rewrote the book to reflect these changes. A subsequent revision was made to reflect the Law changes that came into force in 2003.

As the game has developed in the new century, more demands than ever have been placed on both umpires and scorers to get it right; demands brought about by the increasing examination of decisions scrutinized by the television cameras. This should not be seen as a negative thing; rather it has a benefit, by highlighting, far more often than not, the excellent decisions made by umpires at that level.

This edition has been produced to give help and guidance on what is laid down in the 4th Edition of the 2000 Code of Laws and to explain how the game is to be administered on the field or recorded in the scorebook. It seeks both to educate and to acknowledge the many thousands of umpires and scorers around the world who each make their own contribution to the game.

The book remains, as Tom would have wished, a straightforward account of the Laws and their meaning to umpires and scorers. It is not solely aimed at the officials, however. It is also for the players and spectators worldwide who enjoy the game with their own passion. It does not delve into esoteric points or into unlikely situations.

Acknowledgements

Shortly before the Association of Cricket Umpires and Scorers was dissolved in 2008, its members voted at an SGM that the copyright of *Tom Smith's Cricket Umpiring and Scoring* should pass to Marylebone Cricket Club (MCC). MCC would like to thank the ACU&S, its officers and former members for vesting this responsibility with the Club. The Club's appreciation is shown in particular to Geoff Lowden and Steven Wood for their assistance during the transfer of the copyright.

MCC acknowledges Richie Benaud's contribution with his glowing Foreword to the book. Thanks are also expressed to David Lloyd, Mike Brearley and Simon Taufel for their generous comments about the book, which appear on the back cover.

The members of MCC's Laws sub-committee have devoted a great deal of time to the production of this edition and the Club places on record its gratitude to this group of volunteers. Particular thanks must go to Sheila Hill MBE, who worked tirelessly on the writing, editing and proof-reading of the Laws section. While the scoring section is broadly similar to that in the Jubilee edition, thanks go to Brian Mulholland and Andy Scarlett for their useful contributions to that section.

MCC is appreciative of the help given by the staff at Long Marston Cricket Club, which provided such a picturesque backdrop for most of the photographs in this edition.

Finally, our thanks must be expressed to the staff at Weidenfeld & Nicolson, the publishers, for their efforts.

MCC
Lord's Ground, 2011

The Umpires and Scorers

Although the male gender is used predominantly throughout the text, it must be understood that this is solely for brevity. Both men and women are equally welcome as umpires or scorers. Nothing in this book is to be taken to imply otherwise.

1 TRAINING OF UMPIRES AND SCORERS

The Association of Cricket Umpires was founded by the late Tom Smith in 1953 in response to the fact that the standard of umpiring, at all levels of the non-professional game, was often of very poor quality. The purpose of the Association was to improve the standard of umpiring by education, training and examination and to enhance the status of umpires, also then at a low ebb. Later, the Association became the Association of Cricket Umpires and Scorers with the same aims for scorers as for umpires. Successive editions of this book have, from the outset, formed part of that programme of education. Recently, a new Association has been formed, the England and Wales Cricket Board Association of Cricket Officials, merging ACU&S with a parallel ECB association. The new Association, ECB ACO, now runs the training programmes for umpires and scorers in the UK and Europe.

The game at all levels – junior, club, league, county and international – needs umpires of the highest quality. Scoring, too, is of increasing importance in today's competitive and statistics-hungry world. Although the recruitment and training of umpires and scorers has improved enormously in the last 50 years, there are still far too few of them to cover the many thousands of games of cricket played. Just as ECB has done for the UK and Europe, major cricketing countries have set up their own schemes for the training and development of officials. ICC has recruited these countries to help with such work in countries where resources are not yet sufficient for the task.

MCC assumed responsibility for this book in 2009–10, although it still bears Tom's name at his express wish. Together with MCC's existing Open Learning Manual (OLM), it is offered to umpires and scorers worldwide as an aid to learning and understanding the Laws. It is intended to supplement rather than to replace training courses. Whilst the OLM concentrates on setting out the Laws and what they mean, this book attempts to give umpires an insight into being an umpire on the field of play and to give clear guidance on the practice of the craft of scoring. It is not only for the student, however. It is also a reference for the more experienced. Additionally, it has a role for umpires in helping to promote uniformity of Law interpretation throughout the cricket world.

New editions of the 2000 Code of Laws have been published as various adjustments to the Laws have been made. The 2010 edition incorporates a few Law changes and a major tidying up of detail. This edition of Tom Smith's classic addresses the need for updating in line with the 2010 edition of the Code.

2 NECESSARY QUALIFICATIONS

PHYSICAL QUALIFICATIONS

An umpire needs to have first-class eyesight and acute hearing. Properly prescribed spectacles or contact lenses will correct any defects in natural vision and are perfectly acceptable. Hearing loss can be corrected by hearing aids, once viewed with suspicion but now more readily accepted by players.

An umpire also needs to withstand the strain of long hours in the field. Physical stamina is important but more important still is the need to be able to concentrate throughout long sessions of play. Although not standing or moving about in the field, scorers have precisely the same need for concentration over a long period. Complete concentration is needed to pick up and register even the smallest points of the action. It is indeed often the small points which alert the umpire or scorer to what is about to happen. Concentration by the umpire on every detail will aid good anticipation and correct positioning for making judgments; for the scorer it will mean understanding of events on the field, enabling correct recording.

Whilst natural factors governing susceptibility to fatigue and speed of response are age and health, a less natural one is the effect of alcohol. Umpires and scorers should be very wary of alcohol intake on long, hot, tiring days, when decisions on split-second action are required under heavy pressure, or instant interpretation of what is happening more than 80 yards away is needed.

PERSONAL QUALIFICATIONS

Scorers have to interact with each other and with the players, who will see them as a source of information while the umpires are inaccessibly on the field. Events may happen in rapid succession on the field with barely time to record them. Allowing oneself to get flustered leads only to disaster. A scorer needs to keep calm at the job, whatever the crises, and to remain approachable as a person. He must also have the ability to cope with numbers and a dedication to accuracy of detail.

An umpire must above all be a person of integrity. When under pressure, it is by no means easy to keep calm and to remain completely neutral and unbiased. It is essential to do so. An umpire needs to cope not only with the clinical application of the Laws, but also with the attitudes of the players, which nowadays are often quite aggressive. He must be firm in control of the game without being pedantic or officious. He must not let his absolute impartiality be undermined by the behaviour of the players, nor by the state of the game. He will therefore need a mind able to weigh up evidence quickly. He will need an even temper and good humour to respond wisely to the often hasty and excited actions of the players. He will need confidence in himself to remain calm, fearlessly continuing to control the game in accordance with the Laws. Above all he will need common sense – a rare quality – to deal with both the unexpected event and the awkward player.

TECHNICAL QUALIFICATIONS

It should go without saying that an umpire needs a thorough knowledge of the Laws of cricket. It is the general experience of umpires that however much personal study they have undertaken, however much they have discussed details with others, however many classes they have attended, there is always something to learn. From time to time there will be, as with the 2010 edition of the 2000 Code, new points to learn and changes to old ones to assimilate. Scorers have a less onerous task in that many of the details of the Laws are for the umpires to administer and do not affect scoring. They must, however, know with great accuracy those Laws which do affect scoring, and have complete familiarity with the techniques for recording the events of the game.

Both umpires and scorers must practise their craft assiduously. Theoretical knowledge alone will not make either a good umpire or a good scorer. Every umpire will make mistakes from time to time, just as every player does, whether fielder, bowler, batsman or captain. Theoretical knowledge will help the umpire to avoid mistakes through ignorance of the Law. Only experience will help him to avoid errors in observing the facts, and mistakes in judgment of those facts. In this respect, umpiring and scoring are similar to driving a car. Knowing what to do is only the first stage. Only with practice will it become a practical possibility to interpret traffic conditions, look in the mirror and watch the road ahead, signal, steer and change gear virtually all at the same time. Trainee umpires and scorers must take every opportunity of building up match experience. Even if some of this experience is at quite humble levels it will contribute to an official's skills and help him to deal effectively with more testing matches. Although, of necessity, different in many ways from a normal game of cricket, indoor cricket can provide valuable experience for an umpire. The very fast action within the confined space requires quick reaction and positioning, together with sharp observation as the ball ricochets off the walls.

A very large part of an umpire's match craft nowadays will be handling situations under pressure. The trainee umpire will fortunately not encounter the instant big-screen replay, exposing to spectators in slow motion what he himself had only a split second to see. Many players do not realise that matches at this exalted level are played under special regulations which may differ considerably from the Laws and the regulations in their own local League. Nevertheless, the attitudes of club and youth players are often coloured by what they have seen in high-level matches. They are likely to expect in a club game something of what happens in a Test match! These expectations can create pressure on the umpire, which he must learn to withstand. Confidence in his knowledge of the Laws and of the regulations, if any, that apply in the game he is umpiring, together with the skill and understanding built up through experience, are his best weapons for combating such pressure.

3 THE ROLE OF THE UMPIRE

The word 'umpire', first used certainly as long ago as 1714 but possibly earlier, is a development of the old Middle English word *nompere,* derived from the old French *nomper (nom –* not; *per –* equal). The umpire is to be seen as 'without equal'. He must be part of the game and yet separate from it. He must have a good-humoured rapport with the players and yet be apart from them. He is to be the arbiter dispensing equal-handed justice, whose decisions are accepted without question. Respect for the umpire is one of the requirements of the Spirit of Cricket. Nevertheless an umpire has largely to earn that position of respect. The players will not award it to an umpire who has not shown himself worthy of it.

It follows that the umpire must conduct himself with responsibility and dignity. Although the players can make it difficult to maintain patience and composure, even in extreme cases direct confrontation must be avoided. Incidents of gamesmanship, sometimes amounting to cheating, can occur at any level of the game. The Laws lay down penalties for particular instances of malpractice. These penalties must be applied dispassionately but resolutely.

In considering an appeal, an umpire must not be swayed by its volume or apparent confidence. It is quite normal for the whole team to raise a gleeful shout of 'How's That?', although most of them are in no position to know the facts. The umpire must give to each appeal, whether a concerted one or a quiet enquiry by one player, exactly the same weight of unflustered consideration. Umpires are advised not to offer a justification of their decisions either on or off the field. On the other hand if, after a call of No ball, the bowler asks whether it was his front foot or his back foot, a 'shan't-tell-you' attitude will do nothing for player-umpire relations. It is much wiser to give a simple answer to a polite enquiry – to tell him which foot, or in response to a civil enquiry about LBW to say 'it pitched just outside leg'. At the close of play, explanation of the Law is entirely sensible, but an umpire must not get drawn into an argument about his judgment or that of the other umpire. Loyalty towards a colleague must be absolute.

The umpire who does not make a mistake does not exist. There will be times when, too late, an umpire realises that he has made one. If this happens, it is essential that he puts it out of his mind and continues to apply his utmost concentration to the rest of the game. To lose concentration by worrying about a mistake will only lead to more mistakes. It is also totally out of order for him to think that he can try to be fair by making another 'mistake'. Not only are the consequences of any act of his quite unpredictable, so that he may in fact make matters worse, but he will undermine the players' confidence in him. On the other hand, he must not persist unnecessarily with a decision which he knows to be wrong. If he has miscounted and allowed a seventh ball in an over, there is nothing he can do to 'undo' the seventh ball. The Law allows him, however, to change a mistaken decision promptly. If he gives a batsman out Run out and then realises that the fielder had broken the wicket without having the ball in his hand, he can change the decision and recall the batsman if he does it promptly. He must have the courage to do so. It will earn him greater respect in the long run.

The Law also allows an umpire in doubt to consult his colleague – insists, in fact, that he does so. Consultation is clearly a necessary precaution as well as a wise one if mistakes are to be kept to a minimum. Not to consult would be not only a breach of the Law but an unpardonable lack of good sense. Such consultation can be anything from an eyebrow raised in query to a full conversation. It is obviously paramount that there should be no doubt as to what the question is, nor as to what answer is being given. When there is an appeal, consultation should not arise from reluctance to give a decision, but should be for information that one umpire may be able to supply, because he had a proper view which was denied to the other umpire. For example, the striker's end umpire will have been able to see the breaking of the wicket, which was invisible to the bowler's end umpire because the striker was between him and the stumps. The Law stipulates in some cases that the umpires must consult together, for example in considering the safety or otherwise of the conditions of ground, weather or light. A different reason for consultation will be in some instances of misconduct. In some cases it is mandatory. Where this is not so, it may be necessary but will not be required if the facts are clear. There are situations, however, when it will be prudent to check that the other umpire takes the same view, perhaps as to the deliberateness or otherwise of, for example, a batsman getting in a fielder's way.

This interdependence should extend more widely than asking and answering questions on the field. Not only must the two umpires appointed for a match work together from the start on all aspects of the game, on a basis of absolute mutual confidence, but they will, with the scorers, form a team offering mutual understanding and support as well as factual information. Even if the views of one differ from those of another, this must never be allowed to create constraint or negative feelings.

4 DRESS AND EQUIPMENT

DRESS

A scorer is often judged by the appearance of the score book as well as by its accuracy. Similarly, for the umpire his dress and personal appearance are important. Once upon a time the cartoon image of an umpire was that of a forlorn figure, usually dressed in a grubby, ill-fitting, over-long whitish coat, with crumpled trousers of varying hues, cloth-capped and smothered in player's caps and sweaters. Nowadays, an umpire should be smartly turned out, a man to whom none of the epithets above could apply. The only exception is the cloth cap. That is acceptable providing it is a white one in good condition. This sartorial smartness is not only for his image vis-à-vis the players but for his own self-confidence. Trainee umpires, as well as learning the Laws and acquiring good field technique through experience, should cultivate the highest standards of dress.

An umpire should not expect a white coat to be hanging in the dressing room. If there is one it will probably not come up to expected standards, even of fitting him let alone anything else. He should have his own, fitting him properly, freshly laundered and crisp looking. If the match is under the administration of a controlling body, there may be a 'dress code'. If so, umpires must be aware of its stipulations. In the absence of such rules, it is recommended that, as well as a crisp, clean white coat or jacket, umpires should wear well-pressed black or navy trousers and a white shirt. Women can opt for a plain skirt instead of trousers and a blouse instead of a shirt.

A tie is recommended although nowadays not always regarded as essential; a neat neckline is a must. In very hot weather, rolling up sleeves or not wearing a coat or jacket may be permissible but umpires must be aware of the dangers of exposure to ultraviolet radiation, especially if, in countries where very hot sun is unusual, they are not acclimatised to it.

A wise umpire will not let himself be used as a clothes stand. Carrying the bowler's cap and sweater is a reasonable service. Carrying sweaters for half the team is not. The Law specifies where a fielder's helmet is to be placed if he is not wearing it. It is not for the umpire to carry it.

SUNGLASSES

There is general acceptance nowadays of the need to protect eyes from ultraviolet radiation in strong sunlight. In many cases a cap or hat with a good brim will give sufficient protection. If it does not, it is better to wear sunglasses – particularly if they are tinted or photochromic prescription lenses – than to leave the eyes unprotected and the umpire unable to see when facing the sun.

COUNTERS

One essential duty of the umpire is to count the balls in each over. Every umpire should establish a method of counting with which he feels comfortable and which becomes automatic by usage. If he uses pebbles or other objects as counters, it is advisable to have a spare in an inner pocket where it cannot be confused with the ones in use. He should check that he has six counters at the start of every over. He should have an absolutely rigid system for transferring from 'unused' to 'used' as each ball is delivered. He should have some means of keeping the unused separate from the used if he has to remake the wicket, write notes or do anything else that requires him to use his hands.

CHECKING THE SCORE

Umpires are also required to satisfy themselves of the accuracy of the scores, and to make the final decision should any irresolvable discrepancy occur. This responsibility extends only to the overall totals of runs and wickets – and overs where relevant. It does not refer to the details. On grounds with state-of-the-art scoreboards, they will be able to see each run as it is recorded. Checking that it is correct is instant! Most umpires are denied such luxuries, however, and will have to make their own record of the number of runs, to check each time the scoreboard is changed. Simple 'clickers', where each click advances the display by 1, are available. They are easily operated, usually while the bowler is walking back to his mark, without interfering with other more onerous umpiring duties. It is sensible practice to check occasionally – at the fall of a wicket perhaps – that your colleague's record agrees with yours. It is particularly important in a game where each bowler is permitted only a stated number of overs.

Should an umpire see a mis-match between his record and the scoreboard, he should be circumspect in dealing with it. He should make a written note of the problem. Often action is superfluous because the discrepancy disappears after a short time. However, if it persists he should check with his colleague at a suitable moment. He may discover that he himself is the one at fault. Much embarrassment by wrongly challenging the scorers will then be avoided. If, however, his colleague agrees with him, a quiet word with the scorers when circumstances permit will usually resolve the difficulty. At times it may be more urgent than this procedure admits. Towards the end of the match all should know the correct score. Even then, discretion is better than a public fuss, provided the problem can be sorted out.

WATCH

The Law specifies that the umpires agree which watch or clock is to be used to time the match. They should also agree which timepiece is to be used if the selected one fails. Both umpires should carry a watch and should check it against the agreed master timepiece before the start of the match. They should also check that the scorers' times agree with their own.

PENCIL AND PAPER

These are essential. An umpire may need to make notes of points to discuss later with the scorers, or even to send notes to the scorers, though this would be rare. The main use for writing equipment, however, will be to make notes of the bowlers, batsmen, number of balls, etc., at an interval. These points are set out below and in Part II.

If umpiring in a match where there is a restriction on the number of overs allowed to an individual bowler, the umpire will need some means of recording those overs. Printed cards are available and can be very helpful. They are not obligatory if the umpire has his own efficient system of recording.

LAWS AND REGULATIONS

An umpire should certainly not need to refer either to the Laws or to the Rules specific to that game. However, both should be carried, in case some point arises that can be settled by reference to an official text. The MCC publishes the Laws in a small book designed to fit into an umpire's pocket.

BALLS

The balls to be used in the match will have to be approved by the umpires and captains before the match. The umpires must thereafter have charge of them. If a new ball is to be used after a prescribed number of overs, the umpires will need to take one on to the field at the start of a session in which these overs are likely to be completed. They should carry, or have readily available, at least one spare each, in differing stages of wear, for use as a replacement where the Laws so provide.

BAILS

These should be provided by the Ground Authority. Many umpires carry their own, to guarantee a matching pair. Each should also carry a spare in case of damage or breakage during play.

BOWLER'S MARKER

Bowlers need something to mark the start of their run ups. Such items are usually supplied by the Ground Authority, but it is wise for each umpire to have a marker of his own, to produce if necessary. If there is no marker, the bowler will probably kick out a divot instead – which is undesirable. Markers should always be collected after play, to prevent damage to mowers and other equipment.

DRYING MATERIAL

A piece of cloth or a towel for drying the ball should always be carried, even on a fine day. It may be needed, for instance, to dry the ball after retrieval from long grass which is still wet – or there may even be an unexpected light drizzle.

SUMMARY

The amount an umpire can carry is limited. However, play must not be held up because an umpire is lacking a particular item. Personal items are best left in safe keeping off the field. Those items regarded as essential are:

Counters (with spare)
Means for checking runs if scoreboard will not be sufficient
Watch
Pencil and paper
MCC Law book
Competition or League regulations
Bails (with spares)
Balls (with spares)
Bowler's start marker
Drying material

The equipment essential to a scorer is clearly set out in Part III, the section on scoring.

5 THE UMPIRE'S DUTIES

Although dealt with in some detail under the appropriate Laws in Part II, a summary is set out here, collecting together in one place the instructions scattered throughout Part II.

The umpires will work as part of the team of four officials and also between themselves as a team of two. The striker's end umpire, as well as having some clearly defined responsibilities of his own, must remain alert throughout to be ready at all times to assist and support his busier colleague. Equally, at times the bowler's end umpire will be able to assist the other umpire and must be ready to do so.

DUTIES BEFORE THE MATCH

Law 3 directs the umpires to 'report for duty' at least 45 minutes before the start of a day's play. In practice it is better to arrive earlier. There is much to be done before the match starts. The duties set out below are not necessarily to be done in the order listed.

1   Report to Ground Executive, meet partner and together inspect boundaries and sight-screens.
2   Together inspect pitch, wickets and creases.
3   Check on the availability of covers and wet-weather equipment – especially sawdust.
4   Check with Ground Authority the procedure for outfield mowing, if appropriate.
5   Obtain bails and, if possible, used balls for use as replacements.
6   Meet captains. Confirm hours of play and intervals, timepieces, boundaries and allowances (including whether any obstacle is or is not to be designated a boundary), special conditions. Agree balls and take possession of them.
7   Receive nomination of players.
8   Meet scorers. Inform them of details above. Agree the method by which scorers will acknowledge signals.
9   Check toss is made within the prescribed time limits. Accompany, possibly with colleague, captains on to the field of play for toss to be made.
10 Ensure scorers know result of toss, and decision by winner.
11 Walk out to wicket with colleague at least five minutes before play is due to start. Ensure captains know you are going.
12 Recheck wicket alignment and place bails in position.
13 Discover from which end bowling is to start.
14 Check that there are no more than eleven fielders.

Bowler's end umpire

15 Take the following actions in a suitable order:
> notify the bowler's action and give guard to the striker
> give a marker, if necessary, to the bowler
> help, if necessary, with the alignment of the sight-screen
> give the match ball to the bowler.
16 Make the following checks in a suitable order:
> that the fielding captain has finished setting his field
> that the other umpire is ready
> that the scorers are in position and ready
> that both batsmen are ready
> that the other umpire agrees that time to start has been reached.
17 Call Play.

DUTIES DURING PLAY

Bowler's end umpire

1. Calls Play at the start of the match and on the resumption of play after any interval or interruption.
2. Counts the number of balls in the over.
3. Watches bowler's feet placement during delivery.
4. Watches close fielders for pitch encroachment.
5. Judges whether balls are fast short pitched deliveries or high full pitched deliveries.
6. Observes position of batsmen with regard to crossing on each run, particularly when the action indicates a possible Run out at the other end.
7. Calls and signals No balls within his jurisdiction; calls and signals all Wide balls.
8. Watches for, calls and signals Short runs at his end.
9. Signals all penalty runs to the scorers.
10. Repeats all appropriate signals to the scorers when the ball is dead, including No balls called by the other umpire.
11. Gives final signal of Short runs to the scorers, indicating the number of runs to be recorded, if applicable.
12. Answers appeals for Bowled, Caught, Handled the ball, Hit the ball twice, LBW, Obstructing the field, Timed out and, when it is at his end, Run out.
13. Calls and signals Dead ball when appropriate.
14. Calls Over at the specified time.
15. Signals to scorers when last hour begins.
16. Checks the correctness of the score as play proceeds.
17. Watches for all forms of unfair play and takes appropriate action.
18. Ascertains (if not told) reason for departure of fielder; gives permission for return.
19. Calculates time to elapse before fielder can bowl after return.
20. Calls Time at the start of any interval or interruption and at the end of the match.
21. Together with other umpire decides whether a substitute fielder is justified.
22. Together with other umpire makes decisions as to the fitness of the conditions for play.
23. With other umpire reports as necessary to team Executive and Governing Body.

Striker's end umpire

1. Counts the number of balls in the over as a check to support colleague.
2. Watches all the action of play, to be ready to assist the other umpire at all times.
3. Observes bowler's arm action for fairness of delivery.
4. Checks number of on-side fielders behind the popping crease at the instant of delivery.

5   If applicable, checks number of fielders inside/outside fielding restriction circles.
6   Checks position of wicket-keeper from ball coming into play until it comes into contact with striker, or passes wicket, or striker attempts run.
7   Calls and signals Dead ball when appropriate.
8   Calls and signals No balls within his jurisdiction.
9   Observes position of batsmen with regard to crossing on each run, particularly when the action indicates a possible Run out at the other end, or when his colleague may have to adjudicate on some other dismissal such as Caught.
10 Watches for, calls and signals Short runs at his end.
11 Answers appeals for Hit wicket, Stumped and, when it is at his end, Run out.
12 Watches for all forms of unfair play and takes the specified action.
13 Checks the correctness of the score as play proceeds.
14 Checks timing with colleague, for calculation of time when returning fielder can bowl.
15 Together with other umpire decides whether a substitute fielder is justified.
16 Together with other umpire makes decisions as to the fitness of the conditions for play.
17 With other umpire reports as necessary to team Executive and Governing Body.

DUTIES AT CESSATION OF PLAY

Law 15 makes clear what is to count as an interval. An interruption, when play has to be suspended without prior arrangement, is self-evident. In many cases, of either an interruption or an interval, an over will be in progress and, unless an innings has ended, is to be continued if and when play resumes. Whatever the cause, the bowler's end umpire will call Time. Both sets of bails are to be removed, though this act nowadays has no significance in Law and is often not carried out – though it should be – when the players remain on the field of play for a drinks interval. The list of duties below is divided into those relevant in different situations. It collects together items set out in Part II in the relevant Laws.

Innings to resume after interval or interruption – the following to be noted
1   The time at which Time is called.
2   How many balls, if any, remain in the over and who is bowling it.
3   If over in progress, who bowled the previous over.
4   At which end bowling is to resume. The umpire at that end takes charge of the ball.
5   Which batsmen are at which ends.

The umpires should agree these details and make a written record of them, whether it is an interruption or an arranged interval, even if it is only a drinks interval. It is astonishing how easy it is to forget, for instance, which batsmen were at which end. Umpires may wonder why the previous bowler information is necessary, if an over is in progress at a break in play. It is a precaution against the current bowler being incapacitated during the break. The previous bowler could not finish the over.

Innings to resume after *arranged* interval

6   Unless it is a drinks interval, agree with the other umpire and the scorers the number of runs and wickets and, if relevant, the number of overs.

7   Have creases re-marked if necessary and possible.

8   Have debris removed from the pitch.

9   If the interval is between one day and the next, supervise mowing, sweeping and rolling next morning.

At end of innings

1   Note the time at which Time is called.

2   Agree with the other umpire and the scorers the number of runs and wickets and, if relevant, the number of overs.

3   Supervise any permitted rolling requested by the batting captain – together with associated sweeping or other removal of debris, as applicable.

4   Have creases re-marked.

6 POSITIONING OF UMPIRES

Law 7 directs the umpires to stand where they can best see any act on which their decision may be required. Guidance on where to stand is given in Part II in several Laws.

The major points for the **bowler's end umpire** as the ball is being delivered are –

He must be able to see
• where the bowler's feet land in the delivery stride
• the line between wicket and wicket with both sets of stumps in line
• the flight of the ball after delivery, only swivelling his eyes without head movement.

He must not impede
• the bowler in his run up
• the striker's view of the final part of the bowler's run up.

These requirements mean that he must be far enough back
• to see where the back foot lands
• to be able to see at least the upper part of the near wicket, at the same time as events at the far end
• for a bowler running round from behind him not to come into the striker's view at the last minute. On this point, he will normally ask the bowler to run in front of him rather than behind him, but must judge according to circumstances.

He must also be directly in the line between wicket and wicket (though behind the stumps!).

He will choose what, within these parameters, is most comfortable for himself and for the bowler. He can accede to a bowler's request to move only insofar as he can still meet the conditions above. He must politely but firmly refuse to move outside these limits. Once upon a time, it was thought advisable for the umpire to bend forward during the time of the bowler's run up and delivery. This idea is refuted in more detail in Part II. Bending forward briefly to judge a Run out can, however, be helpful.

Seeing the ball in flight as soon as possible after the bowler's feet have landed is crucial. The umpire must be watching the exact path of the ball, and judging its pace,

for a possible LBW appeal

for a possible touch on the bat

to see whether the ball rises too sharply after pitching

to see whether it is a high full pitched ball

to see whether it is or could have been within the striker's reach

to see whether the batsman makes a genuine attempt to play the ball or to avoid
being hit by it.

He must not let his attention dwell on the bowler's feet once they have landed, even if he has to call No ball for an incorrect foot placement.

If the ball goes out into the field the bowler's end umpire must be ready to move very quickly to a position where he has a side-on view of the wicket and creases to watch for

* completion of each run
* if the wicket is broken, that it is properly and fairly put down
* what is happening to the ball in the field
* when the batsmen cross, if they do.

To see all of this he should be far enough from the stumps to be able to see the wicket and the popping crease at the same time. He will normally go to the same side as the ball so as not to be unsighted by a fielder taking the throw-in, but must not get in the way of that throw-in, both not to disadvantage the fielders and for his own safety. He will break this rule if he is likely to get in the way of a fielder close to the wicket, or if there is a runner. It is explained in Part II, under Law 2, that he must be on the side opposite to the runner, not only to avoid the runner impeding his view of the wicket and creases but also to avoid having the runner behind him, where he cannot judge the runner's being within his ground. Having accustomed himself to going automatically to the side the ball is on, he will find it extremely difficult to change this habit. Great concentration is needed, supplemented by the thought that he must run to the side where his colleague, for exactly the same reasons, is positioned.

In the case of the ball being hit back directly towards the stumps at his end, he will not have time to reach the ideal position. He must get in the best position he can, not impeding the fielder who may be trying to catch the ball or touch it before it hits the stumps, but with at least a diagonal view of the breaking of the wicket and the position of the non-striker. It is more important that he has his head still at the moment of judgment than that he gets a foot or two further away. He will be in even greater difficulties if the bowler exercises his right to attempt to run out the non-striker before entering his delivery stride. A change in the rhythm of sound of the bowler's feet behind him, coupled with an awareness that the non-striker has left his ground, will help to alert him.

Finally, in taking up his position for the delivery of each ball, he must ensure that the other umpire is ready and in a position to observe events. The latter may have had to remake the wicket, or to move across from one side to the other. It would be a bad blunder to allow the ball to come into play without the striker's end umpire ready to see it delivered.

The major points for the **striker's end umpire** as the ball is being delivered are –

He must be able to see
- the bowler's arm action in the delivery swing
- the wicket-keeper's position and actions in relation to the stumps at his end
- that there are no more than two fielders behind the popping crease on the on side at the instant of delivery
- if the wicket is broken, in what manner and by what agency this was done
- where the runner is, if there is one, as well as the creases.

He must not impede
- the fielders.

His position will be square to the wicket, normally at square leg in line with the popping crease. He may find it helpful to move a pace sideways, nearer to the bowling crease, if the wicket-keeper is up close, to check that the latter remains entirely behind the wicket, especially in the event of an attempted catch or stumping. He will go to the off side for one of three reasons:

- there is some impediment to his vision, such as a close short leg fielder blocking his view, or low sun making it difficult to see the creases
- to obtain a different view of the bowler's arm action, if he feels it to be necessary
- there is a runner whom he has placed at square leg, to be out of the fielders' way.

When he moves he is to inform the captain of the fielding side, the striker and the other umpire. All three can be informed with one sufficiently audible call to the captain of the fielding side, at a moment when it will not distract him from his duties as captain.

If the ball goes out into the field, the striker's end umpire must be in a position to see exactly the same four things listed for his colleague at the bowler's end. He will already be square on to the crease and far enough away from the stumps. His only problem is that he may be unsighted by a fielder moving across his line of vision, necessitating a move to one side or the other to see the wicket, the creases and the batsman.

Both umpires will, with experience, be able to set up a rhythm for watching the progress of the ball in play, the completion of each run at his own end and the batsmen crossing. In addition, each will soon learn to recognise when it is imperative for him to watch for the crossing while the other umpire's attention has to be on some other aspect of the action.

7 SIGNALS AND SIGNALLING

A code of signals is laid down in Law 3. These are the means by which the umpires communicate with the scorers. They also have a role in informing the players. The Law sets out, in alphabetical order, the signals that are to be made while the ball is in play. These are, in a different order,

No ball	also to be called
Wide ball	also to be called
Dead Ball	also to be called
Out	

In the first two the ball does not become dead; play continues. The third causes the ball to be dead. The situation, vis-à-vis the ball being dead when Out is signalled, is explained in detail in Part II under Law 23. While the ball is in play the umpire's attention must be directed to what is happening in the field of play, rather than to communicating information to scorers. It is fatal to try to signal to the scorers while the ball is in play. Any of the first three signals made during play is to be repeated to the scorers by the bowler's end umpire, together with any others that may be needed, when the ball is dead. If several signals are made, it is essential that each signal is acknowledged separately. A single acknowledgement is not sufficient to confirm that the scorers have seen all of them.

If several signals are to be given there is an order in which they should be made. The signal for a boundary should be last. It is the event that the scorers are most likely to have seen for themselves and will therefore be expecting to be signalled. They will know that the signalling is not finished until they have seen the one they are expecting. If no signal is given when the ball is dead they will know that any runs they have seen the batsmen complete are to be credited to the striker and that there are no other runs. If this is not the case, the umpire should signal whatever may be necessary in the following order:

1   Penalty runs[1]
2   Short run – this will tell the scorers to deduct one run from the number observed[2]

---

[1] If penalty runs are to the batting side, the patting action must be exaggerated to ensure that there is no confusion with penalty runs to the fielding side.
[2] If more than one run has been short, the number of runs to be recorded must be advised to the scorers in some way.

3   What observed runs (less any Short runs) are to be recorded as

        Runs to the striker (No signal given)

or   No ball extras (No ball[3] followed by Bye signal)

or   No ball + runs to the striker (No ball[3] signal alone)

or   Wides[3]

or   Byes

or   Leg byes

4   Boundary 4[4] or Boundary 6

Dead ball must be inserted at the appropriate point in the sequence. Its message is that all runs the scorers have seen the batsmen make are to be disregarded, but that any runs already signalled are to count. For instance, No ball followed by Dead ball will mean that the one-run penalty for the No ball is to count, but nothing else. For deliberate short running, a signal of Dead ball is more appropriate than Short run. The latter (without any supplementary information) cancels only one run; the former cancels all runs by the batsmen.

---

[3] Signals first given when the ball was in play, now repeated.
[4] If the boundary is for overthrows, the scorers must be advised of the number of runs to be recorded. Whether the allowance is to the striker or to extras will have been covered by previous signals.

PART **II**

The Laws of Cricket
with interpretations

The Preamble – The Spirit of Cricket

Law 1   The Players

Law 2   Substitutes and runners; batsman or fielder leaving the field; batsman retiring; batsman commencing innings

Law 3   The umpires

Law 4   The scorers

Law 5   The ball

Law 6   The bat

Law 7   The pitch

Law 8   The wickets

Law 9   The bowling, popping, and return creases

Law 10   Preparation and maintenance of the playing area

Law 11   Covering the pitch

Law 12   Innings

Law 13   The follow-on

Law 14   Declaration and forfeiture

Law 15   Intervals

Law 16   Start of play; cessation of play

Law 17   Practice on the field

Law 18   Scoring runs

Law 19   Boundaries

Law 20   Lost ball

Law 21   The result

Law 22   The over

Law 23   Dead ball

Law 24   No ball

Law 25   Wide ball

Law 26   Bye and Leg bye

Law 27   Appeals

Law 28   The wicket is down

Law 29   Batsman out of his ground

Law 30   Bowled

Law 31   Timed out

Law 32   Caught

Law 33   Handled the ball

Law 34   Hit the ball twice

Law 35   Hit the wicket

Law 36   Leg before wicket

Law 37   Obstructing the field

Law 38   Run out

Law 39   Stumped

Law 40   The wicket-keeper

Law 41   The fielder

Law 42   Fair and unfair play

THE PREAMBLE – The Spirit of Cricket

Cricket is a game that owes much of its unique appeal to the fact that it should be played not only within its Laws but also within the Spirit of the Game. Any action which is seen to abuse this spirit causes injury to the game itself. The major responsibility for ensuring the spirit of fair play rests with the captains.

I. THERE ARE TWO LAWS WHICH PLACE THE RESPONSIBILITY FOR THE TEAM'S CONDUCT FIRMLY ON THE CAPTAIN.

RESPONSIBILITY OF CAPTAINS
The captains are responsible at all times for ensuring that play is conducted within the Spirit of the Game as well as within the Laws.

PLAYER'S CONDUCT
In the event of a player failing to comply with instructions by an umpire, or criticising by word or action the decisions of an umpire, or showing dissent, or generally behaving in a manner which might bring the game into disrepute, the umpire concerned shall in the first place report the matter to the other umpire and to the player's captain, and instruct the latter to take action.

2. FAIR AND UNFAIR PLAY

According to the Laws the umpires are the sole judges of fair and unfair play. The umpires may intervene at any time and it is the responsibility of the captain to take action where required.

3. THE UMPIRES ARE AUTHORISED TO INTERVENE IN CASES OF:

- Time wasting
- Damaging the pitch
- Dangerous or unfair bowling
- Tampering with the ball
- Any other action that they consider to be unfair

4. THE SPIRIT OF THE GAME INVOLVES **RESPECT** FOR:

- Your opponents
- Your own captain and team
- The role of the umpires
- The game and its traditional values

5. IT IS AGAINST THE SPIRIT OF THE GAME:

- To dispute an umpire's decision by word, action or gesture
- To direct abusive language towards an opponent or umpire
- To indulge in cheating or any sharp practice, for instance:

(a) to appeal knowing that the batsman is not out

(b) to advance towards an umpire in an aggressive manner when appealing

(c) to seek to distract an opponent either verbally or by harassment with persistent clapping or unnecessary noise under the guise of enthusiasm and motivation of one's own side

6. VIOLENCE

There is no place for any act of violence on the field of play.

7. PLAYERS

Captains and umpires together set the tone for the conduct of a cricket match. Every player is expected to make an important contribution to this.

Commentary:

Unlike the Laws which follow it, the Preamble does not set out precise instructions. It is intended to illuminate, rather than to define, the notion of 'the Spirit of Cricket'. There are clear statements of the most basic points of the way players should behave in a game of cricket. These points should not be taken as a full prescription – far from it. They are, however, strong indicators, setting the tone for all aspects of players' behaviour. A game played in this spirit of honesty and respect for others, although hard fought, will both contribute to the enjoyment of players and spectators alike and uphold the status of cricket itself.

Law I The players

I. NUMBER OF PLAYERS

A match is played between two sides, each of eleven players, one of whom shall be captain.

By agreement a match may be played between sides of fewer than, or more than, eleven players, but not more than eleven players may field at any time.

2. NOMINATION OF PLAYERS

Each captain shall nominate his players in writing to one of the umpires before the toss. No player may be changed after the nomination without the consent of the opposing captain.

3. CAPTAIN

If at any time the captain is not available, a deputy shall act for him.

(a) If a captain is not available during the period in which the toss is to take place, then the deputy must be responsible for the nomination of the players, if this has not already been done, and for the toss. See 2 above and Law 12.4 (The toss).

(b) At any time after the nomination of the players, only a nominated player can act as deputy in discharging the duties and responsibilities of the captain as stated in these Laws.

4. RESPONSIBILITY OF CAPTAINS

The captains are responsible at all times for ensuring that play is conducted within the spirit and traditions of the game as well as within the Laws. See The Preamble – The Spirit of Cricket and Law 42.1 (Fair and unfair play – responsibility of captains).

RESPONSIBILITY OF CAPTAINS

The Preamble – The Spirit of Cricket was introduced into the Code of Laws in 2000, in response to growing concern at that time about the deterioration in player behaviour on the field of play. Strenuous efforts by Governing Bodies worldwide – and most particularly by MCC – to increase awareness of and commitment to this 'Code of conduct' by players, officials and administrators have had a welcome effect. The problem is still a serious one, however. Laws 1.4 and 42.1 place the responsibility firmly on the captains for ensuring that play is conducted within the spirit of the game as set out in the Preamble. Should the umpires have any concern that the spirit of the game is not being observed they should immediately and jointly speak to the captain of the side responsible for the offence and require him to take action. Law 42.18 sets out the procedure to be followed for actual breaches of the Spirit of Cricket.

NUMBER OF PLAYERS

Although the Law stipulates eleven players for each side, it can be agreed, for instance in an eight-a-side tournament, that a team will comprise something other than eleven players. If more than eleven are to be in a team, the umpires must ensure that no more than eleven flelders are on the field of play at any one time. In such circumstances, there is no requirement in Law that the same eleven players field throughout an innings.

No minimum number of fielders is laid down. Sometimes special regulations for a match will stipulate that a minimum number must be present for play to take place. If there is no such regulation, umpires must exercise sensible judgment on whether to allow play with a reduced number of fielders. They should certainly not allow start of play to be held up because one or two players of the fielding side have not arrived.

NOMINATION OF PLAYERS

The names of the players of each side must be given, in writing, to one of the umpires before the toss for choice of innings is made. The list must contain no more than eleven players or whatever other number has previously been officially agreed as the number in each team. Once the teams have been thus nominated, no player may be changed, not even to add a new name to an incomplete list, without the specific consent of the opposing captain, except that the umpires may allow (see Law 2.1) a substitute to *act for* a nominated player in fielding.

This Law is the first of many where special regulations in some high-profile games allow procedures at variance with the Laws. In this case it is the replacement of players called at short notice to play in national games. Here, in Law 1, it is a suitable moment to observe that, whilst Governing Bodies can lay down such special regulations, these variations in Law apply only in games under the aegis of the particular Governing Body. Umpires in the recreational game must apply the Laws as written, unless modified by the body actually responsible for the match in question – for example, the League Committee.

THE CAPTAIN

A team has to have a captain. Throughout the Laws, duties and responsibilities are required of such a person. Sometimes the designated captain is not available – possibly he is late arriving; possibly he is out of the game, injured. Nevertheless, procedures cannot be delayed on that account. The umpires must insist that someone acts as deputy for the captain. A responsibility of major importance is nominating the players, which must be done before the toss. There is absolutely no restriction (except the acquiescence of the team) on who may perform this duty. However, if a deputy has to act for the captain in any capacity after the list has been submitted, that deputy must be a nominated player.

FIELD TECHNIQUE

Umpires must insist that both teams are nominated before the toss. They should not wait until the 15-minute deadline is reached, but should take steps well before this to discover who the captains are and whether both are present. If one is not they can then discuss with that team the appointment of a deputy. If the captain arrives in time, no harm is done. If he does not, then the deputy is ready to act and can give in the list in time, before the toss. It is helpful to ensure that copies of the two lists are available to the scorers.

Before Play is called the umpires should check the number of fielders on the field of play. They will not allow more than eleven. If there are fewer than the number nominated, and/or fewer than the number agreed for the teams, they must know the reason for this discrepancy. If they have not already been told they should together check with the fielding captain. It may involve the absence or late arrival of a player. This will have to be dealt with as described in Law 2.

Law 2   Substitutes and runners; batsman or fielder leaving the field; batsman retiring; batsman commencing innings

1. SUBSTITUTES AND RUNNERS

(a) **If the umpires are satisfied that a nominated player has been injured or become ill since the nomination of the players, they shall allow that player to have**
   (i) **a substitute acting for him in the field.**
   (ii) **a runner when batting.**
   Any injury or illness that occurs at any time after the nomination of the players until the conclusion of the match shall be allowable, irrespective of whether play is in progress or not.
(b) **The umpires shall have discretion to allow, for other wholly acceptable reasons, a substitute fielder or a runner to act for a nominated player, at the start of the match, or at any subsequent time.**
(c) **A player wishing to change his shirt, boots, etc. shall leave the field to do so. No substitute shall be allowed for him.**

2. OBJECTION TO SUBSTITUTES

The opposing captain shall have no right of objection to any player acting as a substitute on the field, nor as to where the substitute shall field. However, no substitute shall act as wicket-keeper. See 3 below.

3. RESTRICTIONS ON ROLE OF SUBSTITUTES

A substitute shall not be allowed to bat, bowl or act as wicket-keeper. Note also Law 1.3(b) (Captain).

4. A PLAYER FOR WHOM A SUBSTITUTE HAS ACTED

A nominated player is allowed to bat, bowl or field even though a substitute has previously acted for him.

5. FIELDER ABSENT OR LEAVING THE FIELD

If a fielder fails to take the field with his side at the start of the match or at any later time, or leaves the field during a session of play,

(a) the umpire shall be informed of the reason for his absence.

(b) he shall not thereafter come on to the field of play during a session of play without the consent of the umpire. See 6 below. The umpire shall give such consent as soon as is practicable.

(c) if he is absent for 15 minutes of playing time or longer, he shall not be permitted to bowl thereafter, subject to (i), (ii) or (iii) below, until he has been on the field for at least the length of playing time for which he was absent.

   (i) Absence or penalty for time absent shall not be carried over into a new day's play.

   (ii) If, in the case of a follow-on or forfeiture, a side fields for two consecutive innings, this restriction shall, subject to (i) above, continue as necessary into the second innings, but shall not otherwise be carried over into a new innings.

   (iii) The time lost for an unscheduled break in play shall be counted as time on the field of play for any fielder who comes on to the field at the resumption of play after the break. See Law 15.1 (An interval).

6. PLAYER RETURNING WITHOUT PERMISSION

If a player comes on to the field of play in contravention of 5(b) above and comes into contact with the ball while it is in play,

(a) the ball shall immediately become dead and the umpire shall award 5 penalty runs to the batting side. Additionally, runs completed by the batsmen shall be scored together with the run in progress if they had already crossed at the instant of the offence. The ball shall not count as one of the over.

(b) the umpire shall inform the other umpire, the captain of the fielding side, the batsmen and, as soon as practicable, the captain of the batting side of the reason for this action.

(c) the umpires together shall report the occurrence as soon as possible after the match to the Executive of the fielding side and to any Governing Body responsible for the match, who shall take such action as is considered appropriate against the captain and the player concerned.

7. RUNNER

The player acting as a runner for a batsman shall be a member of the batting side and shall, if possible, have already batted in that innings. The runner shall wear external protective equipment equivalent to that worn by the batsman for whom he runs and shall carry a bat.

8. TRANSGRESSION OF THE LAWS BY A BATSMAN WHO HAS A RUNNER

(a) A batsman's runner is subject to the Laws. He will be regarded as a batsman except where there are specific provisions for his role as a runner. See 7 above and Law 29.2 (Which is a batsman's ground).

(b) A batsman who has a runner will suffer the penalty for any infringement of the Laws by his runner as if he had been himself responsible for the infringement. In particular he will be out if his runner is out under any of Laws 33 (Handled the ball), 37 (Obstructing the field) or 38 (Run out).

(c) When a batsman who has a runner is striker he remains himself subject to the Laws and will be liable to the penalties that any infringement of them demands.

Additionally, if he is out of his ground when the wicket at the wicket-keeper's end is fairly put down by the action of a fielder then, notwithstanding (b) above and irrespective of the position of the non-striker and the runner,

 (i) notwithstanding the provisions of Law 38.2(e), he is out Run out except as in (ii) below. Sections (a), (b), (c) and (d) of Law 38.2 (Batsman not Run out) shall apply.

 (ii) he is out Stumped if the delivery is not a No ball and the wicket is fairly put down by the wicket-keeper without the intervention of another fielder. However, Law 39.3 (Not out Stumped) shall apply.

If he is thus dismissed, runs completed by the runner and the other batsman before the wicket is put down shall be disallowed. However, any runs for penalties awarded to either side shall stand. See Law 18.6 (Runs awarded for penalties). The non-striker shall return to his original end.

(d) When a batsman who has a runner is not the striker

 (i) he remains subject to Laws 33 (Handled the ball) and 37 (Obstructing the field) but is otherwise out of the game.

 (ii) he shall stand where directed by the striker's end umpire so as not to interfere with play.

 (iii) he will be liable, notwithstanding (i) above, to the penalty demanded by the Laws should he commit any act of unfair play.

9. BATSMAN RETIRING

A batsman may retire at any time during his innings when the ball is dead. The umpires, before allowing play to proceed shall be informed of the reason for a batsman retiring.

(a) If a batsman retires because of illness, injury or any other unavoidable cause, he is entitled to resume his innings subject to (c) below. If for any reason he does not do so, his innings is to be recorded as 'Retired – not out'.

(b) If a batsman retires for any reason other than as in (a) above, he may resume his innings only with the consent of the opposing captain. If for any reason he does not resume his innings it is to be recorded as 'Retired – out'.

(c) If after retiring a batsman resumes his innings, it shall be only at the fall of a wicket or the retirement of another batsman.

10. COMMENCEMENT OF A BATSMAN'S INNINGS

Except at the start of a side's innings, a batsman shall be considered to have commenced his innings when he first steps on to the field of play, provided Time has not been called. The innings of the opening batsmen, and that of any new batsman on the resumption of play after a call of Time, shall commence at the call of Play.

This Law explains the circumstances in which a nominated player who is injured, or otherwise unable to take a full part in the game, can have a substitute acting for him as a fielder, or a runner to run for him when he is batting. It also deals with the whole question of the presence or absence of a player during the match.

AFTER THE NOMINATION OF THE TEAMS – SUBSTITUTE OR RUNNER BY RIGHT

The period after the nomination is from that moment onward, until the match is ended, even though during some of that time no play is in progress. A player who falls down the pavilion steps during the lunch interval, injuring his ankle, is just as entitled to a substitute or runner as if the injury had happened while he was actually fielding or batting. If he is to have a runner, he must of course be able to stand at the crease and bat.

It will be for the umpires together to judge that an injury has occurred to a player, or that he has been taken ill, during that period. In the latter case it must be appreciated that the umpires are not medically qualified. They must judge as best they can. The recurrence of a previous injury can count as an injury during the match, providing the umpires are satisfied that some event after the nomination is responsible for the worsening of the injury.

SUBSTITUTE OR RUNNER AT THE UMPIRES' DISCRETION

The umpires should act together in deciding whether a case merits the exercise of their discretion to allow a substitute or runner for a player who does not qualify to have one by right. A player with an artificial leg, or a doctor called away to a case are examples of where this could be considered.

SUBSTITUTES

It is important to understand the difference between a substitute fielder and a replacement for a nominated player. After the teams have been nominated, the opposing captain may, as described in Law 1, allow a nominated player to be *replaced* by another person. Though they may have to remind the captains of the terms of the Law, the umpires have no say in this. They should amend their lists of nominated players, to include the new player *instead* of the replaced one. They will allow any player now on the list, and no others, to take a full part in the game. Any player not on the current list is debarred from taking any part other than simply fielding and then only as a permitted substitute for another player.

In contrast, it is the umpires alone who decide whether a player can have a substitute or runner for whatever reason. The captains have no say. Once a substitute is allowed, there can be no objection as to who it is or where he can field (other than keeping wicket). The umpires will ensure that the restrictions laid on him in Section 3 are observed. If for instance a captain calls on a substitute to bowl, the umpires will remind him that this is not allowed. If the wicket-keeper is injured, then one of the other nominated players must act as keeper. The substitute can do no more than field instead of the one who does so.

If a nominated player has had a substitute, he can nevertheless return as a full player. For example, if a fielder has a badly cut finger, a substitute may act for him while it is treated and bandaged in the pavilion. He is allowed to return and resume as a fielder without restriction except that the umpire must give permission for the actual moment of his return.

FIELDER ABSENT FROM FIELD OF PLAY

A player is counted as absent if, when his side comes on to the field, he is not among the players. This statement must not be taken too literally. If he is simply a moment or two later than the rest of the team, that is of no significance provided he arrives before Play is called. He will also be absent if he leaves the field during a session of play. As is clear from the definitions in Appendix D (see pages 280–3), merely going to retrieve the ball from beyond the boundary is not 'leaving the field'.

Ideally, all the fielders should be within the boundary when the ball comes into play. On smaller club grounds, however, it would be unreasonable to prevent a fielder from starting one or two paces outside to give himself room to walk in towards the wicket. On the other hand, the batsmen are entitled to know where the fielders are when the ball comes into play, so that the striker can judge where to play his shots and both of them can assess whether to attempt a run or not. The umpire will not allow a fielder to start outside the boundary if the batsmen may thereby be deceived. Provided, however, it is obvious that he is there and that he is taking part in the game, such action can be allowed without penalty. He cannot field the ball, however, from a point outside the boundary, not even, as discussed later, if he jumps in the air from such a position.

To be leaving the field, the player must be completely withdrawing from the game. The umpire has to be told, not necessarily by the player himself, the reason for this withdrawal but the question of granting permission does not arise. He will immediately tell his colleague and both will note the time, so that if the fielder returns they will know how long he has been absent. They will together decide whether a substitute can be allowed or not. The bowler's end umpire has to give permission for the fielder to come on to the field again. Both will check the time that this happens.

If a substitute has been fielding meanwhile, he must go off when the original player returns. Permission to return must not be given unless the ball is dead and should be timed so that this fielding change-over does not delay play significantly. On the other hand, umpires must not prolong the length of absence by delaying this consent unnecessarily, since this could affect the player's right to bowl. The end of an over is an obvious time but should not be regarded as the only opportunity. If the returning player positions himself on the boundary nearest to the substitute, the change-over can usually be achieved quite quickly between deliveries. The batsmen need to be made aware of the change in the fielding side.

The penalty if a player returns without permission, *and makes contact with the ball*, is laid down in Section 6. It is quite severe but it must be applied if the situation arises. Once the procedure in Section 6 has been implemented, apart from the reporting to be made after the match, the umpire should take the opportunity to consent to the return of the fielder if that is appropriate.

PLAYER BOWLING AFTER RETURN FROM ABSENCE

Umpires must be clear about the exact time that a fielder is to be counted as absent. Only that part of his absence which was **playing time** is significant. They will have noted the time of his departure, or the start of the innings, if he does not come on with his side. They will also have noted the time of his return. From the difference between these two they must subtract the time for any intervals – not forgetting drinks intervals! – or interruptions in play, since neither of these is playing time. As soon as he has been absent for 15 minutes of playing time, on returning he will face a delay before he can bowl. Non-playing time cannot be used to offset any waiting time, except in the case set out in Section 5(c)(iii). Umpires will do well to study that section. Note that the time he has to wait is often referred to as 'penance time'. There is no official basis for this.

In dealing with calculations for time absent and delay on return, the points to note are:

- The start of the match is not to be treated any differently from any other time.
- If a player is absent on more than one occasion, a separate calculation is made for each absence. The times off the field are not added together but the waiting times are cumulative.
- Only actual playing time counts in any part of the calculation, except in the special case of Section 5, already mentioned.

The following examples demonstrate these points. The first one is somewhat artificial. Multiple absences in such a short span of time are infrequent. It was chosen to illustrate the points, rather than to be realistic.

1. A player leaves the field three times during a session of play – an unlikely occurrence!

He first leaves at 11.25 a.m.		WAITING TIME
Returns 11.48 a.m.	absent 23 minutes	23 minutes
Leaves again 11.59 a.m.	on the field 11 minutes	23 – 11 = 12 minutes
Returns 12.06 p.m.	absent 7 minutes	Less than15 minutes, so no penalty: still 12 minutes
Leaves again 12.14 p.m.	on the field 8 minutes	12 – 8 = 4 minutes
Returns 12.32 p.m.	absent 18 minutes	4 + 18 = 22 minutes

2. A player is late at the beginning of the match and has not arrived by the start of play at 11.00 a.m. He eventually comes on to the field at 12.50 p.m. During this time there has been a drinks interval of 4 minutes.

TIME OFF THE FIELD				ON THE FIELD
From	**Actual time**	**Drinks**	**Playing time**	**Waiting time**
11.00 to 12.50	1 hr 50 min	4 min	1 hr 46 min	1 hr 46 min

He then remains on the field. During the time before he is allowed to bowl, lunch is taken from 1.15 p.m. to 2.00 p.m., and there are drinks at 3 p.m. lasting 5 minutes. This affects his waiting time of 1 hr 46 minutes as follows:

TIME ON THE FIELD			WAITING TIME
12.50 to 1.15	Playing time	25 minutes	reduced to 1 hr 21 min
1.15 to 2.00	Lunch		still 1 hr 21 min
2.00 to 3.00	Playing time	1 hr	reduced to 21 min
3.00 to 3.05	Drinks		still 21 min

At 3.05 p.m. he still has 21 minutes to wait. He could bowl at 3.26 p.m.

3. A player goes off the field at 11.40 a.m. to have a damaged hand (not his bowling hand) X-rayed. At 12.40 p.m. it rains and the players leave the field. Lunch was due from 1 p.m. to 1.40 p.m. but is taken at 12.50 (to 1.30). The injured man returns at 1.15. It is still raining when lunch is over. Play does not resume until 1.55, when he takes the field with the rest of his side. His time off is therefore:

11.40 to 12.40	12.40 to 12.50	12.50 to 1.30	1.30 to 1.55
Playing time	Unscheduled break	Lunch	Unscheduled break
1 hour	10 minutes	40 minutes	25 minutes

Because he comes on to the field with his team on resumption of play at 1.55, he can count the 35 minutes (10 + 25) of unscheduled break towards offsetting his waiting time.

> Absent 1 hour of playing time
> Offset by 35 min unscheduled break   waiting time is 25 min

He could bowl at 2.20 p.m.

FURTHER POINTS TO NOTE

The end of a day's play will wipe the slate clean. If he is absent for the last 45 minutes of play on Monday, but he comes on at the start of play on Tuesday, he could bowl straight away. If he misses the first 20 minutes of play on Tuesday, he would have to wait only 20 minutes after coming on to the field before being allowed to bowl.

This is also true in general at the start of a new innings. If he has waiting time 'left over' at the end of his side's fielding innings, then, in the normal situation in which his side bats before fielding again, that waiting time is cancelled. This does not apply, however, if his side fields again immediately, in the case of a follow-on or forfeiture. The 10 minutes between the two fielding innings is not playing time, so neither adds to his absence nor forms part of his waiting time. If he was absent for the last 20 minutes of the first innings he could not bowl for the first 20 minutes of the follow-on innings, even if he came on to the field at the start of it.

Only time absent <u>as a fielder</u> counts. If a player is injured when batting and is absent for an hour before resuming his innings, this will have no effect on his entitlement to bowl (if fit) when his side fields. Moreover, unlike some high-profile matches, there is no restriction on his position in the batting order if he has been absent as a fielder.

Clearly the scorers can be helpful in recording the times when a fielder leaves the field and subsequently returns. It is, however, the umpires' responsibility to see that the restrictions on bowling after absence are observed. They must be meticulous in noting the times involved.

BATSMAN LEAVING THE FIELD

Umpires would do well to study Section 9 of this Law to see how the reason for a batsman leaving the field affects his right to return and resume his innings. It follows that the umpires must know what that reason is. In any case, whether he is ill or injured, or there is some other reason for his going, either the batsman himself or his captain must inform the umpire at the bowler's end. It is only in the case of 'some other reason' that the opposing captain's consent is required for his return. He must, however, wait in any case until the fall of a wicket or the retirement of another batsman.

RUNNERS

The umpires must ensure that any player acting as a runner is indeed a nominated player of the batting side and that his dress and equipment comply with the requirements laid down in Section 7. Clearly the requirement that he should have already batted cannot be met if one of the opening pair is injured. In that case another batsman must be accepted as runner. To minimise the advantage of his seeing the bowling and getting used to the light, he should not be the next batsman due to come in. To prevent an advantage to the batting side of having a tired runner replaced by a fresh one, he should not be changed for another one unless there is no alternative. This means that he should be from low in the order. Umpires may have to explain these conditions to the captain of the batting side, particularly if he believes that the runner can become the next batsman when a wicket falls.

INNINGS COMMENCING

The instant of stepping on to the field of play applies only to new batsmen coming in during a session of play. At the start of each innings, it is not until Play is called that the innings of the opening batsmen start. When Time is called in any session, the innings of those batsmen already at the wicket will continue in the next session, if their side is still batting. If, however, a new batsman comes in as play resumes, his innings will not start until Play is called to restart after the break, whatever the nature of the break.

BATSMAN WHO HAS A RUNNER

Broadly, a batsman and his runner are regarded as two parts of the same person. The batsman can be out, or penalties can be awarded against the batting side, whether the batsman or the runner is responsible. There are points of difference, however. The question of the batsman attempting a run does not arise, as explained under Law 39, whereas the runner will always be deemed to be attempting a run if he is not within his ground while the ball is in play. The batsman, as striker, can never regard the ground at the bowler's end as his ground. If he himself is run out, no runs other than penalties will be scored, whereas normal scoring of runs applies if his runner is run out. There is more detailed discussion of this under Laws 38 and 39, Run out and Stumped.

FIELD TECHNIQUE

When the striker has a runner, the umpire will have to judge whether or not the runner is within his ground, both for checking on short runs and for a possible Run out. He must therefore position the runner so that he can see the creases and the wicket as well as the runner. Additionally, the runner must not be a hindrance to the fielding side. The most suitable position is usually with the runner at square leg and the umpire on the off side. If, however, there is good reason, such as low sun, for the umpire to be on the leg side, then the positions can be reversed.

The diagram below shows positioning for a right-handed batsmen. It demonstrates that, regardless of which side the ball has gone, the bowler's end umpire must always go to the side that his colleague is on, to avoid the embarrassment of having the runner behind him and therefore not visible.

When the incapacitated batsman is not striker, and so out of the game, he will remain at the wicket-keeper's end while the other batsman is striker. The umpire will need to be aware of what he is doing, so although not always possible, especially if the

U = Umpire
WK = Wicket-keeper
R = Runner;
S = Striker for whom he runs
NS = Non-striker

umpire has reason to move to the off, some position backward of square leg, fairly near the umpire, is usually the best place for him. The runner is then a normal non-striker. If there are two runners, one of them is always to be regarded as the non-striker.

The problems associated with appeals for Run out when there is a runner – or even two runners – on the field are discussed in more detail in Law 38.

Law 3 The umpires

1. APPOINTMENT AND ATTENDANCE

Before the match, two umpires shall be appointed, one for each end, to control the game as required by the Laws, with absolute impartiality. The umpires shall be present on the ground and report to the Executive of the ground at least 45 minutes before the scheduled start of each day's play.

2. CHANGE OF UMPIRE

An umpire shall not be changed during the match, other than in exceptional circumstances, unless he is injured or ill. If there has to be a change of umpire, the replacement shall act only as striker's end umpire unless the captains agree that he should take full responsibility as an umpire.

3. AGREEMENT WITH CAPTAINS

Before the toss the umpires shall
(a) ascertain the hours of play and agree with the captains
    (i) the balls to be used during the match. See Law 5 (The ball).
    (ii) times and durations of intervals for meals and times for drinks intervals. See Law 15 (Intervals).
    (iii) the boundary of the field of play and allowances for boundaries. See Law 19 (Boundaries).
    (iv) any special conditions of play affecting the conduct of the match.
(b) inform the scorers of agreements in (ii), (iii) and (iv) above.

4. TO INFORM CAPTAINS AND SCORERS

Before the toss the umpires shall agree between themselves and inform both captains and both scorers
 (i) which clock or watch and back-up timepiece is to be used during the match.
(ii) whether or not any obstacle within the field of play is to be regarded as a boundary. See Law 19 (Boundaries).

5. THE WICKETS, CREASES AND BOUNDARIES

Before the toss and during the match, the umpires shall satisfy themselves that

(a) the wickets are properly pitched. See Law 8 (The wickets).

(b) the creases are correctly marked. See Law 9 (The bowling, popping and return creases).

(c) the boundary of the field of play complies with the requirements of Laws 19.1 (The boundary of the field of play) and 19.2 (Defining the boundary – boundary marking).

6. CONDUCT OF THE GAME, IMPLEMENTS AND EQUIPMENT

Before the toss and during the match, the umpires shall satisfy themselves that

(a) the conduct of the game is strictly in accordance with the Laws.

(b) the implements of the game conform to the following
   (i) Law 5 (The ball).
   (ii) externally visible requirements of Law 6 (The bat) and Appendix E.
   (iii) either Laws 8.2 (Size of stumps) and 8.3 (The bails) or, if appropriate, Law 8.4 (Junior cricket).

(c) (i) no player uses equipment other than that permitted. See Appendix D. Note particularly therein the interpretation of 'protective helmet'.
   (ii) the wicket-keeper's gloves comply with the requirements of Law 40.2 (Gloves).

7. FAIR AND UNFAIR PLAY

The umpires shall be the sole judges of fair and unfair play.

8. FITNESS FOR PLAY

(a) It is solely for the umpires together to decide whether
   either conditions of ground, weather or light
      or exceptional circumstances
   mean that it would be dangerous or unreasonable for play to take place. Conditions shall not be regarded as either dangerous or unreasonable merely because they are not ideal.

(b) Conditions shall be regarded as dangerous if there is actual and foreseeable risk to the safety of any player or umpire.

(c) Conditions shall be regarded as unreasonable if, although posing no risk to safety, it would not be sensible for play to proceed.

9. SUSPENSION OF PLAY IN DANGEROUS OR UNREASONABLE CONDITIONS

(a) All references to ground include the pitch. See Law 7.1 (Area of pitch).

(b) If at any time the umpires together agree that the conditions of ground, weather or light, or any other circumstances are dangerous or unreasonable, they shall immediately suspend play, or not allow play to start or to recommence.

(c) When there is a suspension of play it is the responsibility of the umpires to monitor conditions. They shall make inspections as often as appropriate, unaccompanied by any players or officials. Immediately the umpires together agree that the conditions are no longer dangerous or unreasonable they shall call upon the players to resume play.

10. POSITION OF UMPIRES

Each umpire shall stand where he can best see any act upon which his decision may be required.

Subject to this over-riding consideration, the bowler's end umpire shall stand where he does not interfere with either the bowler's run up or the striker's view.

The striker's end umpire may elect to stand on the off side instead of the on side of the pitch, provided he informs the captain of the fielding side, the striker and the other umpire of his intention to do so.

11. UMPIRES CHANGING ENDS

The umpires shall change ends after each side has had one completed innings. See Law 12.3 (Completed innings).

12. CONSULTATION BETWEEN UMPIRES

All disputes shall be determined by the umpires. The umpires shall consult with each other whenever necessary. See also Law 27.6 (Consultation by umpires).

13. INFORMING THE UMPIRES

Throughout the Laws, wherever the umpires are to receive information from captains or other players, it will be sufficient for one umpire to be so informed and for him to inform the other umpire.

14. SIGNALS

(a) The following code of signals shall be used by umpires.
   (i) Signals made while the ball is in play
     Dead ball – by crossing and re-crossing the wrists below the waist.
     No ball – by extending one arm horizontally.
     Out – by raising an index finger above the head. (If not out, the umpire shall call Not out.)
     Wide – by extending both arms horizontally.
   (ii) When the ball is dead, the bowler's end umpire shall repeat the signals above, with the exception of the signal for Out, to the scorers.
   (iii) The signals listed below shall be made to the scorers only when the ball is dead.

Boundary 4 – by waving an arm from side to side finishing with the arm across the chest.

Boundary 6 – by raising both arms above the head.

Bye – by raising an open hand above the head.

Commencement of last hour – by pointing to a raised wrist with the other hand.

Five penalty runs awarded to the batting side – by repeated tapping of one shoulder with the opposite hand.

Five penalty runs awarded to the fielding side – by placing one hand on the opposite shoulder.

Leg bye – by touching a raised knee with the hand.

New ball – by holding the ball above the head.

Revoke last signal – by touching both shoulders, each with the opposite hand.

Short run – by bending one arm upwards and touching the nearer shoulder with the tips of the fingers.

All these signals are to be made by the bowler's end umpire except that for Short run, which is to be signalled by the umpire at the end where short running occurs. However, the bowler's end umpire shall be responsible both for the final signal of Short run to the scorers and for informing them as to the number of runs to be recorded.

(b) The umpire shall wait until each signal to the scorers has been separately acknowledged by a scorer before allowing play to proceed.

15. CORRECTNESS OF SCORES

Consultation between umpires and scorers on doubtful points is essential. The umpires shall, throughout the match, satisfy themselves as to the correctness of the number of runs scored, the wickets that have fallen and, where appropriate, the number of overs bowled. They shall agree these with the scorers at least at every interval, other than a drinks interval, and at the conclusion of the match. See Laws 4.2 (Correctness of scores), 21.8 (Correctness of result) and 21.10 (Result not to be changed).

APPOINTMENT AND ATTENDANCE

An umpire may have little or no involvement with either of the teams or may have been appointed by the captain of one of them. Whatever the situation, this Law makes it clear that both umpires must act with the utmost impartiality. They are appointed 'one for each end', not one for each side.

Umpires have many duties – all vital for the smooth and successful conduct of the match – which they are required to undertake before play begins. The Law stipulates that umpires arrive at least 45 minutes before the scheduled start. The prudent umpire will arrive well before that.

DUTIES BEFORE THE TOSS

Organisational duties required of the umpires before the toss for innings are divided into three categories:

- items that they must agree with the two captains
- matters which they decide between themselves and then tell the captains
- tasks in which the captains are not involved.

Performance of these duties requires the umpires and captains to confer before the toss – 'the pre-match conference'.

AGREEMENT WITH CAPTAINS

As some of the items listed in Section 3 will be laid down before the day of the match, 'agreeing' them will mostly be checking between umpires and captains that they all have the same understanding as to the details involved. This is not a formality. It is essential to the avoidance of embarrassing misunderstandings during the game.

The hours of play are the number of days for the match, together with the times for start of play on each day and for close of play on each day. They are not to be confused with times and durations of intervals. Those are temporary cessations of play during the day. Clearly all these times are essential information for the scorers.

The actual balls to be used should be available for captains and umpires to inspect and agree. Law 5 specifies that, having been agreed, the balls are to be given to the umpires and are to remain under their control thereafter. In most one-day recreational cricket there will be only one ball for each innings. The scorers need to know if more than one is to be available, and if so, when a new one can be taken. They do not need to know which actual balls are to be used.

The most neglected of the instructions in this section is probably the agreement as to the allowances for boundaries. Often, it will be assumed that these will be the standard 4 and 6. Often this will be true, but all need to <u>know</u> that this is so. Again, this information is important for the scorers.

Special conditions of play affecting the conduct of the match will include competition rules, such as a limit on the number of overs any one bowler can deliver, limitations of time or number of overs on each innings, and so forth. There may be special conditions peculiar to that particular ground. Whether standard or unusual, all must know and understand them.

UMPIRES TO INFORM CAPTAINS AND SCORERS

The two items listed in Section 4 must be agreed between the two umpires beforehand in order to be passed on to captains at the pre-match conference.

Accurate time-keeping plays an important role at several stages in the match. A pavilion clock in good working order and easy to read accurately is, if available, the most suitable timepiece. The provision of a back-up timepiece is a prudent and necessary precaution against the failure of the one agreed as the master.

An 'obstacle within the field of play' is necessarily a vague description. Examples are a tree, an 'immovable' roller, a concrete strip for the run up to a practice net. It is for the umpires to decide, in line with local customs, whether such an object is to count as boundary or not. The players, through their captains, need to know, as do the scorers.

CREASE MARKINGS, WICKETS, IMPLEMENTS

Before the pre-match conference, umpires will need to make a complete inspection of the field of play. This will include the boundaries and how they are marked, in order to agree these with the captains, and what obstacles there are which may have to be designated as boundaries.

It is essential also that, before the game, umpires check that the creases are correctly marked and the wickets correctly pitched. This will include seeing that stumps and bails are of the correct size. Moreover, while play is in progress, the umpires are responsible for seeing that the players use only the equipment they are permitted to have; that balls, bats, and wicket-keepers' gloves all conform to the Laws. Laws 5, 6, 7, 8, 9 and 40 lay down requirements for each of these 'implements of the game'. There is also additional detail in Appendices A, B, C and E. The umpires' responsibility has, perforce, to be limited to what they can see and reasonably measure. For example, in Law 6 in particular, they will not be able to measure if stickers for manufacturers' logos are too thick, but can tell if a bat is more than 4¼ inches wide at any point.

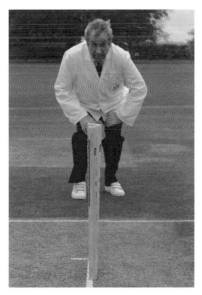

Check from the side as well as from front and back that the stumps are upright and aligned

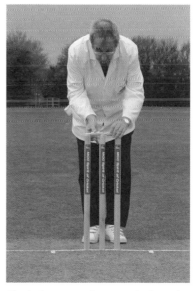

Check that your colleague at the far end has the stumps upright and equally spaced. He will do the same for you

FAIR AND UNFAIR PLAY

Great emphasis is placed on the need for both sides to play within the spirit of the game as well as within the Laws. Both in Law 1 and in Law 42, it is stated that it is the captain's responsibility to see that his side conforms to this ideal. The umpires have the responsibility of judging whether any action is fair or not. It is stated clearly that they are the sole judges of fair and unfair play. Specific acts of unfair play are embodied within a number of Laws, each with relevant instructions for the procedure to be adopted by the umpires. There may, however, be occasions when one umpire sees something which he considers unfair, which is not one of those specific instances. In that situation, he must intervene to stop play by calling and signalling Dead ball and then immediately inform his colleague of the reason for this action. Action thereafter is to be by both umpires jointly.

CHANGE OF UMPIRE

It should be rare for an umpire to be changed. If his becoming ill or injured, or some exceptional circumstance, necessitates a change, it will be for the other umpire to decide on a replacement. The replacement will normally be limited to standing at the striker's end every over. He can, however, take a full part as an umpire if both captains agree to his doing so. The current umpire may need to explain this to the captains.

FITNESS OF GROUND, WEATHER AND LIGHT

In the 2010 edition of the Laws, there is no longer provision for the players to choose whether to play or not when conditions are not very good, but not dangerous. What used to be known as 'offering the light' – telling the batsmen that the umpires considered that the light was poor but play was possible if the batsmen wanted to continue – is no longer allowed. The same applies to ground and weather. The umpires therefore have an even greater responsibility than before in regard to conditions of ground, weather and light. It is essential that they are familiar with their responsibilities under this heading. The paramount consideration is the safety of those on the field of play, players and umpires alike. The umpires are the sole judges of whether each of the conditions of the ground underfoot, of the weather overhead or of the surrounding light is safe for play to take place. It is not to be deemed dangerous merely because it is dull and overcast. If, however, the light is so poor, possibly exacerbated by a dark background of, for example, trees, that players or umpires are unable to pick up soon enough the flight of a ball coming towards them – then that is dangerous. Equally, if it is a bit wet and it is necessary to dry the ball fairly often, it is not dangerous. If the ground is so wet and soft that players cannot maintain a reasonable foothold, when bowling, when playing the ball, when running between wickets or when fielding the ball – then that is dangerous. Umpires must judge how bad conditions are and must agree together whether conditions are dangerous or not. They must not allow play to take place in dangerous conditions, whatever the wishes of the captains may be.

Whilst not suspending play unless conditions warrant it, they must, if in doubt, err on the side of caution, and suspend play earlier rather than later.

There could be other situations where it would be dangerous for play to take place – a large swarm of bees 'invading' the field of play, for instance – or unreasonable, but not dangerous for play to take place – for example, waiting for professional paramedics to come to administer to a player who has collapsed on the field of play. The same considerations apply to such situations as to ground, weather and light. If conditions are dangerous or unreasonable, umpires must not allow play to take place.

Their first duty in this respect is to check the conditions before the day's play. Although the selection and preparation of the pitch before the toss is entirely a matter for the ground staff, umpires have authority to pronounce at any time, even before the toss, on the fitness of conditions and must do so. When play is to resume after an interval, again, the umpires must ensure that conditions are safe for this to happen.

Once the umpires have decided that play is not to take place, they must keep a watch on conditions to see if they improve. The state of the game may influence the teams differently about wanting to start play. The umpires must entertain no such considerations. They will carry out periodic inspections, concerned only with whether conditions are safe for play, and unaccompanied by any player or team official. Once the umpires agree between themselves that conditions are no longer dangerous, play is to resume regardless of the wishes of the players.

POSITION OF UMPIRES

The ability to see the action that is taking place is paramount. If a bowler requests that an umpire stands closer to, or further from, the stumps, the umpire should acquiesce only as far as is possible without impairing this ability. If a bowler in his follow-through runs in front of the umpire he may contravene the Law but will certainly block the umpire's view. The umpire must not simply accept that he cannot see what is happening. He must quickly step to one side. He will not be able to adjudge LBW from an off-line position, but must see the many other matters for which he is responsible. The same applies to the umpire standing at the striker's end when a fielder crosses his path. When the batsmen are running, the bowler's end umpire must move round quickly to get a side-on view of the creases, of the putting down of the wicket, and, if necessary, of the crossing or otherwise of the batsmen. He needs to be as far from the wicket as he can get in the time. He must not impede the fielders; nor impede the throw-in – not only to avoid being hit himself, but so as not to disadvantage the fielding side. There is more detailed discussion of this under Law 28.

UMPIRES CHANGING ENDS

Umpires will not change ends during a one-innings match. They will change ends only when both sides have had one completed innings. What constitutes a completed innings – not to be confused with the completion of the match – is discussed under Law 12.

UMPIRES CONSULTING

Not only is it permissible to ask your colleague for help, the Law obliges umpires to consult in a number of situations. These range from agreeing about the safety or otherwise of conditions to questions of fact. For example, it may be that the bowler's end umpire cannot see how the wicket was broken because the striker has remained squarely in front of it. His colleague can supply this information. Such consultation is not feebleness on the part of an umpire; it is essential to ensure that decisions are made only on the most accurate and complete evidence available.

SIGNALS TO SCORERS

These are fully explained in Law and illustrated on pages 45–8. Signals should be made as stated. They are the means by which the umpire informs the scorers of vital facts about the progress of play. They must be entirely clear, without personal idiosyncratic variations or flourishes.

The Law also lays down when signals are to be made. Initial signals made while the ball is in play are merely to inform the players. Apart from the signal for Out, all are to be repeated to the scorers by the bowler's end umpire when the ball is dead. The other signals are not made at all until the ball is dead. They are all to be made by the bowler's end umpire, with the one exception of Short run. This is not made until the ball is dead, but may be by either umpire and is accompanied by a call. It will depend on the end, or ends, at which short running occurred. If both umpires have seen a short run, they must confer to see whether two separate runs were short, or whether the short running was in one and the same run. To avoid all doubt for the scorers, the bowler's end umpire should give a final signal and tell them the actual number of runs scored. Separate acknowledgements for each signal by at least one scorer are essential if the umpire is to be satisfied that the information has been received in full.

CORRECTNESS OF SCORES

The widely used dictum that 'the umpires are responsible for the score' is a misinterpretation of the Law. Their responsibility is to <u>satisfy themselves</u>, throughout the game that the score is correct. The Law requires that they check with the scorers at intervals. In order for this to be viable, they need to know what the score should be. There are mechanical devices on the market by which runs can be recorded as they occur. A note of the score at the end of every over should then be made, and at the same time a check that this agrees with the scoreboard. The umpires must check with each other at the first opportunity if either of them thinks the scoreboard is incorrect. If they agree that it is not right, and it is not put right in the next over or so, the problem must be sorted out. As far as is possible, play should not be held up to do so. The fall of a wicket or a bowling change may provide the necessary pause in play.

Dead ball

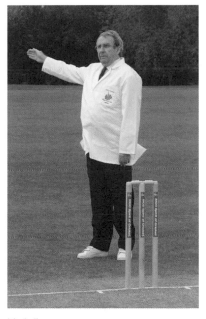

No ball

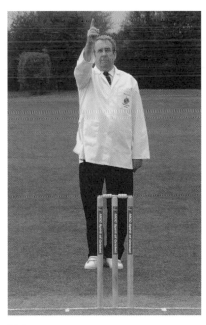

Out

Wide

Boundary 4 – moving one arm back and forth as shown above, ending with the arm across the chest

Boundary 6

Bye

Commencement of last hour. The wrist is well raised to be clearly visible to the scorers

Five penalty runs to the fielding side. The hand stays on the shoulder

Five penalty runs to the batting side. The patting movement must be exaggerated, to make it clear

Leg bye, made sideways on to the scorers, rather than facing them

New ball, held high for maximum visibility

Revoke last signal

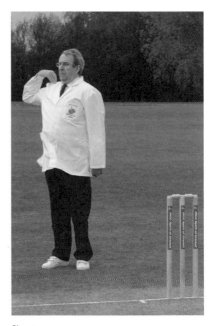

Short run

At the end of each innings and, of course, at the end of the match, the umpires and scorers must agree as to the final scores, wickets and, if relevant, overs. If there is any discrepancy, this must be sorted out between umpires and scorers. If agreement cannot be reached, it is the umpires who decide what is to be recorded.

Law 4   The scorers

I. APPOINTMENT OF SCORERS

Two scorers shall be appointed to record all runs scored, all wickets taken and, where appropriate, number of overs bowled.

2. CORRECTNESS OF SCORES

The scorers shall frequently check to ensure that their records agree. They shall agree with the umpires, at least at every interval, other than drinks intervals, and at the conclusion of the match, the runs scored, the wickets that have fallen and, where appropriate, the number of overs bowled. See Law 3.15 (Correctness of scores).

3. ACKNOWLEDGING SIGNALS

The scorers shall accept all instructions and signals given to them by umpires. They shall immediately acknowledge each separate signal.

There should be no difficulty in understanding this Law. As for umpires, two are to be appointed. They should constantly check with each other that their records agree. Just as it is important that umpires give them clear signals, it is important that they acknowledge those signals, each separately.

As well as the checks laid down for each interval (except drinks), they should take the earliest opportunity to clarify with the umpires any doubtful points. For example, that a batsman is dismissed will be obvious. The method of dismissal may not be.

Law 5   The ball

I. WEIGHT AND SIZE

The ball, when new, shall weigh not less than $5\frac{1}{2}$ ounces/155.9 g, nor more than $5\frac{3}{4}$ ounces/163 g, and shall measure not less than $8\frac{13}{16}$ in/22.4 cm, nor more than 9 in/22.9 cm in circumference.

2. APPROVAL AND CONTROL OF BALLS

(a) **All balls to be used in the match, having been approved by the umpires and captains, shall be in the possession of the umpires before the toss and shall remain under their control throughout the match.**

(b) **The umpire shall take possession of the ball in use at the fall of each wicket, at the start of any interval and at any interruption of play.**

3. NEW BALL

Unless an agreement to the contrary has been made before the match, either captain may demand a new ball at the start of each innings.

4. NEW BALL IN MATCH OF MORE THAN ONE DAY'S DURATION

In a match of more than one day's duration, the captain of the fielding side may demand a new ball after the prescribed number of overs has been bowled with the old one. The Governing Body for cricket in the country concerned shall decide the number of overs applicable in that country, which shall not be less than 75 overs.

The umpire shall inform the other umpire and indicate to the batsmen and the scorers whenever a new ball is taken into play.

5. BALL LOST OR BECOMING UNFIT FOR PLAY

If, during play, the ball cannot be found or recovered or the umpires agree that it has become unfit for play through normal use, the umpires shall replace it with a ball which has had wear comparable with that which the previous ball had received before the need for its replacement. When the ball is replaced the umpire shall inform the batsmen and the fielding captain.

6. SPECIFICATIONS

The specifications as described in 1 above shall apply to men's cricket only. The following specifications will apply to

    (i) **Women's cricket**
       Weight: from $4^{15}/_{16}$ ounces/140 g to $5^5/_{16}$ ounces/151 g
       Circumference: from $8^1/_4$ in/21.0 cm to $8^7/_8$ in/22.5 cm

    (ii) **Junior cricket – Under 13**
       Weight: from $4^{11}/_{16}$ ounces/133 g to $5^1/_{16}$ ounces/144 g
       Circumference: from $8^1/_{16}$ in/20.5 cm to $8^{11}/_{16}$ in/22.0 cm

There are two aspects to this Law – the measurements to which balls must conform and responsibility for their use during the match.

Section 1, together with Section 6, lays down the specifications. At higher level matches, scales in the changing room and ball gauges are often used to check the weight and size of balls. Gauges consist of two rings. One prevents too large a ball from passing through; the other will not prevent one that is too small from going through. At lower levels, umpires without such devices may have to trust the manufacturers to produce balls conforming to Law. Fortunately, this is usually the case with reputable manufacturers.

APPROVAL AND CONTROL

At the pre-match conference, it must first be agreed how many balls are to be used. It is normal in a one-day match for there to be a new ball for each side's innings. This is often laid down in regulations for the match but is otherwise not obligatory. It may be agreed that the same ball will be used in both innings. Unless there is such an agreement, however, if a captain requests a new ball at the start of an innings, the other captain has no power to prevent this. Section 4 lays down regulations for taking new balls into use in matches of more than one day. Few umpires will need to apply these. Umpires, captains and scorers must all be aware how many balls are to be used and, if relevant, at what point in the match a new one may be introduced.

The umpires must check, as far as is within their power, that the balls to be used are within the Law. The captains must agree to their being used. Most importantly, the umpires must then take possession of these balls. Ideally, there should also be a supply of used balls, in case the ball in use has to be replaced at any time. These should also be agreed by umpires and captains and kept by the umpires.

During play, the umpire must take possession of the ball at the fall of every wicket, at every interval or interruption. It should be the umpire who will be at the end from which the next delivery is to be made. These should not be the only occasions when an umpire looks at the ball. Law 42.3 instructs that they should make frequent and irregular inspections of the ball. The fact that irregular inspections are specified should help to deter players from tampering with the ball. Frequent inspections mean that umpires will know how much wear a ball has received if it has to be replaced with one of similar wear.

REPLACING THE BALL IN USE

A ball could be lost if, for example, there is dense undergrowth surrounding the ground. Similarly, an example of its becoming irrecoverable is its getting stuck in the high branches of a tree. It can become unfit for play if it loses its shape, or some mishap damages the seam or the surface. It will be the umpires jointly who decide, independently of the players, that it is unfit for play. The umpires will together choose, from those available, a ball as near as possible to the original one before it was lost or became unfit. If, however, the lost or unfit ball is wet, they will replace it with a dry one of otherwise similar wear. Merely changing the ball is not the only action required if the umpires consider that the ball has been deliberately damaged. That is dealt with under Law 42.3.

When a ball is changed, the fielding captain and batsmen should be informed.

FIELD TECHNIQUE

Each umpire should carry a used spare ball on the field. If there are two that have received different wear, it is more likely to be possible to match the condition of the ball in use if it has to be replaced. It will certainly save time if a ball can be replaced without the umpires having to go off the field.

In matches of more than one day, in which a new ball is to be taken into use at some point, it will be prudent for one umpire to take a new ball on to the field at the start of a session in which the new ball becomes due.

Both umpires should also carry with them a cloth for drying in case the ball should get wet.

Law 6 The bat

1. THE BAT

The bat consists of two parts, a handle and a blade.

2. MEASUREMENTS

All provisions in sections 3 to 6 below are subject to the measurements and restrictions stated in Appendix E.

3. THE HANDLE

(a) **One end of the handle is inserted into a recess in the blade as a means of joining the handle and the blade. The part of the handle that is then wholly outside the blade is defined to be the upper portion of the handle. It is a straight shaft for holding the bat. The remainder of the handle is its lower portion used purely for joining the blade and the handle together. It is not part of the blade but, solely in interpreting 5 and 6 below, references to the blade shall be considered to extend also to the lower portion of the handle where relevant.**

(b) **The handle is to be made principally of cane and/or wood, glued where necessary and bound with twine along the upper portion.**

(c) **Providing 7 below is not contravened, the upper portion may be covered with materials solely to provide a surface suitable for gripping. Such covering is an addition and is not part of the bat. Note, however, 8 below.**

(d) **Notwithstanding 4(c) and 5 below, both the twine binding and the covering grip may extend beyond the junction of the upper and lower portions, to cover part of the shoulders as defined in Appendix E.**

4. THE BLADE

(a) **The blade comprises the whole of the bat apart from the handle as defined above. The blade has a face, a back, a toe, sides and shoulders. See Appendix E.**

(b) The blade shall consist solely of wood.

(c) No material may be placed on or inserted into either the blade or the lower portion of the handle other than as permitted in 3(d) above and 5 and 6 below, together with the minimal adhesives or adhesive tape used solely for fixing these items, or for fixing the handle to the blade.

5. COVERING THE BLADE

All bats may have commercial identifications on the blade. Type A and Type B bats may have no other covering on the blade except as permitted in 6 below. Type C bats may have a cloth covering on the blade. This may be treated as specified in 6 below.

Such covering is additional to the blade and is not part of the bat. Note, however, 8 below.

6. PROTECTION AND REPAIR

Providing neither 4 above nor 7 below is contravened,

(a) solely for the purposes of
> either   (i)   protection from surface damage to the face, sides and shoulders of the blade
> or (ii)   repair to the blade after damage

material that is not rigid, either at the time of its application to the blade or subsequently, may be placed on these surfaces. Any such material shall not extend over any part of the back of the blade except in the case of (ii) above and then only when it is applied as a continuous wrapping covering the damaged area.

(b) solid material may be inserted into the blade for repair after damage other than surface damage. Additionally, for protection from damage, for Types B and C, material may be inserted at the toe and/or along the sides, parallel to the face of the blade.
The only material permitted for any insertion is wood with minimal essential adhesives.

(c) to prevent damage to the toe, material may be placed on that part of the blade but shall not extend over any part of the face, back or sides of the blade.

(d) the surface of the blade may be treated with non-solid materials to improve resistance to moisture penetration and/or mask natural blemishes in the appearance of the wood. Save for the purpose of giving a homogeneous appearance by masking natural blemishes, such treatment must not materially alter the colour of the blade.

Any materials referred to in (a), (b), (c) or (d) above are additional to the blade and not part of the bat. Note, however, 8 below.

7. DAMAGE TO THE BALL

(a) For any part of the bat, covered or uncovered, the hardness of the constituent materials and the surface texture thereof shall not be such that either or both could cause unacceptable damage to the ball.

(b) Any material placed on any part of the bat, for whatever purpose, shall similarly not be such that it could cause unacceptable damage to the ball.

(c) For the purposes of this Law, unacceptable damage is deterioration greater than normal wear and tear caused by the ball striking the uncovered wooden surface of the blade.

8. CONTACT WITH THE BALL

In these Laws,

(a) reference to the bat shall imply that the bat is held in the batsman's hand or a glove worn on his hand, unless stated otherwise.

(b) contact between the ball and

either   (i)   the bat itself

   or (ii)   the batsman's hand holding the bat

   or (iii) any part of a glove worn on the batsman's hand holding the bat

   or (iv) any additional materials permitted under 3, 5 or 6 above

shall be regarded as the ball striking or touching the bat or being struck by the bat.

In 2008, a major revision of this Law introduced very detailed specifications to which bats must conform, from how far the twine binding on the handle can extend to the microscopic thickness allowed for manufacturers' identification stickers. It is clearly impractical for the umpire on the field to check all these complex details. It is the primary responsibility of manufacturers to see that bats comply with the Law. Section 6 of Law 3, however, stipulates that umpires should check externally visible features of bats.

LENGTH AND WIDTH

A bat more than 38 inches long is rarely, if ever, found. There have been in recent years, however, bats more than 4¼ inches wide, even without any binding. A bat should be measured if either umpire suspects it may be too wide, but there is certainly no need to measure every bat brought to the crease. Gauges for checking the width of a bat are available. Otherwise, some simpler measuring device – such as a tape measure – though not absolutely accurate, will probably be sufficient at least to confirm that suspicion.

OTHER FEATURES

Umpires should also check, as far as practicable, if the blade is solely of wood and that any covering is not likely to damage the ball, by being abrasive or likely to crack.

TYPES OF BAT

In most non-professional cricket, any of the three types A, B and C will be allowed, though cloth-covered bats (Type C) may not be allowed at higher levels of the recreational game. Other bats will usually be restricted to special forms of cricket for young players. In any case a bat bought before the new regulations took effect can be used until the end of its natural life. Bat types should not therefore present umpires with a great problem.

BAT OR PERSON

In a number of Laws, whether the ball struck the striker's bat or his person is an important factor. Section 8, together with the definitions in Appendix D, makes it clear that a hand holding the bat is to be regarded as part of the bat. Moreover the whole of a glove worn on the hand equally counts as part of the bat. If a glove is held rather than worn, or the hand is not holding the bat, then either will become part of his person. To be holding the bat, the batsman has to have some part of a glove he is wearing, or his bare hand, in contact with the bat.

Law 7 The pitch

I. AREA OF PITCH

The pitch is a rectangular area of the ground 22 yards/20.12 m in length and 10 ft/3.05 m in width. It is bounded at either end by the bowling creases and on either side by imaginary lines, one each side of the imaginary line joining the centres of the two middle stumps, each parallel to it and 5 ft/1.52 m from it. See Laws 8.1 (Width and pitching) and 9.2 (The bowling crease).

2. FITNESS OF PITCH FOR PLAY

The umpires shall be the sole judges of the fitness of the pitch for play. See Laws 3.8 (Fitness for play) and 3.9 (Suspension of play in dangerous or unreasonable conditions).

3. SELECTION AND PREPARATION

Before the match, the Ground Authority shall be responsible for the selection and preparation of the pitch. During the match, the umpires shall control its use and maintenance.

4. CHANGING THE PITCH

The pitch shall not be changed during the match unless the umpires decide that it is dangerous or unreasonable for play to continue on it and then only with the consent of both captains.

5. NON-TURF PITCHES

In the event of a non-turf pitch being used, the artificial surface shall conform to the following measurements.
Length – a minimum of 58 ft/17.68 m
Width – a minimum of 6 ft/1.83 m
See Law 10.8 (Non-turf pitches).

Note that the area of ground defined in Law 7 is the pitch, not the wicket. That is the stumps and bails. In cricket jargon, 'wicket' is commonly used for the pitch and for the wicket. Umpires must be clear as to the difference between them. The wicket is a set of three wooden sticks with two bits of wood on top. The pitch is the closely specified piece of ground between the two wickets.

SELECTION, PREPARATION AND MAINTENANCE
Before the match, selection and preparation of the pitch is entirely a matter for the ground staff. Once the toss has been made, however, the umpires must control its use and maintenance. The ground staff will still carry out the mechanical tasks of mowing and rolling, but the umpires are to supervise that this is done within the Laws as set out in Law 10. Even though this responsibility does not pass to the umpires until the toss, they should nevertheless inspect the pitch well before the match is to start, to check both that it conforms to Law and that it is fit for play – that is, that it would not be unreasonable or dangerous for play to take place on it, as discussed under Law 3.

MEASUREMENTS
There is an excellent diagram in Appendix B, showing all the measurements and how they relate to the crease markings. The latter are the subject of Law 9. It will seldom be necessary for umpires to measure the length of the pitch. With experience, the umpire will develop the ability to make a good visual assessment. After a few matches in the season, markings on previously used pitches can be a help. If, however, it is thought that the length of the pitch may be incorrect, proper measurement should be made. Pacing it out is far too inaccurate to be of the slightest use.

Any errors should be corrected if possible. If it is not possible, both captains should be made fully aware of the situation.

CHANGING THE PITCH DURING A MATCH
This is not allowed, unless the umpires pronounce the one in use to be unfit – that is, unreasonable or dangerous, for play. Even then, the two captains must agree to

continuing the game on another pitch. It is unlikely that there will be another pitch properly prepared, although on some grounds there will be an artificial pitch which can be used.

If either or both captains decide that they do not wish to use another pitch, this would not be considered a refusal to play. The options then would be either that the match is abandoned or that it is decided to wait in the hope that conditions will improve sufficiently for play to restart on the original pitch.

Law 8 The wickets

1. WIDTH AND PITCHING

Two sets of wickets shall be pitched opposite and parallel to each other at a distance of 22 yards/20.12 m between the centres of the two middle stumps. Each set shall be 9 in/22.86 cm wide and shall consist of three wooden stumps with two wooden bails on top. See Appendix A.

2. SIZE OF STUMPS

The tops of the stumps shall be 28 in/71.1 cm above the playing surface and shall be dome shaped except for the bail grooves. The portion of a stump above the playing surface shall be cylindrical apart from the domed top, with circular section of diameter not less than 1 in/3.49 cm nor more than 1½ in/3.81 cm. See Appendix A.

3. THE BAILS

(a) The bails, when in position on top of the stumps,
   (i) shall not project more than ½ in/1.27 cm above them.
   (ii) shall fit between the stumps without forcing them out of the vertical.
(b) Each bail shall conform to the following specifications. See Appendix A.

Overall length	4⁵⁄₁₆ in/10.95 cm
Length of barrel	2⅛ in /5.40 cm
Longer spigot	1 in/3.49 cm
Shorter spigot	¹³⁄₁₆ in/2.06 cm

4. JUNIOR CRICKET

In junior cricket, the same definitions of the wickets shall apply subject to the following measurements being used.

Width	8 in/20.32 cm
Pitched for under 13	21 yards/19.20 m
Pitched for under 11	20 yards/18.29 m
Pitched for under 9	18 yards/16.46 m
Height above playing surface	27 in/68.58 cm

Each stump

Diameter	not less than 1¼ in/3.18 cm
	nor more than 1⅜ in/3.49 cm

Each bail

Overall	3¹³⁄₁₆ in/9.68 cm
Barrel	1¹³⁄₁₆ in/4.60 cm
Longer spigot	1¼ in/3.18 cm
Shorter spigot	¾ in/1.91 cm

5. DISPENSING WITH BAILS

The umpires may agree to dispense with the use of bails, if necessary. If they so agree then no bails shall be used at either end. The use of bails shall be resumed as soon as conditions permit. See Law 28.4 (Dispensing with bails).

This Law defines the shape and size of the stumps and of the bails, as well as the dimensions of the wicket as a whole. These are all clearly illustrated in Appendix A. Umpires are not expected to go out with callipers and measuring tapes, but should not hesitate to check any items which appear not to conform to Law.

Matters that umpires should always check are:

- that the wickets are aligned end to end and parallel to each other
- that stumps are of the correct shape and are correctly sited, with the back edge of the marking through the centres of the stumps
- that the stumps are driven firmly into the ground, and are equally spaced, upright and parallel to each other. Watering of the stump holes will give extra firmness if the ground is crumbling or better grip if the ground is hard
- that the bails fit into the grooves and do not force the tops of the stumps apart
- that, if possible, the bails at each end are a matching pair
- that the ball will not pass between the stumps.

Both umpires should carry a spare bail in case one breaks. Some will carry a spare pair, to ensure having a matching pair if replacement is necessary.

DISPENSING WITH BAILS

If the bails are continually being blown off during play, not only is this an irritant, unfairly breaking concentration for both batsmen and fielders, but it slows up play. Heavy bails made of *lignum vitae* can be purchased. If they are available, they are often sufficient to cure the problem, if it is caused by a strong wind. It is not always that the difficulty is caused by a high wind. It may be the result of poor bail grooves.

Whatever the cause of the problem, if heavy bails do not solve it, the umpires should agree to dispense with bails. This decision, which is for the umpires alone to make, should not be taken lightly. It creates extra responsibility for the umpires in judging whether or not the wicket has been put down. That problem is discussed in Law 28. Here it should be noted that bails should be dispensed with at both ends, if at all. If conditions improve, bails should be replaced at both ends as soon as possible.

Law 9   The bowling, popping and return creases

1. THE CREASES

A bowling crease, a popping crease and two return creases shall be marked in white, as set out in 2, 3 and 4 below, at each end of the pitch. See Appendix B.

2. THE BOWLING CREASE

The bowling crease, which is the back edge of the crease marking, shall be the line through the centres of the three stumps at that end. It shall be 8 ft 8 in/2.64 m in length, with the stumps in the centre.

3. THE POPPING CREASE

The popping crease, which is the back edge of the crease marking, shall be in front of and parallel to the bowling crease and shall be 4 ft/1.22 m from it. The popping crease shall be marked to a minimum of 6 ft/1.83 m on either side of the imaginary line joining the centres of the two middle stumps and shall be considered to be unlimited in length.

4. THE RETURN CREASES

The return creases, which are the inside edges of the crease markings, shall be at right angles to the popping crease at a distance of 4 ft 4 in/1.32 m either side of the imaginary line joining the centres of the two middle stumps. Each return crease shall be marked from the popping crease to a minimum of 8 ft/2.44 m behind it and shall be considered to be unlimited in length.

The umpires should always check the crease markings before the pre-match conference. Even experienced groundsmen have been known to make occasional errors, both in measurement and in alignment! As with the pitch itself and the wickets, umpires will, with experience, become better able to judge visually if the creases are not correct. The most frequently encountered errors are the return creases not being marked to their full 8 feet back from the popping crease and the wickets not being centred between the return creases. Any mistakes should be corrected if possible. If it is not possible then the captains must be made fully aware of the difficulty.

CREASES AND CREASE MARKINGS

The crease markings are the lines painted on the ground. The creases are the back or inside edges of those lines. They are clearly marked on the diagram in Appendix B. The Law makes a clear distinction between the two. The creases are the exact lines to be used in judgments under Law 24 (No ball) and Law 29 (Batsman out of his ground).

Although the Law stipulates that the lines must be white, it imposes no restrictions on the width of the markings. Whilst the bowling crease is to be 8 ft 8 in long, for the popping crease and the return creases the stated lengths are only the minimum that must be marked. They actually extend, respectively, to the boundary on either side and the boundary behind the wicket. This must not be forgotten by umpires judging the position of the feet in Law 24.

The bowling crease no longer has any significance for bowling. Its importance is in relation to the wicket. The centres of the stumps are to be on the crease, not in the middle of the crease marking.

RE-MARKING OF CREASES

Sections of the popping crease are often quickly obliterated by the bowler's front foot. It is, however, essential that there is a clear line for the umpire to judge the position of the bowler's front foot for No balls. Although in Law 10 it will be seen that creases may be re-marked when either umpire considers it necessary, umpires should take any possible remedial action to restore the popping crease temporarily, until an opportunity arises for the ground staff to repaint them fully, without holding up play unduly. Scoring a line with the edge of a boot or a bail is effective but may have to be done for every delivery.

Using a bail for a temporary repair to the popping crease – vital to the judgment of No balls

Law 10   Preparation and maintenance of the playing area

1. ROLLING

The pitch shall not be rolled during the match except as permitted in (a) and (b) below.

(a) **Frequency and duration of rolling**

During the match the pitch may be rolled at the request of the captain of the batting side, for a period of not more than 7 minutes, before the start of each innings, other than the first innings of the match, and before the start of each subsequent day's play. See (d) below.

(b) **Rolling after a delayed start**

In addition to the rolling permitted above, if, after the toss and before the first innings of the match, the start is delayed, the captain of the batting side may request that the pitch be rolled for not more than 7 minutes. However, if the umpires together agree that the delay has had no significant effect on the state of the pitch, they shall refuse such request for rolling of the pitch.

(c) **Choice of rollers**

If there is more than one roller available the captain of the batting side shall choose which one is to be used.

(d) **Timing of permitted rolling**

The rolling permitted (maximum 7 minutes) before play begins on any day shall be started not more than 30 minutes before the time scheduled or rescheduled for play to begin. The captain of the batting side may, however, delay the start of such rolling until not less than 10 minutes before the time scheduled or rescheduled for play to begin, should he so wish.

(e) **Insufficient time to complete rolling**

If, when a captain declares an innings closed, or forfeits an innings, or enforces the follow-on, there is insufficient time for the pitch to be rolled for 7 minutes, or if there is insufficient time for any other reason, the batting captain shall nevertheless be permitted to exercise his option to have such rolling. The time by which the start of the innings is delayed on that account shall be taken out of normal playing time.

2. CLEARING DEBRIS FROM THE PITCH

(a) **The pitch shall be cleared of any debris**

(i) before the start of each day's play. This shall be after the completion of mowing and before any rolling, not earlier than 30 minutes nor later than 10 minutes before the time or any rescheduled time for start of play.

(ii) between innings. This shall precede rolling if any is to take place.

(iii) at all intervals for meals.

(b) The clearance of debris in (a) above shall be done by sweeping, except where the umpires consider that this may be detrimental to the surface of the pitch. In this case the debris must be cleared from that area by hand, without sweeping.

(c) In addition to (a) above, debris may be cleared from the pitch by hand, without sweeping, before mowing and whenever either umpire considers it necessary.

3. MOWING

(a) Responsibility for mowing
All mowings which are carried out before the match shall be the sole responsibility of the Ground Authority.
All subsequent mowings shall be carried out under the supervision of the umpires.

(b) The pitch and outfield
In order that throughout the match the ground conditions should be as nearly the same for both sides as possible,
(i) the pitch
(ii) the outfield
shall be mown on each day of the match on which play is expected to take place, if ground and weather conditions permit.
If, for reasons other than conditions of ground or weather, complete mowing of the outfield is not possible, the Ground Authority shall notify the captains and umpires of the procedure to be adopted for such mowing during the match.

(c) Timing of mowing
(i) Mowing of the pitch on any day shall be completed not later than 30 minutes before the time scheduled or rescheduled for play to begin on that day, before any sweeping prior to rolling. If necessary, debris may be removed from the pitch before mowing, by hand, without sweeping. See 2(c) above.
(ii) Mowing of the outfield on any day shall be completed not later than 15 minutes before the time scheduled or rescheduled for play to begin on that day.

4. WATERING THE PITCH

The pitch shall not be watered during the match.

5. RE-MARKING CREASES

Creases shall be re-marked whenever either umpire considers it necessary.

6. MAINTENANCE OF FOOTHOLES

The umpires shall ensure that the holes made by the bowler and batsmen are cleaned out and dried whenever necessary to facilitate play.

In matches of more than one day's duration, the umpires shall allow, if necessary, the re-turfing of footholes made by the bowler in his delivery stride, or the use of quick-setting fillings for the same purpose.

7. SECURING OF FOOTHOLDS AND MAINTENANCE OF PITCH

During play, umpires shall allow the players to secure their footholds by the use of sawdust provided that no damage to the pitch is caused and that Law 42 (Fair and unfair play) is not contravened.

8. NON-TURF PITCHES

Wherever appropriate, the provisions set out in 1 to 7 above shall apply.

Much of this Law will apply only in higher grade matches, where play extends to more than one day. However, even at fairly humble levels of the game, rolling of the pitch is often available and, in addition to the pre-match rolling by the ground staff, will take place between innings.

RESPONSIBILITY OF UMPIRES

Until the toss, decisions about mowing, sweeping, watering and covering the pitch are entirely the responsibility of the Ground Authority – whoever that may be. This does not mean that the umpires have no interest until the toss. Not only do they have a responsibility to check that the creases and wickets are in accordance with Law but they are also the sole judges of the fitness of the pitch for play. It is not necessary for the toss to have taken place for them to decide that it would be unreasonable or dangerous for play to take place on it and so to forbid play to start.

Once the toss has taken place, all the activities listed above, although still carried out by the Ground Authority, are controlled by the umpires. The Law lays down both the restrictions imposed and what is permitted. This is the ideal to be aimed at. In many cases, in a one-day game there will be neither the equipment nor the personnel to achieve these conditions. Umpires must see that what is possible does take place and that no action of pitch or ground maintenance contravenes the Law.

The chart on page 65 summarises the points of the Law.

The captain of the side winning the toss will have based his decision whether to bat or to field partly on his estimation of the pitch. This is the reason that no rolling is allowed before the first innings of the match, unless there is a delay after the toss. If there is such a delay and the captain of the side due to bat then requests that the pitch be rolled, the umpires must decide together what effect that delay has had on the state of the pitch. If there has been a sudden heavy downpour before the call of Play, this will almost certainly change its condition and rolling could be allowed. If, however, one of the opening batsmen ricks his ankle on the way to the crease, there would be a short delay in which nothing significant happens to the pitch. In this case, the umpires would refuse the request for rolling. It is to be noted that the concession of allowing the batting captain to request rolling after the toss applies only if the delay occurs between the toss and the call of Play.

DAMAGE TO THE PITCH

Since the players cannot avoid walking or running on the pitch in appropriate circumstances, some damage is unavoidable, especially in damp conditions when the ground is soft. Specific, or even deliberate, damage is dealt with in Law 42. Here, umpires should note their responsibility for minimising this unavoidable damage in several ways under this Law.

- The use of sawdust will help bowlers and batsmen to avoid the sliding which could impair their performance. It will also reduce scarring of the ground.
- The batsmen may legitimately prod down divots on which the ball could land but must not be allowed to bang the bat on the ground with undue force.
- If, in dry conditions, the surface is breaking up, the umpires will not allow sweeping to worsen the condition.
- The bowler's footholes should be cleaned out and dried as far as possible. In matches of more than one day's duration, the ground staff will be able to fill them overnight with quick-setting fillings, or even turf.

ROLLING CAUSING DELAY

A prime right of the batting captain is to have the pitch rolled before the start of his side's innings and to choose which roller, if there is a choice. If he opts to have rolling, this must be preceded by clearing debris from the pitch, normally by sweeping. The rolling will normally be followed by re-marking creases. It is extremely rare for a captain to opt for less than the maximum 7 minutes rolling. Hence it is a very tight schedule to bring on the equipment and to do all this in the 10 minutes between innings. Often the players will come on to the field, and the preliminaries of giving guard, etc. will be done, while the roller is being driven off. Play will of course not start until it is off the field! It follows that, although there is just time if a prompt start is made, if there is any delay at all there may not be sufficient time to complete this routine. The Law gives a captain the right to declare at any time during his side's innings when the ball is dead, or to forfeit an innings before it starts – possibly during the 10 minutes. He may also enforce a follow-on and take a few minutes to decide to do so. If any such circumstance means that there is insufficient time for the rolling to be completed, the umpires must accept the situation. If the rolling has to continue past the official time for resumption of play, then no extra time is added on elsewhere. The 3 or 4 minutes delay is simply lost playing time. This provision is not to be taken as licence for slowness in doing the rolling in normal circumstances. The same will apply if a decision to enforce a follow-on is taken. See Law 13.

PREPARATION AND MAINTENANCE OF THE PITCH

	First day	Subsequent days	Before time for start of play		
			Start		Finish
			Not earlier than	Not later than	Not later than
Mowing					
Outfield		each morning (if possible)			15 minutes
Pitch		each morning			30 minutes

Rolling the pitch If batting captain requests it. Maximum of 7 minutes for each occasion

	First day	Subsequent days	Not earlier than	Not later than	
	not before first innings	each morning	30 minutes	10 minutes †	
	between toss and start of play, if start delayed*				
	before subsequent innings	between innings			

Sweeping may be used to clear debris as below, **but NOT before mowing** and **NOT if detrimental to surface of pitch**

Clearing debris from the pitch. No sweeping before mowing

	First day	Subsequent days	Not earlier than	Not later than	
	before start of play	before start of play	30 minutes	10 minutes †	
	between innings, before rolling	between innings, before rolling			
	at all intervals	at all intervals			
		Additionally, **by hand**, before mowing and whenever umpires consider necessary			

Re-marking creases   Whenever either umpire considers necessary

Watering the pitch   AT NO TIME DURING THE MATCH

---

* but **not** if umpires consider delay has had no significant effect

† Batting captain can *request* that start of rolling be delayed until 10 minutes before start time

65

MOWING NOT POSSIBLE

The Law makes provision for difficulties in mowing the outfield every day, such as the breakdown of the machinery required. The umpires and captains must know what alternative arrangements – perhaps for partial mowing – have been made. The umpires should check that this information is forthcoming.

RE-MARKING CREASES

Creases are important for many judgments that the umpires have to make. It is therefore essential that the markings are clear. There is no restriction in Law on when they may be re-marked. It is to be done whenever either umpire considers it necessary. It is likely that both sets of creases will need re-marking at the same time, but the Law does not insist on this.

They should, if possible, be re-marked between innings. There are other opportunities when re-marking can be done without delaying the progress of play. If necessary an umpire can, as explained in Law 9, do a makeshift marking himself, until such an opportunity arises.

The chart summarises the main points. It does not include the initial preparation by the ground staff, except for the time by which rolling and mowing must finish before the match.

NON-TURF PITCHES

Clearly strictures about mowing will not apply, but re-marking of creases and clearing of debris might well be relevant. If the undersurface is hard earth, rather than concrete, even rolling might be appropriate. Umpires must apply this Law as befits the circumstances.

They should also check whether there are any special regulations arising out of the use of a non-turf pitch. One possible example is that Wides may be defined in terms of not pitching on the artificial surface.

Law 11   Covering the pitch

1. BEFORE THE MATCH

The use of covers before the match is the responsibility of the Ground Authority and may include full covering if required.

However, the Ground Authority shall grant suitable facility to the captains to inspect the pitch before the nomination of their players and to the umpires to discharge their duties as laid down in Laws 3 (The umpires), 7 (The pitch), 8 (The wickets), 9 (The bowling, popping and return creases) and 10 (Preparation and maintenance of the playing area).

2. DURING THE MATCH

The pitch shall not be completely covered during the match unless provided otherwise by regulations or by agreement before the toss.

3. COVERING THE BOWLERS' RUN UPS

Whenever possible, the bowlers' run ups shall be covered in inclement weather, in order to keep them dry. Unless there is agreement for full covering under 2 above the covers so used shall not extend further than 5 ft/1.52 m in front of each popping crease.

4. REMOVAL OF COVERS

(a) If after the toss the pitch is covered overnight, the covers shall be removed in the morning at the earliest possible moment on each day that play is expected to take place.

(b) If covers are used during the day as protection from inclement weather, or if inclement weather delays the removal of overnight covers, they shall be removed promptly as soon as conditions allow.

AGREEMENT TO THE USE OF COVERS

Once a rarity in club cricket, an increasing number of grounds can now offer some form of covering for the pitch. Umpires will discover, in their general inspection tour on arrival, what covers, if any, there are. This Law lays down both procedures and priorities for their use.

What covering is done before the match is, as with all pitch preparation, a matter for the Ground Authority. The only restriction on the extent and timing of its use is that players and umpires must be granted access before the toss, to inspect the pitch. It would clearly be inappropriate to insist on this unless the weather was fine. Once the toss has taken place, the umpires are responsible for overseeing covering throughout the match.

Although in Law, covering of the whole pitch during the match is not allowed, it may be permitted under Special Regulations for the competition. Even without a Special Regulation, captains and umpires may agree to have full covering, if it is available. There is no obligation to make such an agreement. It is essential that umpires clarify the position at the pre-match conference.

COVERING BOWLERS' RUN UPS

If any covers are available, then they must be used firstly to protect the bowlers' run ups. Even at Test Match grounds, the covers may not be long enough for the complete run up of some bowlers. At club grounds they will certainly fall very far short! The vital part that needs covering is the last few strides before delivery, in the vicinity of the bowling and popping creases. Unless there is agreement for complete covering, the covers are permitted to extend only as far as 5 feet (1.52 m) in front of the popping crease. This extension may have to fall short of the maximum in order to get a decent amount of the pre-delivery run up covered. Umpires must judge sensibly how to deploy the coverage available. There is no restriction on how far behind the wicket covers may extend.

REMOVAL OF COVERS

To keep loss of playing time to a minimum, covers should be removed as soon as it is fine enough for play to start after an interruption for rain.

In matches of more than one day, covers may well be used to protect the pitch from possible rain overnight. These, too, should be removed as early as practicable providing the weather is fine. 'Practicable' means at a time at which it is reasonable to expect ground staff to be available.

FIELD TECHNIQUE

If there is a sudden downpour, getting the covers on to the pitch quickly will be important for keeping the pitch as dry as possible, thus maximising the time for subsequent play. In their pre-match inspection, umpires should not only find out what covers are available, they also should ascertain how they are to be brought on to the pitch and by whom, so that everyone is ready to act promptly if need arises.

In deciding a time for resumption of play after an interruption for rain, umpires should allow time for removal of covers.

Law 12 Innings

1. NUMBER OF INNINGS

(a) **A match shall be one or two innings for each side according to agreement reached before the match.**

(b) **It may be agreed to limit any innings to a number of overs or to a period of time. If such an agreement is made then**

  (i) **in a one-innings match a similar agreement shall apply to both innings.**

  (ii) **in a two-innings match similar agreements shall apply to**

    either the first innings of each side

    or the second innings of each side

    or both innings of each side.

For both one-innings and two-innings matches, the agreement must also include criteria for determining the result when neither of Laws 21.1 (A Win – two-innings match) or 21.2 (A Win – one-innings match) applies.

2. ALTERNATE INNINGS

In a two-innings match each side shall take their innings alternately except in the cases provided for in Law 13 (The follow-on) or in Law 14.2 (Forfeiture of an innings).

3. COMPLETED INNINGS

A side's innings is to be considered as completed if
- (a) the side is all out
- or (b) at the fall of a wicket or the retirement of a batsman, further balls remain to be bowled but no further batsman is available to come in
- or (c) the captain declares the innings closed
- or (d) the captain forfeits the innings
- or (e) in the case of an agreement under 1(b) above,
    - either (i) the prescribed number of overs has been bowled
        - or (ii) the prescribed time has expired

as appropriate.

4. THE TOSS

The captains shall toss for the choice of innings, on the field of play and in the presence of one or both of the umpires, not earlier than 30 minutes, nor later than 15 minutes before the scheduled or any rescheduled time for the match to start. Note, however, the provisions of Law 1.3 (Captain).

5. DECISION TO BE NOTIFIED

As soon as the toss is completed, the captain of the side winning the toss shall notify the opposing captain and the umpires of his decision to bat or to field. Once notified, the decision cannot be changed.

NUMBER AND LIMITATION OF INNINGS

Whether a match is played over one or two innings for each side will normally be either determined by the Regulations governing the match, or will have been agreed well in advance of the start of the match. It is clearly essential that all concerned have this information. The Regulation or agreement may include a limitation on the time or the overs allowed for any, or all, of the innings. The Law stipulates that similar arrangements must apply to both sides.

The umpires must ensure, before the toss is made, that both captains and they themselves are aware of any limitations that have been laid down, or agreed, together with all the possible consequences. It may be, for example, that any overs or time not taken up by the side batting first will be added to the number of overs or time for the side batting second.

ALTERNATE INNINGS

If a match is of two innings for each side, the only two situations in which innings are not to alternate are those of a follow-on or a forfeiture. These are discussed in Laws 13 and 14 respectively.

COMPLETED INNINGS

The outcome of a match may depend on whether an innings is completed or not. There are other occasions when it is important to know if an innings has been completed. Section 3 sets out clearly the criteria for an innings to be considered completed. Apart from the side being all out, the situation of there being no further batsmen to come in, although further balls remain to be bowled, will occur if a batsman has retired at some point in the innings and either is unable to resume his innings, or is not permitted to do so by the opposing captain. The same would be true if the last batsman, having been injured earlier, was unable to come in at the fall of the 9th wicket.

THE TOSS

It is usual for the captains to make the toss for choice of innings on or near the pitch to be used. The Law merely requires that it be on the field of play. It is, however, necessary for one of the umpires to be present at the toss, to see that it is fairly conducted. It is not necessary, though not forbidden, for both umpires to be present.

The Law lays down time limitations for the toss – not earlier than 30 minutes, nor later than 15 minutes before the time set for play to start. Umpires must insist that the toss is made within these time limits so as to enable a prompt start for the match. If it has been decided that, for any reason, usually bad weather, it is necessary to defer the originally agreed time for start of play, then unless the toss has already taken place, the timings will apply to the new start time.

If either captain is not available when the toss is to be made, the umpires must call upon that side to appoint a deputy to do this. This deputy must be a nominated player.

The captain who wins the toss will, virtually immediately, have to declare to the other captain and the umpire his choice of batting first or fielding first. Once he has stated his choice, there are no circumstances in which it can be changed.

FIELD TECHNIQUE

The same points of technique apply to the toss as to the nomination of teams, as discussed under Law 1. If the umpires have taken early steps to ensure the nomination is done in time, then, if required, a deputy will also be ready to make the toss. It may well be necessary to remind captains that the time for the toss is approaching. In the case of a delayed start, it may also be necessary to tell the captains that a decision to bat or to field cannot be changed, even if it was made some hours before the rescheduled start time.

Law 13 The follow-on

1. LEAD ON FIRST INNINGS

(a) **In a two-innings match of 5 days or more, the side which bats first and leads by at least 200 runs shall have the option of requiring the other side to follow their innings.**

(b) **The same option shall be available in two-innings matches of shorter duration with the minimum leads as follows.**
   (i) **150 runs in a match of 3 or 4 days;**
   (ii) **100 runs in a 2-day match;**
   (iii) **75 runs in a 1-day match.**

2. NOTIFICATION

A captain shall notify the opposing captain and the umpires of his intention to take up this option. Law 10.1(e) (Insufficient time to complete rolling) shall apply.

3. FIRST DAY'S PLAY LOST

If no play takes place on the first day of a match of more than one day's duration, 1 above shall apply in accordance with the number of days remaining from the actual start of the match. The day on which play first commences shall count as a whole day for this purpose, irrespective of the time at which play starts.

Play will have taken place as soon as, after the call of Play, the first over has started. See Law 22.2 (Start of an over).

ENFORCING THE FOLLOW-ON

A follow-on can arise only in matches of two innings for each side. It occurs when each side has completed one innings. It requires the side batting first to have scored more runs than the side batting second, by at least the number stated in Section 1. In this situation, the captain of the side batting first has the power to ask the opposing side to 'follow their innings' – that is to bat again immediately. He is not obliged to use this power. If he does use it, the Law stipulates that he must notify the opposing captain and the umpires of his intention to do so. Usually, all will be aware that the difference in scores is large enough to make a follow-on possible. Hence it will be sensible for him to notify his intention whether that is to enforce the follow-on, or not to do so.

In the case of a follow-on, the interval between innings should be 10 minutes as normal, but sometimes, when the captain notifies his decision, there may be insufficient time to complete rolling. This situation has been discussed under Law 10 Section 1(e).

The scorers will need to be informed as to whether there is to be a follow-on or not.

CHANGING THE DURATION OF THE MATCH

The lead required for a follow-on to be possible depends on the number of days the match is to last. This number may be affected by loss of playing time.

The moment that play is deemed to have taken place will determine the duration of the match. Play will have taken place as soon as the bowler starts his run up or, if he has no run up, his bowling action for the first delivery of the match. The number of days then remaining, counting the starting day as a whole day, whenever during the day play actually starts, is that to be taken for calculating the lead required for a follow-on. This number will not alter, even if subsequently more whole days are lost. A 5-day match in which play first takes place after lunch on the third day counts as a 3-day match, even if the fourth day is washed out. If, according to the definition above, play takes place on the first day, the match will be considered as remaining at its originally scheduled length, however many days' play are actually achieved.

Law 14   Declaration and forfeiture

1. TIME OF DECLARATION

The captain of the side batting may declare an innings closed, when the ball is dead, at any time during the innings.

2. FORFEITURE OF AN INNINGS

A captain may forfeit either of his side's innings at any time before the commencement of that innings. A forfeited innings shall be considered to be a completed innings.

3. NOTIFICATION

A captain shall notify the opposing captain and the umpires of his decision to declare or to forfeit an innings. Law 10.1(e) (Insufficient time to complete rolling) shall apply.

DECLARATION

The captain of the batting side may declare his side's innings closed at any time during the innings, whether play is in progress or not. If play is in progress, the ball must be dead. Following a declaration, the opposing captain is entitled to have the pitch rolled for a maximum of 7 minutes. If a declaration is made so late as to prevent completion of rolling before the time for the next innings to start, the umpires must still allow the rolling, if requested, as already discussed under Section 1(e) of Law 10.

Even if rolling is not requested, it may not be possible to start the next innings on time, as time will have to be taken for players to put on the appropriate equipment.

There are competitions in which Special Regulations may set restrictions on declaring, or even forbid it in some circumstances.

FORFEITURE

In a two-innings match either captain may forfeit – that is, forgo – either of his side's innings. It may be that time has been lost to rain and both captains agree to forgo one innings, thereby effectively reducing the game to a one-innings match. The captain of the side batting first may decide to risk forgoing his second innings because his side have not achieved sufficient lead to enforce a follow-on but he believes that it may be possible to dismiss his opponents for fewer runs than the lead that has been established.

The same conditions apply to a forfeiture as to a declaration. The side next to bat has the right to have the pitch rolled for a maximum of 7 minutes. This rolling must be allowed if requested, even if playing time is lost.

Both an innings declared closed and a forfeited innings are to be regarded as completed innings.

FIELD TECHNIQUE

When a captain declares an innings closed, or forfeits an innings, umpires should ensure that the opposing captain and the scorers are informed. It is essential that the groundsman is told as soon as possible, so that there is minimum delay in rolling the pitch, if the captain requests this, and re-marking the creases. As already explained, some loss of playing time may be inevitable in these circumstances. Every effort must be made to start the new innings as soon as possible to reduce this loss to a minimum.

Law 15   Intervals

1. AN INTERVAL

The following shall be classed as intervals.
- (i) **The period between close of play on one day and the start of the next day's play.**
- (ii) **Intervals between innings.**
- (iii) **Intervals for meals.**
- (iv) **Intervals for drinks.**
- (v) **Any other agreed interval.**

All these intervals shall be considered as scheduled breaks for the purposes of Law 2.5 (Fielder absent or leaving the field).

2. AGREEMENT OF INTERVALS

(a) Before the toss
    (i) the hours of play shall be established.
    (ii) except as in (b) below, the timing and duration of intervals for meals shall be agreed.
    (iii) the timing and duration of any other interval under 1(v) above shall be agreed.

(b) In a one-day match no specific time need be agreed for the tea interval. It may be agreed instead to take this interval between innings.

(c) Intervals for drinks may not be taken during the last hour of the match, as defined in Law 16.6 (Last hour of match – number of overs). Subject to this limitation, the captains and umpires shall agree the times for such intervals, if any, before the toss and on each subsequent day not later than 10 minutes before play is scheduled to start.

See also Law 3.3 (Agreement with captains).

3. DURATION OF INTERVALS

(a) An interval for lunch or tea shall be of the duration agreed under 2(a) above, taken from the call of Time before the interval until the call of Play on resumption after the interval.

(b) An interval between innings shall be 10 minutes from the close of an innings until the call of Play for the start of the next innings, except as in 4, 6 and 7 below.

4. NO ALLOWANCE FOR INTERVAL BETWEEN INNINGS

In addition to the provisions of 6 and 7 below,

(a) if an innings ends when 10 minutes or less remains before the time agreed for close of play on any day, there shall be no further play on that day. No change shall be made to the time for the start of play on the following day on account of the 10-minute interval between innings.

(b) if a captain declares an innings closed during an interruption in play of more than 10 minutes duration, no adjustment shall be made to the time for resumption of play on account of the 10-minute interval between innings, which shall be considered as included in the interruption. Law 10.1(e) (Insufficient time to complete rolling) shall apply.

(c) if a captain declares an innings closed during any interval other than an interval for drinks, the interval shall be of the agreed duration and shall be considered to include the 10-minute interval between innings. Law 10.1(e) (Insufficient time to complete rolling) shall apply.

5. CHANGING AGREED TIMES OF INTERVALS

If, at any time during the match,
> either playing time is lost through adverse conditions of ground, weather or light or in exceptional circumstances,
> or the players have occasion to leave the field other than at a scheduled interval,

the time of the lunch interval or of the tea interval may be changed if the two umpires and both captains so agree, providing the requirements of 3 above and 6, 7, 8 and 9(c) below are not contravened.

6. CHANGING AGREED TIME FOR LUNCH INTERVAL

(a) If an innings ends when 10 minutes or less remains before the agreed time for lunch, the interval shall be taken immediately. It shall be of the agreed length and shall be considered to include the 10-minute interval between innings.

(b) If because of adverse conditions of ground, weather or light, or in exceptional circumstances, a stoppage occurs when 10 minutes or less remains before the agreed time for lunch, then, notwithstanding 5 above, the interval shall be taken immediately. It shall be of the agreed length. Play shall resume at the end of this interval or as soon after as conditions permit.

(c) If the players have occasion to leave the field for any reason when more than 10 minutes remains before the agreed time for lunch then, unless the umpires and captains together agree to alter it, lunch will be taken at the agreed time.

7. CHANGING AGREED TIME FOR TEA INTERVAL

(a) (i) If an innings ends when 30 minutes or less remains before the agreed time for tea, the interval shall be taken immediately. It shall be of the agreed length and shall be considered to include the 10-minute interval between innings.

(ii) If, when 30 minutes remains before the agreed time for tea, an interval between innings is already in progress, play will resume at the end of the 10-minute interval, if conditions permit.

(b) (i) If, because of adverse conditions of ground, weather or light, or in exceptional circumstances, a stoppage occurs when 30 minutes or less remains before the agreed time for tea, then unless
> either there is an agreement to change the time for tea, as permitted in 5 above
> or the captains agree to forgo the tea interval, as permitted in 10 below

the interval shall be taken immediately. The interval shall be of the agreed length. Play shall resume at the end of the interval or as soon after as conditions permit.

(ii) If a stoppage is already in progress when 30 minutes remains before the agreed time for tea, 5 above will apply.

8. TEA INTERVAL – 9 WICKETS DOWN

If either 9 wickets are already down when 2 minutes remains to the agreed time for tea,

or the 9th wicket falls within this 2 minutes, or at any time up to and including the final ball of the over in progress at the agreed time for tea,

then, notwithstanding the provisions of Law 16.5(b) (Completion of an over), tea will not be taken until the end of the over that is in progress 30 minutes after the originally agreed time for tea, unless the players have cause to leave the field of play or the innings is completed earlier.

For the purposes of this section of Law, the retirement of a batsman is not to be considered equivalent to the fall of a wicket.

9. INTERVALS FOR DRINKS

(a) If on any day the captains agree that there shall be intervals for drinks, the option to take such drinks shall be available to either side. Each interval shall be kept as short as possible and in any case shall not exceed 5 minutes.

(b) Unless, as permitted in 10 below, the captains agree to forgo it, a drinks interval shall be taken at the end of the over in progress when the agreed time is reached. If, however, a wicket falls or a batsman retires within 5 minutes of the agreed time then drinks shall be taken immediately.

No other variation in the timing of drinks intervals shall be permitted except as provided for in (c) below.

(c) If an innings ends or the players have to leave the field of play for any other reason within 30 minutes of the agreed time for a drinks interval, the umpires and captains together may rearrange the timing of drinks intervals in that session.

10. AGREEMENT TO FORGO INTERVALS

At any time during the match, the captains may agree to forgo the tea interval or any of the drinks intervals. The umpires shall be informed of the decision.

When play is in progress, the batsmen at the wicket may deputise for their captain in making an agreement to forgo a drinks interval in that session.

11. SCORERS TO BE INFORMED

The umpires shall ensure that the scorers are informed of all agreements about hours of play and intervals and of any changes made thereto as permitted under this Law.

This Law identifies which breaks in play are to be classed as intervals, how such intervals may be varied or cancelled and the restrictions placed on certain intervals. Many matches will be governed by Special Regulations which will define when intervals may be taken. Where intervals are not specified in Regulations, they must be agreed before the toss, in compliance with this Law. In either case, it is essential that umpires, captains and scorers all know, before the toss, the timing and duration of all intervals. Details are set out in Section 2.

INTERVAL BETWEEN INNINGS
The interval between innings is not a matter of agreement. No flexibility is allowed. It has to start as an innings ends and must be of 10 minutes duration. There is provision, in a one-day match, for the tea interval to be taken between innings. The normal 10-minute interval will then be incorporated into the tea interval.

There are other occasions when the 10-minute interval is to be subsumed into another break in play. These are

(a)   an innings ending within 10 minutes of time for close of play. There will be no further play that day. Play will resume at the scheduled time on the following day – subject to conditions being safe for play.

(b)   the batting captain declaring his side's innings closed
   • during an interruption of more than 10 minutes duration.
     In this case the new innings will start as soon as umpires consider that conditions are no longer unreasonable or dangerous
   • during any interval other than a drinks interval.
     In this case the new innings will start at the time agreed for the end of the interval.

   In both these cases, the captain of the side about to bat is entitled to have up to 7 minutes rolling. If he chooses this option, the umpires must allow the rolling, even though playing time may be lost, as discussed in Section 1(e) of Law 10.

DURATION OF INTERVALS
The umpires should make every effort to ensure that intervals are limited to the length of time agreed, measured from the call of Time to start the interval up to the call of Play for resumption of play after the interval. There are many situations, discussed in the following text, where the time for starting an interval can be changed. In no circumstances can the duration of an agreed interval be changed.

Although the timing of a declaration or forfeiture, or some other cause, may mean that the 10-minute interval between innings is insufficient, once the 10 minutes has expired, the interval is at an end. The remaining time is playing time, which cannot be made up unless the delay is caused by the umpires investigating a possible refusal to play. This is dealt with in Law 21.

ALTERATION OF INTERVALS

The hours of play are times for start of play and for close of play on each day. Start of play may have to be delayed if conditions are unreasonable or dangerous. There is special provision in Section 3 of Law 21 for altering time for close of play. These two situations apart, hours of play are not to be altered.

For lunch and tea, there are several situations where the time for the start of the interval may be changed by agreement between umpires and captains. These situations are dealt with below. In no case, however, may the duration of these intervals be changed.

FORGOING INTERVALS

The captains are permitted to agree between themselves to forgo the tea interval on any day, or one or more of the agreed drinks intervals. This must be jointly agreed. If either captain does not wish to forgo any particular interval, then that interval will take place. They must of course notify the umpires if they come to such an agreement. The umpires should ensure that the scorers also know. The captains are not permitted to forgo the lunch interval, even if they both wish to do so.

LUNCH AND TEA INTERVALS

Section 5 sets out a general provision for altering the time of either the lunch interval or the tea interval. It requires that not only both captains but also both umpires agree to the change. This prevents one captain exploiting a situation to disadvantage the other side. Umpires will see that the agreed change is not only sensible, but is possible within the capabilities of the catering staff to make such a change at short notice.

For example, suppose lunch has been arranged for 40 minutes at 1.30 p.m. At 12.30 p.m. there is heavy rain, which is obviously going to continue for some time. It would clearly save a waste of playing time if lunch could be taken at once, in the hope that by 1.10 conditions will have improved. It would, however, be impracticable to expect that at short notice lunch could be ready an hour before it was due. It might be practicable, in consultation with the catering staff, to have it brought forward to 1 p.m.

Again, suppose an innings ends at 4.19, with tea scheduled for 4.30. It would save time to take tea at once, because the 10-minute interval would be absorbed into the tea interval. The fact that both captains have to agree to any change gives the fielding captain the right to insist on starting the new innings at 4.29, in order to get one over in before another break.

The umpires must ensure that agreements to change the time of intervals in such circumstances are on the one hand practicable and on the other hand do not force either captain into an arrangement against his will.

CHANGING THE TIME OF THE LUNCH INTERVAL

In contrast to Section 5, which gives criteria for altering lunch or tea generally, Section 6 deals with specific cases where the starting time for the lunch interval is to be altered. The critical time is 10 minutes before lunch is due. Any stoppage, or the end of an innings at that time, or closer to the agreed time than that, will mean that lunch is to be taken at once. This is not subject to agreement, but must be followed as stated. The 10-minute interval between innings will be absorbed into the lunch interval.

Players leaving the field, at the end of an innings, or for a stoppage, or for any other reason, earlier than 10 minutes before the agreed time for lunch means that lunch is to be taken at the agreed time. In this case, however, agreement between captains and umpires to alter this, as described above, is allowed.

CHANGING THE TIME OF THE TEA INTERVAL – END OF INNINGS AND STOPPAGES

In every case the captains can agree to forgo the tea interval. In every case the critical time for decisions about altering the timing of the tea interval is 30 minutes before tea is due.

A *stoppage* may occur <u>before this time</u>. If the stoppage is still in progress at the 30-minute deadline then an agreement between captains and umpires as detailed above is permitted. Otherwise tea will be taken at the agreed time.

If an *innings ends* <u>before this time</u>, such an agreement is not permitted. Play will resume after the 10-minute interval, even if that interval is already in progress at the 30-minute deadline. Tea will be taken at the agreed time.

The following two provisions apply to times at or after the 30-minute deadline. If at exactly 30 minutes before tea is due, or between then and the end of the over in progress at the due time

- players have to leave the field for any reason other than the end of an innings – for example a *stoppage* for weather – tea will be taken immediately but captains and umpires are allowed to agree otherwise
- an *innings ends*, the tea interval will be taken at once and will absorb the 10-minute interval between innings. Captains and umpires are not permitted to agree otherwise.

Section 8 sets out a special provision which relates to <u>2 minutes</u> before tea is due. This section sets out clearly the situations in which tea will be delayed.

Note that how early the 9th wicket falls is immaterial. If tea is due at 4 p.m., the 9th wicket falling at 3 p.m. will qualify. The criteria are that it should <u>either</u> be *already* down when 2 minutes remains, <u>or</u> *fall* before the completion of the over in progress when the agreed time for tea is reached.

Tea is due at 4 p.m. Tea will be deferred in the following cases:

- the 9th wicket falls at 3 p.m. A new over starts at 3.58 and is completed at 4.01. The 10th wicket has still not fallen.
- a new over starts at 3.57. Only 8 wickets are down. The 9th wicket falls at 3.59 on the 4th ball of the over.
- a new over starts at 3.59. Only 8 wickets have fallen. At 4.02 the 9th wicket falls on the 5th ball of this over.

Play will continue and tea will then be taken when the innings ends – the fall of the 10th wicket is most likely but maybe the captain will declare, or even the winning runs will be scored! Tea would also have to be taken if the players are forced off the field by a sudden thunderstorm or the like. However, tea is not to be postponed indefinitely. Section 8 lays down the deadline, which is not exactly 30 minutes after the original time, but the end of the over then in progress. If in the examples above play is still in progress at 4.30, and 2 balls of an over have been bowled, then the very latest that tea can be taken is *the end of that over.*

Note that this section of Law applies only to 9 wickets actually falling. A batsman retiring does not count as one of the 9 wickets. Moreover it <u>must be 9</u> wickets. If the team is one player short, it does not apply to 8 wickets falling.

It is also worth repeating that all the above provisions are subject to the captains' right to agree to forgo the tea interval.

DRINKS INTERVALS

Unlike other agreements between captains, whether or not to have drinks intervals must be agreed afresh on each day of the match. Once made, one captain cannot decide unilaterally to cancel a drinks interval. It can be cancelled only if the captains *agree* to do so. Note that on the field of play, the batsmen at the wicket are allowed to deputise for their captain in making such a decision.

Umpires should see that the strictures on timing set out in Section 9 are observed. Notice also that, if there is an interruption, rearrangement of a drinks interval can be only by captains and umpires together.

SCORERS

The whole of Law 15 is about agreement and possible alteration of timings relating to the match. It is essential that at every stage the scorers are kept fully informed.

Law 16   Start of play; cessation of play

I. CALL OF PLAY

The bowler's end umpire shall call Play at the start of the match and on the resumption of play after any interval or interruption.

2. CALL OF TIME

The bowler's end umpire shall call Time when the ball is dead on the cessation of play before any interval or interruption and at the conclusion of the match. See Laws 23.3 (Call of Over or Time) and 27 (Appeals).

3. REMOVAL OF BAILS

After the call of Time, the bails shall be removed from both wickets.

4. STARTING A NEW OVER

Another over shall always be started at any time during the match, unless an interval is to be taken in the circumstances set out in 5 below, if, walking at his normal pace, the umpire has arrived at his position behind the stumps at the bowler's end before the time agreed for the next interval, or for the close of play, has been reached.

5. COMPLETION OF AN OVER

Other than at the end of the match,
(a) if the agreed time for an interval is reached during an over, the over shall be completed before the interval is taken, except as provided for in (b) below
(b) when less than 2 minutes remains before the time agreed for the next interval, the interval will be taken immediately if
either (i) a batsman is dismissed or retires
    or (ii) the players have occasion to leave the field
whether this occurs during an over or at the end of an over. Except at the end of an innings, if an over is thus interrupted it shall be completed on the resumption of play.

6. LAST HOUR OF MATCH – NUMBER OF OVERS

When one hour of playing time of the match remains, according to the agreed hours of play, the over in progress shall be completed. The next over shall be the first of a minimum of 20 overs which must be bowled, provided that a result is not reached earlier and provided that there is no interval or interruption in play.

The bowler's end umpire shall indicate the commencement of this 20 overs to the players and to the scorers. The period of play thereafter shall be referred to as the last hour, whatever its actual duration.

7. LAST HOUR OF MATCH – INTERRUPTIONS OF PLAY

If there is an interruption in play during the last hour of the match, the minimum number of overs to be bowled shall be reduced from 20 as follows.

(a) The time lost for an interruption is counted from the call of Time until the time for resumption as decided by the umpires.

(b) One over shall be deducted for every complete 3 minutes of time lost.

(c) In the case of more than one such interruption, the minutes lost shall not be aggregated; the calculation shall be made for each interruption separately.

(d) If, when one hour of playing time remains, an interruption is already in progress

    (i) only the time lost after this moment shall be counted in the calculation

    (ii) the over in progress at the start of the interruption shall be completed on resumption and shall not count as one of the minimum number of overs to be bowled.

(e) If, after the start of the last hour, an interruption occurs during an over, the over shall be completed on resumption of play. The two part-overs shall between them count as one over of the minimum number to be bowled.

8. LAST HOUR OF MATCH – INTERVALS BETWEEN INNINGS

If an innings ends so that a new innings is to be started during the last hour of the match, the interval starts with the end of the innings and is to end 10 minutes later.

(a) If this interval is already in progress at the start of the last hour then, to determine the number of overs to be bowled in the new innings, calculations are to be made as set out in 7 above.

(b) If the innings ends after the last hour has started, two calculations are to be made, as set out in (c) and (d) below. The greater of the numbers yielded by these two calculations is to be the minimum number of overs to be bowled in the new innings.

(c) Calculation based on overs remaining.

    (i) At the conclusion of the innings, the number of overs that remain to be bowled, of the minimum in the last hour, to be noted.

    (ii) If this is not a whole number it is to be rounded up to the next whole number.

    (iii) Three overs, for the interval, to be deducted from the resulting number to determine the number of overs still to be bowled.

(d) Calculation based on time remaining.

    (i) At the conclusion of the innings, the time remaining until the agreed time for close of play to be noted.

    (ii) 10 minutes, for the interval, to be deducted from this time to determine the playing time remaining.

    (iii) A calculation to be made of one over for every complete 3 minutes of the playing time remaining, plus one more over if a further part of 3 minutes remains.

9. CONCLUSION OF MATCH

The match is concluded

(a) as soon as a result as defined in sections 1, 2, 3, 4 or 5(a) of Law 21 (The result) is reached.

(b) as soon as both
    (i) the minimum number of overs for the last hour are completed
    and (ii) the agreed time for close of play is reached
    unless a result is reached earlier.

(c) in the case of an agreement under Law 12.1(b) (Number of innings), as soon as the final innings is completed as defined in Law 12.3(e) (Completed innings).

(d) if, without the match being concluded, either as in (a) or in (b) or in (c) above, the players leave the field for adverse conditions of ground, weather or light, or in exceptional circumstances, and no further play is possible.

10. COMPLETION OF LAST OVER OF MATCH

The over in progress at the close of play on the final day shall be completed unless

either (i) a result has been reached

or (ii) the players have occasion to leave the field. In this case there shall be no resumption of play except in the circumstances of Law 21.9 (Mistakes in scoring) and the match shall be at an end.

11. BOWLER UNABLE TO COMPLETE AN OVER DURING LAST HOUR OF MATCH

If, for any reason, a bowler is unable to complete an over during the last hour, Law 22.8 (Bowler incapacitated or suspended during an over) shall apply. The separate parts of such an over shall count as one over of the minimum to be bowled.

The call of Play begins a session of play. The call of Time terminates one. These calls have considerable significance for the game. For example there are restrictions, set out in Law 17, imposed on players once Play has been called. Although many times during the course of play the ball becomes dead, or is called dead, these occasions do not have the same finality as the call of Time. Once Time has been called, no incident can have any significance for the match apart from some specifically stated exceptions which apply 'at any time in the match'. An example is the banning of practice on the pitch. The significance of a call of Time is discussed further in Law 27.

CALL OF PLAY

The first call of Play starts the match. A call of Play is to be made subsequently to restart play whenever it has been in abeyance, for whatever reason, whether an interruption or an interval. An interruption is an unscheduled break in play – usually but not always for conditions of ground, weather or light. It could for example be caused by the umpires having to investigate a delay in the appearance of a new batsman after the fall of a wicket. The definition of an interval is set out in Law 15. There are four specific types of interval and one general one. Inexperienced umpires sometimes forget that taking drinks is just as much an interval as the break for lunch. None must be forgotten.

FIELD TECHNIQUE – CALL OF PLAY

When going out to the pitch to start the match, the umpires will check that the field is cleared of spectators, players and miscellaneous obstructions. They should walk out 5 minutes before the time agreed for play to start. On some grounds there is a bell which can be rung to alert players. If there is no '5-minute bell', it will be necessary to ensure in some other way that the players know that the umpires are about to go out to the pitch.

The umpires will agree at which ends they will stand, and recheck the alignment of the stumps and place the bails in position as the players follow them out. It is usually obvious from which end the bowling is to begin. If not, this must be ascertained. The umpire at that end must then take the following actions:

- enquire as to the bowler's mode of delivery – i.e. right-handed or left-handed, from over or round the wicket
- notify the bowler's action and give guard to the striker
- give a marker, if necessary, to the bowler
- give the match ball to the bowler.

It is by no means part of an umpire's duty, but if the sight-screen needs to be moved, it may be helpful for him to assist by standing with the appropriate arm upraised in the approximate place from which the ball will be delivered.

The umpire must also make the following checks:

- that the number of fielders does not exceed eleven
- that the fielding captain has finished setting the field
- that his colleague is ready
- that the scorers are in position and ready
- that both batsmen are ready
- that his colleague agrees that time for start of play has been reached.

The experienced umpire at the striker's end will be looking for the enquiry that he is ready, having checked that field setting does not involve more than two on-side fielders behind the popping crease. See Law 41.

The listing of these items does not imply that they have to be in that order, though it will be seen that there is a natural logic in it. For example, the point at which to hand the match ball to the bowler can be varied to suit the circumstances. However, the check that the players and fellow officials are ready must come last. Many umpires will want to check that the striker is ready immediately before calling Play.

When the checks are completed and the umpires agree that the scheduled time for start of play has been reached, the bowler's end umpire will call Play. The call must be made clearly so that players of both sides are aware that the match has started and play is about to begin. The exact time that Play is called should be noted by both umpires, so that they have an accurate record of what is playing time and what is not.

All these checks are important. Probably the two most often neglected by inexperienced umpires are checking that the other umpire is ready and checking that the scorers are ready. Events on the first delivery may be missed if play commences before the striker's end umpire is ready. Moreover, to start without anyone to record the progress of play would be a serious, probably disastrous, lapse by the umpires. A frequently used signal for this check with the scorers, although none is laid down, is for the umpire to raise one arm high above his head, in the way he would signal Byes if play were in progress. An acknowledgement from the scorebox will indicate that all is in order.

Most of the start-of-match routine will be necessary at each call of Play. There will be small exceptions. For example after an interval for drinks the umpires and players will already be on the field of play and there will be no set time for play to resume. It will begin as soon as the checks reveal that everyone is ready. The umpire must do what is appropriate to each situation.

CALL OF TIME

This is also the responsibility of the bowler's end umpire. Just as Play is called to start the match and to re-start after any break in play, so Time is called to end play before any break and at the end of the match. 'Any break' includes interruptions as well as intervals. It is just as important to call Time when all are dashing off the field for a sudden heavy downpour as it is when the break is a more sedate departure for lunch or at the end of an innings. Again, the umpire must not neglect to call Time before a drinks interval as well as at other intervals. After Time is called, the bails are to be removed. Nowadays this is a symbolic act; it has no significance for the game. It is quite in order for a friendly wicket-keeper to bring them to the umpire at that end if going to the pavilion takes him in that direction, as long they were not removed until Time had been called. The appropriate umpire should also take possession of the match ball.

FIELD TECHNIQUE – CALL OF TIME

(a) **Before an interval**

Time is not to be called until the ball is dead. Unless the reason for the call is the end of an innings, it is necessary for the umpires to check that the moment for the call has arrived. It is clearly inappropriate to do such checking while the ball is in play. It must be done, slightly ahead of time, when the ball is dead. When an agreed interval is approaching, possible checks, which can be made unobtrusively are

- at the start of an over that he agrees there will not be time for more than this over
- during an over, while the ball is dead between deliveries, that the 2-minute deadline discussed below has been reached
- if necessary, a final 'fail-safe' check, by a small mime of lifting the bails before actually doing so.

(b) For any break

For a break not at the end of an innings, if play resumes after the interval, it must do so with the game in exactly the same state as it was when the break began. Umpires should note, agree with each other and write down:

- at which end the bowling will resume; the umpire at that end should take possession of the ball
- who is bowling and at which ends
- at which end each batsman (or the not out batsman, as the case may be) should be
- how many balls remain in the over, if relevant
- the exact time at which the break began. For an agreed interval this will determine when it is to end. For an interruption it will be needed to determine how much playing time is lost.

At the end of an innings, only the last of these, the time, is necessary. However, except for drinks, at any interval as opposed to an interruption, the umpires are to check with the scorers that they agree the number of runs scored, the number of wickets that have fallen and, if relevant, the number of overs bowled. It is therefore prudent to have checked with each other first.

If the break is an interruption, it may be after consultation to agree that conditions are bad enough to warrant a suspension of play. There will be plenty of time to make these notes. It may be a wild dash, grabbing the bails on the way, because of a sudden cloudburst. The notes must be made, even if done when the shelter of the pavilion is reached.

COMPLETING THE OVER IN PROGRESS

1 During the match

The current over will always be finished unless an innings ends during the course of it. Section 5 sets out when an over is to be completed before starting an interval and when it will not be completed until after the interval. If a batsman is out or retires when an interval is nearly due, the umpire should check himself and with his colleague whether the time remaining until the agreed time for the interval is 2 minutes or more, or whether it is less than 2 minutes. If it is less than 2 minutes, he will call Time and remove and the bails. The interval will be taken. This is to happen even if the wicket falls on the last ball of an over and the other umpire could have been in place in time for another over to start. Otherwise play will continue. Of course, if an innings ends, there is no option but to take either the 10-minute interval, or lunch or tea, or close of play, whichever of these is appropriate.

2 At the end of the match

Here there is no option. If a result is reached, the match is at an end, unless the belief that a result has been reached turns out to be a mistaken one. That situation is discussed in Law 21. Setting aside this possibility, if the players are obliged to leave the field in mid-over, it may already be clear that this was to be the last over. If that is not so, then the loss of time during the interruption may mean that it becomes the last over. In either of these two situations, play will not resume, and this over will be left unfinished. In all other situations, the over in progress at the end of a match will be completed, in the absence of a result, even if this means a new batsman coming in after time has been reached.

STARTING A NEW OVER

1 During the course of play – not at the fall of a wicket

When it is getting near time for an interval at the end of a session, the umpires will check with each other as to the time remaining. If at the end of an over time has already been reached, Time will be called. If, however, there is even a short time remaining, the umpires will walk to their positions for the next over. This is to be done 'at their normal pace'. It follows that a 'normal pace' must have been established during the course of the match. When the umpire who was at the striker's end arrives at his new position behind the stumps, a further check on the time is to be made. If time has still not been reached, even by a small margin, a new over will be started. There might be a delay in starting it. For example the captain may decide to change the field setting. The striker may be facing his first ball at that end and require guard. Such delay has no bearing on starting the over, neither would fielders rushing (or conversely, dawdling) to get to their new positions. The only criterion is whether or not time has been reached when the umpire arrives at his position behind the stumps.

The situation at the fall of a wicket has been dealt with under 'completing the over in progress'.

2 At the end of the match

If the length of the final innings is limited to a number of overs, a new over will always be started until all these overs are completed, unless a result is reached earlier, or conditions make play impossible.

Even if the match (not the innings) is one limited by time, during the last hour the number of overs becomes the first deciding factor. Unless the match comes to a premature conclusion, the minimum number of overs as calculated must be bowled, and no question of time for starting another over or not can arise. Once that minimum number of overs is achieved, then exactly the same routine will be applied as that described in 1. The first time check will be at the end of the last over of the minimum number required. It will be rare for there to be any time remaining at this point, but it could happen. Note, however, that the fall of a wicket, either during the course of an over, or at the end of an over, will not alter the decision as to whether another over is to be bowled. If, when the umpire arrives at his position behind the stumps, the agreed time for close of play has not been reached, in the absence of a result, another over will be started.

THE LAST HOUR OF THE MATCH

Sections 6, 7 and 8 deal with this very important feature of the closing stages of a match (not an innings) limited by time – the last hour. The last hour begins, not one hour before the agreed time for close of play, but at the start of the next over after that moment. Once begun, a minimum of 20 overs is to be bowled, unless the match reaches a conclusion sooner, or time is lost for an interruption or interval. Often it takes significantly longer than one hour to complete the overs. Sometimes more than 20 overs are bowled before time is reached. The latter is virtually unheard of in these days of slow over rates. The situation is not helped by some local Leagues condoning this laggardly play by setting a target of fewer than 20 overs in the last hour. The Law requires 20, and specifies that, even if they take an hour and a half to complete, or if 23 overs are achieved in the hour, this final period of play is to be known as the last hour.

Umpires and scorers need to be clear that the match will not be concluded, unless a result is reached sooner, until the minimum number of overs has been bowled and time for close of play has been reached.

Suppose close of play has been agreed for 7.30 p.m. An over is in progress at 6.30 p.m., so the last hour does not begin until 6.32 and there is no interruption or interval thereafter. This does not change the time for close of play. It is still 7.30. If 20 overs are completed by 7.23, then play will continue until the end of the over in progress at 7.30. If, on the other hand, at 7.30 only 17.4 overs of the minimum 20 have been bowled, then play will continue until the full 20 have been bowled.

That it is time for the last hour to begin should be agreed between the umpires exactly as for the call of Time before an interval. The umpire who is at the bowler's end for the first of the 20 overs will announce it to the players and signal to the scorers. The scorers will record the passage of the overs, but the umpires must themselves both keep a check.

LOSS OF TIME IN THE LAST HOUR

If playing time is reduced, either by interruptions to play or by an interval between innings, there will be a reduction in the minimum number of overs to be bowled. The principles which govern the calculations are set out in detail in the Law and illustrated in the four examples on pages 89–92. Two of those principles may need emphasising.

The following examples illustrate the points, though some may not be very realistic.

EXAMPLE 1

1 Close of play is agreed for 6.30. 2 The first over of the minimum 20 begins at 5.32.
3 At 5.39, 2.2 overs (2 overs and 2 balls) have been bowled. 4 There is then an interruption of 5 minutes for rain.
5 Play is resumed at 5.44.

				Lose 1 over	
1.	5.30		One hour remains		
2.	5.32		Last hour starts		Minimum of **20** overs remain
3.	5.39	2.2	overs have been bowled		Minimum of **17.4** overs remain
4.			**Interruption** of 5 minutes	Lose 1 over	
5.	5.44		Play resumes		Minimum of **16.4** overs remain
		0.4	over bowled to complete broken over		Minimum of **16** overs remain

Notice that

- although the last hour does not start until 5.32 p.m., this has no effect on any calculation
- in column 2, the 2.2 overs and 0.4 overs together make 3 overs achieved, partly before the interruption, the rest by completing the broken over after the interruption
- in column 4 only 1 over is lost. The 5 minutes lost is only one complete period of 3 minutes. The remaining 2 minutes are ignored
- the achieving of 3 overs shown in column 2 and the loss of 1 over shown in column 4 together make 4 overs, which tallies with the final statement that 16 overs must still be bowled.

EXAMPLE 2

Exactly the same as above, but now with a second interruption

1 Close of play is agreed for 6.30.   2 The first over of the minimum 20 begins at 5.32.

3 At 5.39, 2.2 overs (2 overs and 2 balls) have been bowled.   4 There is then an interruption of 5 minutes for rain.

5 Play is resumed at 5.44.   6 The broken over is completed and   7 a further 5.1 overs are bowled.

8 There is then a second interruption of 10 minutes.

1.	5.30		One hour remains		
2.	5.32		Last hour starts		Minimum of **20** overs remain
3.	5.39	2.2	overs have been bowled		
4.			**Interruption** of 5 minutes	Lose **1** over	
5.	5.44		Play resumes		Minimum of **16.4** overs remain
6.		0.4	over bowled to complete broken over		Minimum of **16** overs remain
7.		5.1	further overs are bowled		Minimum of **10.5** overs remain
8.			Interruption of 10 minutes	Lose **3** overs	
			Play resumes		Minimum of **7.5** overs remain
		0.5	over bowled to complete broken over		Minimum of **7** overs remain

In column 2, a total of 9 overs are shown as bowled (2.2 + 0.4 = 3; 5.1 + 0.5 = 6; total 9). In column 4, 4 overs (1, then 3) have been lost. These all total 13 overs. The minimum number remaining out of 20 is thus 7. Note that the two interruptions are not aggregated to make 15 minutes. They are treated separately.

EXAMPLE 3

An interruption is already in progress when the last hour is reached

1 Close of play is agreed for 6.30.
2 At 5.10 rain holds up play, with 2 balls of an over still to be bowled.
3 Play resumes at 5.38.

2.	5.10		Interruption starts		
1.	5.30		One hour remains		Minimum of **20** overs remain
3.	5.38		Play resumes		
			8 minutes lost	Lose **2** overs	Minimum of **18** overs remain
	5.40	0.2	over bowled to complete broken over (not part of minimum number)		Minimum of **18** overs remain

The irregular numbering on the left is intentional. It corresponds with events which are described in a logical sequence but are considered in time sequence. Notice here that

- although the interruption lasted 28 minutes only 8 minutes came after 5.30, in the last hour
- the over in progress at the interruption is still the over in progress when 1 hour of playing time remains. The last hour does not start until the **next** over after it. Therefore although this over must be completed on resumption, it does not form part of the minimum 20 overs.

Example 4

An innings ends and a new innings is started during the last hour

1 Last hour starts at 5.33.

2 At 5.45 the captain declares, after 3.4 overs of the last 20 have been bowled. The calculation is for the number of overs for the next innings.

OVERS calculation

1.	5.33		Last hour starts		Minimum of **20** overs remain
2.	5.45	3.4	overs bowled		Minimum of **16.2** overs remain
3.			Innings ends: round up overs left to next whole number		Minimum of **17** overs remain
			Interval of 10 minutes	Lose 3 overs	Minimum of **14** overs remain

TIME calculation

	5.45	**Innings ends**	45 minutes remains
		Interval (= 10 minutes)	35 minutes remains = 12 overs
	5.55	**New innings starts**	

The larger number is 14. A minimum of 14 overs to be allocated for new innings.

Notice that

- the time calculation is needed only because a new innings *ended* in the last hour
- if the 16.2 overs remaining at the end of the innings had been exactly 16, it would not have been rounded up
- in the time calculation, 35 minutes is 33 + 2 minutes – i.e. 11 overs and 2 minutes. In contrast to the overs calculation an over is *added on* for the surplus 2 minutes.

It is clearly impossible to do instantaneous calculations at the moment of calling Play. An interval between innings is always to be counted as 10 minutes. This will determine in advance the time for resumption. In the case of an interruption, the umpires must decide the time for resumption before going back on to the field, so that they can make a prior calculation, agree it with the scorers and inform the captains. In deciding this time, they will take account of how long it will take to remove covers, as well as the usual time taken for all to be ready for the call of Play. After either an interval or an interruption, if for any reason – adjustments to the sight-screen perhaps – the start of play varies slightly from the theoretical time set, no revision of the calculation is to be made. If, of course, the start after resumption is held up because of adverse conditions, then the loss of time counts as an interruption and a calculation has to be made accordingly.

The second principle to note especially is that starting a new innings during the last hour does not of itself change the method of calculation. It is only when an innings *ends* during the last hour that the two calculations are to be made.

The exact recording of times at each stage is essential. To minimise the possibility of mistakes each umpire makes a calculation and agrees it with his colleague. Both should then agree it with the scorers who will also have made their own calculation.

CONCLUSION OF MATCH

Umpires need to be clear about when a match – as opposed to any one particular innings – is concluded. The criteria are set out in Section 9. Obviously, achieving a result will conclude a match. If a result is not reached in a match limited solely by hours of play, the criteria for determining whether the match is concluded are discussed above under 'Last hour of match'. If, however, the match is one where it has been agreed to limit some or all innings to a number of overs, or to a specified length of time, deciding that the match is concluded will involve some of the terms of that agreement. Umpires should ensure that they know what those terms are before the start of the match.

Law 17 Practice on the field

1. PRACTICE ON THE PITCH

There shall be no practice of any kind, at any time on any day of the match, on the pitch or on either of the two strips parallel and immediately adjacent to the pitch, one on either side of it, each of the same dimensions as the pitch.

2. PRACTICE ON THE REST OF THE SQUARE

There shall be no practice of any kind on any other part of the square on any day of the match, except before the start of play or after the close of play on that day. Practice before the start of play

(a) must not continue later than 30 minutes before the scheduled time or any rescheduled time for play to start on that day.

(b) shall not be allowed if the umpires consider that it will significantly impair the surface of the square.

3. PRACTICE ON THE OUTFIELD

(a) All forms of practice are permitted on the outfield
> before the start of play or after the close of play on any day

or during the lunch and tea intervals

or between innings

providing the umpires are satisfied that such practice will not cause significant deterioration in the condition of the outfield.
Such practice must not continue later than 5 minutes before the time for play to commence or to resume.

(b) Between the call of Play and the call of Time

  (i) no one may participate in practice of any kind on the field of play, even from outside the boundary, except the fielders as defined in Appendix D and the batsmen at the wicket. Any player involved in practice contravening this Law shall be considered to have himself contravened the Law and will be subject to the penalty in 4 below.

  (ii) there shall be no bowling or batting practice on the outfield. Bowling a ball, using arm action only, to a player in the outfield is not to be regarded as bowling practice but shall be subject to (b) (iii) and (c) below. However, a bowler deliberately bowling a ball thus on to the ground will contravene Law 42.3 (The match ball – changing its condition).

  (iii) other practice shall be permitted, subject to the restriction in (i) and (ii) above,

  either at the fall of a wicket

  or during other gaps in play for legitimate activities, such as adjustment of the sight-screen.

(c) (i) Practice at the fall of a wicket must cease as soon as the incoming batsman steps on to the square.

  (ii) Practice during other legitimate gaps in play must not continue beyond the minimum time required for the activity causing the gap in play.

  If these time restrictions are not observed, umpires shall apply the procedures of Law 42.9 (Time wasting by the fielding side).

4. PENALTY FOR CONTRAVENTION

If a player contravenes 1, 2, 3(b)(i) or 3(b)(ii) above, he shall not be allowed to bowl until

either at least one hour has elapsed

  or there has been at least 30 minutes of playing time

since the contravention, whichever is sooner.

If the contravention is by the bowler during an over, he shall not be allowed to complete that over. It shall be completed by another bowler, who shall neither have bowled any part of the previous over nor be allowed to bowl any part of the next over.

5. TRIAL RUN UP

A bowler is permitted to have a trial run up subject to the provisions of 3 and 4 above.

PRACTICE ON THE FIELD

This Law differentiates between the three areas, the pitch and its immediate neighbouring strips, the rest of the square and the outfield, namely the rest of the field of play. It sets out clearly when and where batting practice or bowling practice, or other forms of practice are or are not allowed in each area. Umpires must see that players comply with the provisions of the Law.

Players will often practise throwing and catching the ball during a lull in play. In recent years, this has tended to lead to waste of playing time. However, as long as they do this practice only while there is some other necessary activity, such as the captain re-setting the field for a new bowler, or the sight-screen being moved, this is legitimate. It is common for a bowler to bowl the ball to a fellow fielder at the beginning of a new spell. If this is done while the striker is taking a new guard, or the sight-screen is being moved, no time is being wasted. The umpires must be ready to require the bowler to start the over as soon as such other legitimate activities are completed. A short comment to the bowler in good time will probably prevent the more severe action in Law 42.9 becoming necessary.

If, however, fielders fail to comply with the time limitations, the umpire should implement the procedure set out in Law 42.9, initially giving a first and final warning to the captain of the fielding side.

PRACTICE ON THE SQUARE

Practice on the square, excluding the pitch and its two adjacent strips, is restricted to after the close of play or earlier than 30 minutes before the time for start of play. Any running, or even walking, on the square will cause some damage to the surface, but in good conditions this will not be significant. Umpires must not allow practice on the square, even at a time when it is legitimate, if they consider that the damage will be significant. This may be because the surface is damp and soft. It may be because the surface is very dry and easily scuffed up.

If players contravene this Law by practising on the square at a time when it is not permitted, or by practising on the pitch or adjacent strips at any time, those players will be prevented from bowling in the match for a period which is clearly set down in Section 4.

If the time for start of play is changed, the time '30 minutes before time for start of play' will refer to the newly agreed time.

PRACTICE ON THE OUTFIELD

Much pre-match practice takes place on the outfield. Players will also often practise before play re-starts after the lunch interval. This is permitted, but time limits are set for it. The only other restriction is that it should not cause undue damage. The outfield usually has a more robust surface than the square. Nevertheless, in very damp conditions, significant damage could be caused. Umpires must not allow this.

Between the call of Play and the call of Time – that is while a session of play is in progress – practice must be restricted to legitimate gaps in play such as moving the sight-screen, or a new batsman coming in. Recently a practice has crept in of a coach on the boundary helping fielders with throwing, bowling and catching. The Law now, from 2010 onwards, specifically forbids such a person to be involved. It is clearly laid down that no one except the current players can be involved in this practice. Although batting practice is forbidden (as well as bowling practice), batsmen at the wicket are not excluded. This does not mean that they are expected to indulge in fielding practice! It is for the removal of doubt if they become inadvertently involved in fielders' practice by, for example, picking up a ball that has strayed and returning it to a fielder.

Another form of practice that has become prevalent is bowling the ball hard into the ground. The Law now also forbids this. If a bowler wants to loosen his shoulder in this way, he must do so without releasing the ball, otherwise he will be guilty of 'action to change the condition of the ball' (see Law 42.3). Reminding captains of this restriction at the pre-match conference would be sensible. Bowling a ball on the full to a fielder is, however, acceptable if there is a suitable gap in play.

TRIAL RUN UP

It is inevitable that play will be held up if there is a change of bowler. The captain of the fielding side is entitled to a reasonable time for re-arranging the field, though the umpire should intervene if he considers he is taking overlong to do this. The striker is entitled to ask for the sight-screen to be moved if the new bowler's action is to be from the other side of the wicket. While such a temporary hold up is occurring, the bowler is entitled to have a trial run up if he wishes. He is not allowed a trial run up if there is no convenient and legitimate gap in play. Again, Law 42.9 is to be implemented if he breaches the time limitations. If he allows it to extend on to any part of the pitch, his trial run up will have included practice on the pitch; he will be in breach of Section 1. He will therefore be subject to the penalty in Section 4. The umpire should perhaps warn him of this risk. Suggesting that he runs from the bowling crease in the other direction is a ploy often used.

Law 18 Scoring runs

1. A RUN

The score shall be reckoned by runs. A run is scored

(a) so often as the batsmen, at any time while the ball is in play, have crossed and made good their ground from end to end.

(b) when a boundary is scored. See Law 19 (Boundaries).

(c) when penalty runs are awarded. See 6 below.

(d) when Lost ball is called. See Law 20 (Lost ball).

2. RUNS DISALLOWED

Notwithstanding 1 above, or any other provisions elsewhere in these Laws, the scoring of runs or awarding of penalties will be subject to any provisions that may be applicable, for the disallowance of runs or for the non-award of penalties.

3. SHORT RUNS

(a) A run is short if a batsman fails to make good his ground in turning for a further run.

(b) Although a short run shortens the succeeding one, the latter if completed shall not be regarded as short. A striker setting off for his first run from in front of his popping crease may do so also without penalty.

4. UNINTENTIONAL SHORT RUNS

Except in the circumstances of 5 below,

(a) if either batsman runs a short run, the umpire concerned shall, unless a boundary is scored, call and signal Short run as soon as the ball becomes dead and that run shall not be scored.

(b) if, after either or both batsmen run short, a boundary is scored the umpire concerned shall disregard the short running and shall not call or signal Short run.

(c) if both batsmen run short in one and the same run, this shall be regarded as only one Short run.

(d) if more than one run is short then, subject to (b) and (c) above, all runs so called shall not be scored.
If there has been more than one Short run, the umpire shall inform the scorers as to the number of runs to be recorded.

5. DELIBERATE SHORT RUNS

(a) Notwithstanding 4 above, if either umpire considers that either or both batsmen deliberately run short at his end, the umpire concerned shall, when the ball is dead, inform the other umpire of what has occurred.

The bowler's end umpire shall then

   (i) warn both batsmen that the practice is unfair and indicate that this is a first and final warning. This warning shall apply throughout the innings. The umpire shall so inform each incoming batsman.

 (ii) whether a batsman is dismissed or not, disallow all runs to the batting side from that delivery other than any runs awarded for penalties.

(iii) return the batsmen to their original ends.

(iv) inform the captain of the fielding side and, as soon as practicable, the captain of the batting side of the reason for this action.

 (v) inform the scorers as to the number of runs to be recorded.

(b) If there is any further instance of deliberate short running by any batsman in that innings, the umpire concerned shall, when the ball is dead, inform the other umpire of what has occurred and the procedure set out in (a) (ii), (iii) and (iv) above shall be repeated. Additionally the bowler's end umpire shall

   (i) award 5 penalty runs to the fielding side

 (ii) inform the scorers as to the number of runs to be recorded

(iii) together with the other umpire report the occurrence as soon as possible after the match to the Executive of the batting side and to any Governing Body responsible for the match, who shall take such action as is considered appropriate against the captain and the player or players concerned.

6. RUNS AWARDED FOR PENALTIES

Runs shall be awarded for penalties under 5 above and Laws 2.6 (Player returning without permission), 24 (No ball), 25 (Wide ball), 41.2 (Fielding the ball), 41.3 (Protective helmets belonging to the fielding side), and 42 (Fair and unfair play).

7. RUNS SCORED FOR BOUNDARIES

Runs shall be scored for boundary allowances under Law 19 (Boundaries).

8. RUNS SCORED FOR LOST BALL

Runs shall be scored when Lost ball is called under Law 20 (Lost ball).

9. RUNS SCORED WHEN A BATSMAN IS DISMISSED

When a batsman is dismissed, any runs for penalties awarded to either side shall stand. No other runs shall be credited to the batting side, except as follows.

If a batsman is

(a) dismissed Handled the ball, the batting side shall also score the runs completed before the offence.

(b) dismissed Obstructing the field, the batting side shall also score the runs completed before the offence.

If, however, the obstruction prevented a catch from being made, no runs other than penalties shall be scored.

(c) dismissed Run out, the batting side shall also score the runs completed before the wicket was put down.

If, however, a striker who has a runner is himself dismissed Run out, no runs other than penalties shall be scored. See Law 2.8 (Transgression of the Laws by a batsman who has a runner).

10. RUNS SCORED WHEN THE BALL BECOMES DEAD OTHER THAN AT THE FALL OF A WICKET

When the ball becomes dead for any reason other than the fall of a wicket, or is called dead by an umpire, unless there is specific provision otherwise in the Laws,

(a) any runs for penalties awarded to either side shall be scored. Note, however, the provisions of Laws 26.3 (Leg byes not to be awarded) and 41.4 (Penalty runs not to be awarded).

(b) additionally the batting side shall be credited with

(i) all runs completed by the batsmen before the incident or call

and (ii) the run in progress if the batsmen had already crossed at the instant of the incident or call. Note specifically, however, the provisions of Laws 34.4(c) (Runs scored from ball lawfully struck more than once) and 42.5(f) (Deliberate distraction or obstruction of batsman).

11. BATSMAN RETURNING TO ORIGINAL END

(a) When a batsman is dismissed, the not out batsman shall return to his original end

(i) if the striker is himself Run out in the circumstances of Law 2.8(c) (Transgression of the Laws by a batsman who has a runner).

(ii) for all other methods of dismissal other than those in 12(a) below.

(b) Other than at the fall of a wicket, the batsmen shall return to their original ends in the cases of, and only in the cases of,

(i) a boundary.

(ii) disallowance of runs for any reason.

(iii) a decision by the batsmen at the wicket to do so under Law 42.5(g) (Deliberate distraction or obstruction of batsman).

12. BATSMAN RETURNING TO WICKET HE HAS LEFT

(a) When a batsman is dismissed
   (i) Caught, Handled the ball or Obstructing the field,
   (ii) Run out other than as in 11(a) above,
   the not out batsman shall return to the wicket he has left, but only if the batsmen had not already crossed at the instant of the incident causing the dismissal.

(b) Except in the cases of 11(b) above, if while a run is in progress the ball becomes dead for any reason other than the dismissal of a batsman, or is called dead by an umpire, the batsmen shall return to the wickets they had left, but only if they had not already crossed in running when the ball became dead.

This Law explains how the batsmen can score a run and how they can fail to score a run. It includes several of the cases where the runs they make are not allowed. It summarises when runs that have not been made by the batsmen are to accrue to the batting side. It also states what runs, if any, are to be allowed when a batsman is dismissed. It is therefore at the very heart of the game of cricket.

There are three main ways in which runs are scored. The batsmen run; runs are awarded for boundaries; runs are awarded as penalties, either against the fielding side, or conceded to the fielding side by the batting side. The extremely rare situation of Lost ball being called is a fourth way. All of these are set out in detail in individual Laws.

RUNS NOT ALLOWED

Before considering the many ways in which runs can be scored or awarded, due note must be taken of Section 2. There are certain situations in which runs by the batsmen are to be cancelled or penalties otherwise due are not to be awarded. Section 2 of this Law makes it clear that whenever a Law speaks of runs to be scored or penalties to be awarded, the statement is to be understood as accompanied by the phrase 'subject to any disallowance of runs or penalties that may apply'. It avoids the necessity of making this statement in each case, although it is always implicit in that Law. For example, a run is scored if the batsmen 'cross and make good their ground from end to end', but that run will be disallowed if it was an illegal attempt to score Leg byes.

The Law specifies that runs will not be allowed, or will be actively disallowed if

- a striker who has a runner is himself dismissed Run out (Law 2.8)
- either batsman deliberately runs short (Section 5 of this Law, 18)
- Leg byes are attempted without the striker having tried either to play the ball or to avoid being hit by the ball (Law 26.3)[†]
- a batsman is dismissed Caught (Law 32.5)
- the batsmen run after a legitimate second stroke when there has been no overthrow (Law 34.4)

- the batsmen run after a legitimate second stroke when the first stroke did not satisfy the conditions for Leg byes to be allowed (Law 34.4)
- a batsman is dismissed for obstructing a catch (Law 37.5)
- after due warning, a batsman damages the pitch (Law 42.14).

In the situations marked thus[†], even awards of 5 penalty runs are not to be allowed; in others it is only runs made by the batsmen that are to be cancelled. Umpires and scorers must study each relevant Law to be clear what runs are allowed or disallowed. They must further understand that any such disallowance will over-ride any award of runs. In addition to the example of illegal Leg byes above, another example is the deletion of all runs when a batsman is out Caught. Although the batsmen may have completed a run and perhaps even started another, the dismissal of the striker by a fair catch will cancel the completed run.

WHEN THE BATSMEN SCORE A RUN BY RUNNING

It is important to understand that a run is not completed until both batsmen have run and crossed and each has grounded his bat or some part of his person behind the popping crease at his new end. It is this grounding behind the popping crease that is essential for the completion of the run.

Grounding alone is not sufficient, nor is being behind the crease but not grounded. Whenever the batsmen run, each umpire must be in a position to watch that every run is properly completed. This means that the bowler's end umpire must move away from the wicket to a position where he can observe the creases and the wicket from the side. This is discussed further in Law 38.

SHORT RUNNING

The key words in Section 3 are 'in turning for a further run'. If a batsman fails to complete a run, but does not start out for another one, he leaves himself vulnerable to being run out, but is not to be considered as running short. Equally, if he does turn for another run, then whatever may happen on the next run is not affected by this one. It is the one he fails to complete before setting out again that is short and so not to be counted. The Law also states what is taken for granted by players – the striker receiving the ball in front of his popping crease may run from that point without causing that first run to be short.

A simple mistake is penalised only by the loss of the uncompleted run, and even that sanction is not imposed if the ball goes to the boundary. Since it is a failed turn round that constitutes a short run, it follows that two runs must be attempted before one can be short. If in this case both umpires call and signal Short run when the ball is dead, it must be for the first run. Only one run will be deducted. The scorers will understand this and no consultation between umpires is necessary, though it should be checked with the scorers at the next interval. If, however, three (or more) runs have been attempted, and both umpires call and signal, consultation will be necessary to determine whether it was the same run short at both ends or whether it was the first at one end and the second at the other. In the former case only one run is to be deducted; in the latter case two will not be counted. The scorers will need to be informed – as will be the case if one umpire sees two short runs at his end.

This is not a case of runs being disallowed. It is an example of the principle that, with certain exceptions, only completed runs count.

DELIBERATE SHORT RUNNING

Deliberate short running could occur at any time but it is more likely towards the end of an innings, when it could be important to the batting side both to score runs and for a particular batsman to keep the strike. The dishonest manoeuvre of deliberately running short leads not only to cancellation of all runs, other than penalties, from that delivery but also to a warning and, for any repetition, to a 5-run penalty and report to higher authority. Moreover, the ball going to the boundary does not cancel the penalty, either at first or at any repetition. The cancellation of all runs means of course that the batsmen are to return to their original ends. This is stated categorically in the Law, together with the instruction that it is to apply 'whether a batsman is dismissed or not'. This very specific wording means that instructions laid down in Sections 11 and 12, about where the not out batsman should go, will not apply. The not out batsman will go to his original end; the new batsman will go to the other end.

The decision that it was deliberate must be made with due seriousness, but an umpire must not shrink from it. Help from his colleague is unlikely to be available; he will have been watching the touch-down at his end. Nevertheless, the umpires should act in concert if a report is to be made. Note also that while either umpire may have seen the short running at his end, it is the bowler's end umpire who will issue the warning and, if it comes to that, the penalty. In all procedures involving warning and/or penalty runs, all the action is to be taken either by the bowler's end umpire or, occasionally, by both umpires together. Reports are always to be made jointly.

OTHER SCORING OF RUNS

Scoring of runs for boundaries – or by the award of penalties – or when Lost ball is called are all dealt with under the appropriate Laws. Sections 6, 7 and 8 list what those Laws are.

BATSMEN CROSSING

Taken in conjunction with Law 29, it will be seen that when the batsmen cross they exchange ends. For example, after crossing on the first run the striker now has the bowler's end as his end, since he is now nearer to that end than the non-striker is. This principle applies in every case and so can be useful in deciding if they have crossed if there are any unusual circumstances.

Whether the batsmen had already crossed or not at the crucial moment is an important consideration in the awarding of runs, in deciding which batman is out and in deciding whether or not batsmen will continue to the ends they were approaching or be sent back. It is obvious in most cases, if it is remembered that batsmen who are level have not yet crossed.

In addition to watching the crease for the completion of runs, umpires must also watch whether the batsmen have crossed or not when they are running. It is not as difficult as it sounds.

SENDING BATSMEN BACK – OR NOT
If the ball becomes dead for any reason when the batsmen are running, it is important that they are then directed to the correct ends. There are two situations to consider.

1 Ball becomes dead without either batsman being dismissed
There are several situations in which this can occur. Two examples from many are the ball hitting a helmet on the ground, and the umpire calling Dead ball for a case of serious injury to a player or umpire.

The general principle here, in Section 12(b), is that each batsman goes to *his* end. This is *his* ground, as defined in Law 29.2. That is if, at the instant pinpointed in the Law, the batsmen had already crossed they will continue to the ends they were approaching. If they had not already crossed, they go back to the ends they have just left. Section 11(b) sets out the only three exceptions to this principle. In two of these three cases the batsmen are to go to their *original* ends – where they were when the ball came into play. The third is a special case, with its own instructions.

CASES FOR RETURN TO ORIGINAL ENDS
A boundary. The unusual situation of the batsmen running more than the boundary allowance is not included as an exception. The reason for this and details of other boundary situations, including boundary overthrows, are dealt with under Law 19 (Boundaries).

Disallowance of runs. This does not apply to situations where incomplete runs are not counted, such as accidental Short runs, but to situations where all runs by the batsman are to be disallowed. These are:
- deliberate short running – described above
- attempt to run when Leg byes are not to be allowed – see Laws 26 and 34
- attempt to run after a legitimate second stroke when there is no overthrow – see Law 34
- batsman damaging the pitch – see Law 42.14
- batsman attempting to steal a run – see Law 42.16. In this case although no run will have been completed to be disallowed, the batsmen will have crossed. Nevertheless they are to be returned to their original ends.

The case of a batsman who has a runner, although relevant to this list, is included in the list of dismissals shown below.

Decision under Law 42.5(g). In this case of deliberate obstruction by the fielding side, the batsmen have the right to choose which of them will face the next delivery. The umpire's only responsibility is therefore to see that the batsmen know this. A question 'Which ends do you want to go to?', if necessary, will achieve this.

2 Batsman dismissed

Section 11(a) sets out the cases in which the Not out batsman will return to his original end. Section 12(a) sets out the cases in which he will go to *his* end as determined by the batsmen having crossed or not. The chart lists the various cases:

DISMISSAL OF A BATSMAN

The not out batsman will	
Return to/stay at original end	*Go on if crossed* *Go back if not*
Bowled	
	Caught
	Handled the ball
Hit the ball twice	
Hit wicket	
LBW	
	Obstructing the field
	Run out (except next case)
Striker who has a runner himself run out	
Stumped	
Timed out	

It will be seen that, except for the striker who has a runner, those on the left are situations where in normal circumstances there is no opportunity for runs to be taken.

FIELD TECHNIQUE

The need for the umpires to watch the completion of each run is clear. To do that, the bowler's end umpire must move to one side where he can have a view of the creases and of the wicket. He will normally move to the side where the ball has been struck. See Law 38. As well as watching for the batsman grounding behind the crease, he must also know what is happening to the ball and what the fielders are doing. He must, however, not neglect the batsmen to follow the progress of the ball. An umpire must be able to adjudicate on any action at his end, such as an attempted Run out, and also assist his colleague with information on other events. In addition, the umpires must know whether or not the batsmen have already crossed at the appropriate moment. This moment might be the completion of a catch, the breaking of the wicket for a successful Run out, the fielder's throw in the case of a boundary overthrow, or the ball crossing the boundary. If from observing the run of play an umpire sees that an attempted Run out may be imminent at the other end, then it will be for him to watch for the batsmen crossing or not, while his colleague is judging the Run out. With a little practice, a rhythm can be built up to watch what is happening in the field, to glance back at the crease at the right moment for the touch-down and then look to see the batsmen cross. At the same time, of course, he must try not to get into the path of the throw-in.

SCORERS

This Law and the next demand the maximum cooperation and communication between umpires and scorers. The scorers have to divine what is going on by what they can see from a great distance, sometimes unable to hear any calls by the umpire. As well as the points where the Law instructs the umpires to inform the scorers – such as in short running – the umpire should assist in every situation where there could be doubt.

Law 19 Boundaries

1. THE BOUNDARY OF THE FIELD OF PLAY

(a) Before the toss the umpires shall agree the boundary of the field of play with both captains. The boundary shall if possible be marked along its whole length.
(b) The boundary shall be agreed so that no part of any sight-screen is within the field of play.
(c) An obstacle or person within the field of play shall not be regarded as a boundary unless so decided by the umpires before the toss. See Law 3.4 (To inform captains and scorers).

2. DEFINING THE BOUNDARY – BOUNDARY MARKING

(a) Wherever practicable the boundary shall be marked by means of a white line or a rope along the ground.
(b) If the boundary is marked by means of a white line,
    (i) the inside edge of the line shall be the boundary edge.
    (ii) a flag, post or board used merely to highlight the position of a line marked on the ground must be placed outside the boundary edge and is not itself to be regarded as defining or marking the boundary. Note, however, the provisions of (c) below.

(c) If a solid object is used to mark the boundary, it must have an edge or a line to constitute the boundary edge.

  (i) For a rope, which includes any similar object of curved cross section, lying on the ground, the boundary edge will be the line formed by the innermost points of the rope along its length.

  (ii) For a fence, which includes any similar object in contact with the ground but with a flat surface projecting above the ground, the boundary edge will be the base line of the fence.

(d) If the boundary edge is not defined as in (b) or (c) above, the umpires and captains must agree before the toss what line will be the boundary edge. Where there is no physical marker for a section of boundary, the boundary edge shall be the imaginary straight line on the ground joining the two nearest marked points of the boundary edge.

(e) If a solid object used to mark the boundary is disturbed for any reason during play then, if possible, it shall be restored to its original position as soon as the ball is dead. If it is not possible then,

  (i) if some part of the fence or other marker has come within the field of play, that part shall be removed from the field of play as soon as the ball becomes dead.

  (ii) the line where the base of the fence or marker originally stood shall define the boundary edge.

3. SCORING A BOUNDARY

(a) A boundary shall be scored and signalled by the bowler's end umpire whenever, while the ball is in play, in his opinion,

  (i) the ball touches the boundary, or is grounded beyond the boundary.

  (ii) a fielder with some part of his person in contact with the ball, touches the boundary or has some part of his person grounded beyond the boundary.

(b) The phrases 'touches the boundary' and 'touching the boundary' shall mean contact with

  either (i) the boundary edge as defined in 2 above

  or (ii) any person or obstacle within the field of play which has been designated a boundary by the umpires before the toss.

(c) The phrase 'grounded beyond the boundary' shall mean contact with

  either (i) any part of a line or solid object marking the boundary except its boundary edge

  or (ii) the ground beyond the boundary edge

  or (iii) any object in contact with the ground beyond the boundary edge.

4. BALL BEYOND THE BOUNDARY

A ball may be caught, subject to the provisions of Law 32, or fielded after it has crossed the boundary, provided that
  (I) the first contact with the ball is by a fielder either with some part of his person grounded within the boundary, or whose final contact with the ground before touching the ball was within the boundary.
  (ii) neither the ball, nor any fielder in contact with the ball, touches or is grounded beyond the boundary at any time during the act of making the catch or of fielding the ball.
The act of making the catch, or of fielding the ball, shall start from the time when the ball first comes into contact with some part of a fielder's person and shall end when a fielder obtains complete control both over the ball and over his own movement and has no part of his person touching or grounded beyond the boundary.

5. RUNS ALLOWED FOR BOUNDARIES

(a) Before the toss, the umpires shall agree with both captains the runs to be allowed for boundaries. In deciding the allowances, the umpires and captains shall be guided by the prevailing custom of the ground.
(b) Unless agreed differently under (a) above, the allowances for boundaries shall be 6 runs if the ball having been struck by the bat pitches beyond the boundary, but otherwise 4 runs. These allowances shall still apply even though the ball has previously touched a fielder. See also (c) below.
(c) The ball shall be regarded as pitching beyond the boundary and 6 runs shall be scored if a fielder
    (i) has any part of his person touching the boundary or grounded beyond the boundary when he catches the ball.
    (ii) catches the ball and subsequently touches the boundary or grounds some part of his person beyond the boundary while carrying the ball but before completing the catch. See Law 32 (Caught).

6. RUNS SCORED

When a boundary is scored,
(a) any runs for penalties awarded to either side shall be scored.
(b) the batting side, except in the circumstances of 7 below, shall additionally be awarded whichever is the greater of
    (i) the allowance for the boundary
    (ii) the runs completed by the batsmen together with the run in progress if they had already crossed at the instant the boundary is scored.
(c) When the runs in (ii) above exceed the boundary allowance they shall replace the boundary for the purposes of Law 18.12 (Batsman returning to wicket he has left).

7. OVERTHROW OR WILFUL ACT OF FIELDER

If the boundary results from an overthrow or from the wilful act of a fielder the runs scored shall be

  (i) **any runs for penalties awarded to either side**

and (ii) the allowance for the boundary

and (iii) the runs completed by the batsmen, together with the run in progress if they had already crossed at the instant of the throw or act.

Law 18.12(b) (Batsman returning to wicket he has left) shall apply as from the instant of the throw or act.

AGREEING THE BOUNDARY

Probably the most crucial part of the application of this Law will take place before play starts, when first the umpires inspect the ground and subsequently agree with the captains what the boundary of the field of play is. On some grounds the boundary will be clear and will be suitably marked by a line or a rope. On others it will be a patchwork of a stretch of wall, an area of long grass, a piece of picket fence where only the main posts are in contact with the ground, a length of beech hedge, and so on.

Just as the creases are edges, so the boundary is an edge. It is the dividing line between the field of play and the world outside. At every point round the field there must be a *boundary edge* to be this dividing line, even if in some parts it is a line to be imagined on the ground.

The best form of boundary. The umpires can see it and can see if the ball or fielders touch or breach it

It might be wise here to agree the boundary as the start of the rough ground at the edge of the grass. If however, the fence is the boundary, the boundary edge would be a series of short lines where each upright meets the ground, joined from one to the next by imaginary straight lines.

Note that the wire netting does not quite touch the ground, so cannot define the boundary edge.

Section 2 of this Law sets out in great detail what that edge is to be for various possible types of marking. If in any section of the field none of those types of marking exists, it is essential that there is clear agreement, understood and accepted by both captains, as to what is to constitute the boundary edge in that section. When the ball is trickling towards the long grass, there must be a clear definition of when it has reached the boundary.

Umpires should note the procedure if some part of a physical boundary collapses and intrudes into the field of play.

SIGHT-SCREENS

The boundary edge must be agreed so that each sight-screen is wholly outside. On a small ground this may necessitate indenting the boundary in that area. If there is no white line and no rope then it is helpful if at least boards can be put across in front of the screen. If there is such an indentation, then there must be clear agreement, acceptable to both captains, about what is to happen if the screen has to be moved during play. If there is enough room, it is desirable to have a big enough indentation to accommodate the screen in both positions.

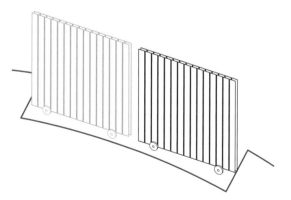

Since, however, the reason for the indentation is lack of space, it may not be sensible to take out yet more of the field of play. Umpires must use their judgment, when agreeing the boundary with the captains. Although it is not ideal to move the indentation if the screen is moved, it is not contrary to Law.

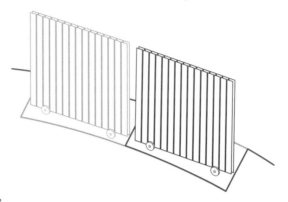

OBSTACLES

There may be some grounds, in company with the famous one at Canterbury, where there is a tree entirely within the field of play. Grounds in public parks may be at risk of people unconnected with the game walking across the field. Spectators may spill on to the outfield. The umpires must decide before the toss whether or not such objects or persons are to be regarded as a boundary. Having made a decision, they will inform the captains. If such an item is to be a boundary, then as soon as the ball in play touches it, a boundary is scored and the ball, of course, becomes dead. If it is not a boundary, then the ball remains in play after contact with it. Note, however, that trees bordering the ground with foliage overhanging the field of play are catered for within the Law, since the whole of the tree is 'an object in contact with the ground outside the boundary edge'. As soon as the ball touches the foliage, a boundary is scored.

ALLOWANCES

The traditional allowances of four and six runs will apply in most cases. The six is awarded only if the ball has been struck by the bat and only if it is grounded beyond the boundary when it lands. It is permitted to agree different allowances. A market garden with acres of glass could be a good reason for discouraging hits over the fence, by having an allowance much lower than six. In making such judgments, local customs are to be observed. Local customs could well include conditions in the club's insurance policy! All agreements about boundary allowances must be between umpires and captains. Most importantly, once agreement is made, the scorers must be informed.

SCORING A BOUNDARY

A boundary will be scored whenever the ball makes contact with the boundary or with the world outside the field of play, beyond the boundary edge. Where there is a physical marking – be it white line, rope, fence, tufted grass or whatever – it is to be appreciated that only the innermost edge of the object is the boundary edge. Hence, every part of the marking *other* than this innermost edge is part of the world outside the field of play. A ball hitting a boundary fence has made contact with something outside the boundary.

As soon as the ball touches the rope, a boundary is scored

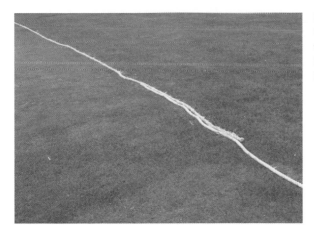

The boundary is the inner edge of the rope, so the lowest point of the rope is outside the boundary. When the ball touches **any part** of the rope – even the frayed part, as on the right – it has touched something in contact with the ground beyond the boundary. A boundary has been scored

If the ball lands on the rope it has been grounded beyond the boundary. If it has not been previously grounded a Boundary 6 is scored

No problem here

If a fielder, who has any part of his person in contact with the ball, touches or goes beyond the boundary edge, it is to be considered that the ball itself has done so. A boundary will have been scored thereby. The boundary edge is sacrosanct. Once breached by the ball, on its own or in contact with a fielder, a boundary is scored.

He is clearly 'grounded outside the boundary'

... but also is if merely touching it ...

... in any way

If a boundary is scored because a fielder touches or goes beyond the boundary while in contact with the ball, and if that ball has not previously been grounded inside or outside the boundary, then 6 runs are scored. This will always be 6 runs, even though the allowance has been agreed as something other than 6.

He is touching the fence. A boundary has been scored – 4 if the ball has already been grounded, 6 if it hasn't

Any part of the fence, except its boundary edge, is outside the boundary. A boundary has been scored – 6 if the ball has not yet been grounded, 4 otherwise

Umpires should also study carefully the comments in Law 32 on catching and fielding at the boundary.

Umpires must be clear about the meaning of all the phrases in Section 3. They define in detail what is meant by 'touching the boundary' and 'grounded beyond the boundary'. They are crucial to the scoring of a boundary and the runs awarded for it. Note, in particular, that 'pitching beyond the boundary' does not necessarily imply landing on the ground, as long as there is contact with some object that is in contact with ground in the world outside the field of play. A ball landing on the pavilion roof has pitched beyond the boundary. Conversely, until the ball comes into contact with

The ball has passed over the fence; it has not yet touched anything grounded outside. A boundary has not been scored. The ball is still in play.

The same is true even though it has passed through the fence.

In Law 19 it does not matter that the ball has crossed the boundary. Neither the ball nor the fielder is grounded beyond the boundary; the ball is still in play and can be fielded or caught

something beyond the boundary, a boundary has not been scored. The ball is still in play. It can be fielded or even caught if other conditions are right.

RUNS SCORED

Although Section 5 is of principal interest to scorers, umpires must also note and understand its provisions, since they have to satisfy themselves as to the correctness of the scores.

If the ball reaches the boundary when No ball or Wide has been called, then the boundary allowance is added to the one-run penalty.

If the batsmen run more than the number allowed for the boundary, before the ball reaches it, then they will score as many as they have run. It should be noted that the run in progress will count as one they have run if they had already crossed by the time the ball reached the boundary. If, for instance, they had run four and crossed on the fifth at the moment the ball crossed the line, not only would they have all five runs, but the score would no longer be regarded as a boundary (although the ball would nevertheless become dead), and would therefore not entail returning them to their original ends. Any penalties would not be affected.

OVERTHROWS

In the normal situation, when a boundary is scored, the allowance replaces any runs that the batsmen may have completed. Exceptionally, if they have run and crossed on more than the allowance, these runs replace the allowance, as discussed above. If, however, the ball crosses the boundary as the result of an overthrow, both the batsmen's runs and the allowance are counted.

An overthrow is difficult to define, but easy to see on the field. Generally speaking, it is a throw by a fielder that gives the batsmen opportunity to score further runs. A ball thrown by a fielder that goes over the boundary, whether thrown to hit the stumps and missing, or slipping out of his hand and going over the boundary behind him, is a boundary overthrow. If there is an obstacle within the field of play that has been designated a boundary, a fielder's throw hitting it will be a boundary overthrow.

Often the ball will travel a long way from the throw before it goes over the edge. Meanwhile the batsmen may have completed further runs. The runs that count and the ends to which the batsmen are to go are determined by *where they were when the ball was thrown* – another important reason for the umpires to watch for the batsmen crossing on every run. There may be more than one throw. A fielder misses the stumps. The batsmen run on. Another fielder picks up the ball on the far side and throws it. This time it goes to the boundary unhindered. The counting of runs and decision on going back or not is to be taken from the moment of the last throw – the second one in this example.

WILFUL ACT OF FIELDER

It is rare for a fielder wilfully to kick the ball over the boundary in the mistaken belief that by giving away a boundary he can dictate which batsman will take next strike. Nevertheless, if he does so, then it counts as a boundary overthrow exactly as above. The words wilful and act are both significant. It will not count as a boundary overthrow if he accidentally pushes the ball over, nor if he deliberately refrains from stopping the ball to let it cross the boundary under its own impetus.

FIELD TECHNIQUE

1 Judging a boundary

It will often be difficult for an umpire to know whether the ball actually reached and crossed the boundary edge or not. He will be a long way from it. His colleague may have been nearer to that bit of boundary and could help. It is prudent, when inspecting the ground before the match, to note any landmarks near the boundary, such as advertisement boards, seating, flagpoles etc., which help to pinpoint where the line actually is. The honesty of a fielder's answer to a direct question must be a matter of judgment. The umpire must do his best, using all evidence available.

2 Signalling to the scorers

When a boundary is scored, there may be other signals to be made to the scorers as well as the boundary. Perhaps a No ball has been called or there are other penalties. Although for a six or a Wide there will be no ambiguity, they will certainly want to know in the case of a No ball whether the ball came off the bat or not. The way to tell them that is to give the Bye signal to show that there was no contact between bat and ball. If there is no Bye signal, the scorers will understand that the ball came off the bat.

The umpire should make each signal separately, maintaining a standard recognised order, so that the scorers know when the sequence is finished. The scorers will then not look for any more signals after a boundary. To take a complicated example – a No ball from which a boundary is scored and on which 5 penalty runs are awarded against the fielding side. When the ball is dead signal as follows:

signal the 5-run penalty	5 penalty runs always come first
signal the No ball	No ball or Wide come first otherwise
either – an upraised arm like a Bye	No ball always needs 'Off
(not off the bat)	the bat' or not
or – omit signal here (off the bat)	
give the boundary signal	Boundary always comes last

Each of these signals must be separately acknowledged.

Law 20   Lost ball

I. FIELDER TO CALL LOST BALL

If a ball in play cannot be found or recovered, any fielder may call Lost ball. The ball shall then become dead. See Law 23.1 (Ball is dead). Law 18.12(b) (Batsman returning to wicket he has left) shall apply as from the instant of the call.

2. BALL TO BE REPLACED

The umpires shall replace the ball with one which has had wear comparable with that which the previous ball had received before it was lost or became irrecoverable. See Law 5.5 (Ball lost or becoming unfit for play).

3. RUNS SCORED

(a) Any runs for penalties awarded to either side shall be scored.
(b) The batting side shall additionally be awarded
either (i) the runs completed by the batsmen, together with the run in progress if they had already crossed at the instant of the call,
or (ii) 6 runs,
whichever is the greater.
These shall be credited to the striker if the ball has been struck by the bat, but otherwise to the total of Byes, Leg byes, No balls or Wides as the case may be.

Many think this Law a quaint and unnecessary survival from the past, when there were no boundaries and very long grass surrounded the area that had been mown. However, it can still apply today. Balls have been known to fall down goalpost sockets. A ball can be stuck in the branches of a tree, wholly within the field of play, which has not been designated a boundary.

There are two important points. One is that the ball must be lost or become irrecoverable *while in play* – that goalpost socket must be inside the boundary. Lodging in a tree which *has* been declared a boundary would not count. The ball would be dead. The other point is that it is a fielder, not an umpire, who must call Lost ball. A farcical situation could arise if the fielding side does not realise this and so the batsmen keep on running while frantic attempts are made to recover the ball. Umpires must use common sense in dealing with such a situation. The point at which the umpire intervenes, if he does, will affect the number of runs. If it is too soon the batsmen are disadvantaged. If it is too late the fielding side is disadvantaged.

RUNS SCORED
The batsmen can continue running, if they want to, until the call of Lost ball. The ball then immediately becomes dead. Section 3 specifies how many runs the batting side will get. If the batsmen do not run they will get 6. If they run 3 and cross on the 4th, they will get 6. If they run 10 they will get 10! These runs will be credited to the striker if the ball came off his bat. Otherwise they will be scored as the appropriate extras. Any penalties will, as usual, be scored as extras.

BALL TO BE REPLACED

On the call of Lost ball, once the ball is dead umpires should bring a replacement ball into use, so that play can resume without prolonging the delay further. Should the original ball subsequently be found, they must consider whether or not to bring it back into use. The wear on the replacement is unlikely to have been an exact match of the original, so if the original is found after only a short time, it is probably better to revert to that one. If however, some time has elapsed, then the replacement will have received further wear to which the original one has not been subject. Then the replacement ball should continue in use. Umpires must exercise judgment, in consultation with each other, as to which course of action will be best.

BATSMEN'S ENDS

The ends to which the batsmen go after a call of Lost ball are determined by the number they have *actually* run at the instant of the call. For example if they have run 4 and crossed on the 5th, they will not return to their original ends, even though they are awarded 6 runs. The umpire will probably have to guide them on this. Once they have run 6 or more there is no conflict in the numbers. The number they have run will then be the number scored.

Law 21 The result

1. A WIN – TWO-INNINGS MATCH

The side which has scored a total of runs in excess of that scored in the two completed innings of the opposing side shall win the match. See Law12.3 (Completed innings). Note also 6 below.

2. A WIN – ONE-INNINGS MATCH

The side which has scored in its one innings a total of runs in excess of that scored by the opposing side in its one completed innings shall win the match. See Law12.3 (Completed innings). Note also 6 below.

3. UMPIRES AWARDING A MATCH

Notwithstanding any agreement under Law 12.1(b) (Number of innings),
(a) a match shall be lost by a side which
    either (i) concedes defeat
      or (ii) in the opinion of the umpires refuses to play
    and the umpires shall award the match to the other side.
(b) if an umpire considers that an action by any player or players might constitute a refusal by either side to play then the umpires together shall ascertain the cause of the action. If they then decide together that

this action does constitute a refusal to play by one side, they shall so inform the captain of that side. If the captain persists in the action the umpires shall award the match in accordance with (a) above.

(c) if action as in (b) above takes place after play has started and does not constitute a refusal to play,

    (i) playing time lost shall be counted from the start of the action until play recommences, subject to Law 15.5 (Changing agreed times for intervals).

    (ii) the time for close of play on that day shall be extended by this length of time, subject to Law 3.9 (Suspension of play in dangerous or unreasonable conditions).

    (iii) if applicable, no overs shall be deducted during the last hour of the match solely on account of this time.

4. MATCHES IN WHICH THERE IS AN AGREEMENT UNDER LAW 12.1(B)

For any match in which there is an agreement under Law 12.1(b) (Number of innings), if the result is not determined in any of the ways stated in 1, 2 or 3 above, then the result shall be as laid down in that agreement.

5. ALL OTHER MATCHES – A TIE OR DRAW

(a) A Tie

The result of a match shall be a Tie when the scores are equal at the conclusion of play, but only if the side batting last has completed its innings.

(b) A Draw

A match which is concluded as defined in Law 16.9 (Conclusion of match), without being determined in any of the ways stated in (a) above or in 1, 2, or 3, above, shall count as a Draw.

6. WINNING HIT OR EXTRAS

(a) As soon as a result is reached as defined in 1, 2, 3, 4 or 5(a) above, the match is at an end. Nothing that happens thereafter, except as in Law 42.17(b) (Penalty runs), shall be regarded as part of it. Note also 9 below.

(b) The side batting last will have scored enough runs to win only if its total of runs is sufficient without including any runs completed by the batsmen before the completion of a catch, or the obstruction of a catch, from which the striker could be dismissed.

(c) If a boundary is scored before the batsmen have completed sufficient runs to win the match, the whole of the boundary allowance shall be credited to the side's total and, in the case of a hit by the bat, to the striker's score.

7. STATEMENT OF RESULT

If the side batting last wins the match without losing all its wickets, the result shall be stated as a win by the number of wickets still then to fall.

If, without having scored a total of runs in excess of the total scored by the opposing side, the side batting last has lost all its wickets, but as the result of an award of 5 penalty runs its total of runs is then sufficient to win, the result shall be stated as a win to that side by Penalty runs.

If the side fielding last wins the match, the result shall be stated as a win by runs.

If the match is decided by one side conceding defeat or refusing to play, the result shall be stated as Match Conceded or Match Awarded, as the case may be.

8. CORRECTNESS OF RESULT

Any decision as to the correctness of the scores shall be the responsibility of the umpires. See Law 3.15 (Correctness of scores).

9. MISTAKES IN SCORING

If, after the players and umpires have left the field in the belief that the match has been concluded, the umpires discover that a mistake in scoring has occurred which affects the result then, subject to 10 below, they shall adopt the following procedure.

(a) If, when the players leave the field, the side batting last has not completed its innings and

either (i) the number of overs to be bowled in the last hour, or in that innings, has not been completed

or (ii) the agreed time for close of play, or for the end of the innings, has not been reached

then, unless one side concedes defeat, the umpires shall order play to resume.

Unless a result is reached sooner, play will then continue, if conditions permit, until the prescribed number of overs has been completed and either time for close of play has been reached or the allotted time for the innings has expired, as appropriate. The number of overs and time remaining shall be taken as they were at the call of Time for the supposed conclusion of the match. No account shall be taken of the time between that moment and the resumption of play.

(b) If, at this call of Time, the overs have been completed and no playing time remains, or if the side batting last has completed its innings, the umpires shall immediately inform both captains of the necessary corrections to the scores and to the result.

10. RESULT NOT TO BE CHANGED

Once the umpires have agreed with the scorers the correctness of the scores at the conclusion of the match – see Laws 3.15 (Correctness of scores) and 4.2 (Correctness of scores) – the result cannot thereafter be changed.

CORRECTNESS OF RESULT

The umpires have a responsibility to ensure that the result is correct. They are required to check with the scorers at intervals and again at the end of the match. Such checks are valueless unless they know what the score should be. To this end they must each keep a tally of runs as they occur, throughout the match, checking with each other at convenient points – fall of wicket, drinks, etc. Mechanical devices, similar to a car's milometer, that move on one run at each click can be helpful. If the scoreboard appears to be incorrect, it may soon be put right. If not, having agreed with each other, they must sort out the discrepancy with the scorers as soon as possible, trying to avoid a hold up in play. If there are any queries that can't be resolved by discussion then the umpires must decide what the score should be. This is discussed more fully a little later.

THE RESULT OF A MATCH

A straightforward win by one side getting more runs than the other is clear. It is important to realise that for such a win, the losing side must have completed its innings or, in a two-innings match, both its innings. It should be noted from Section 7 how these results are to be stated in the scoring record, as a win by runs, or a win by wickets. In a two-innings match it is possible for a side to score enough runs to win in one innings, although its losing opponents must have batted twice. In this case, it is traditional to state the result as a win by an innings and the number of runs in excess of its opponent's aggregate.

Increasingly, however, matches are played under special regulations in which situations other than such a straightforward win are not covered by Law. Those responsible for such matches are required to give details of how the result is to be determined in these other situations. In this case, umpires must make sure before the match that they understand these details. They may have to settle a dispute as to the result.

Unless special regulations apply, if the side batting last does not score more than its opponents, but is not all out, then the match is a Draw, even if the scores are equal. Only when the side batting last is all out when the final scores are level is the result a Tie. A Draw is not strictly a result. It is a match which is concluded but in which a result has not been reached. Law 16 deals with how a match is concluded.

The special and rare cases of a win by Penalty runs, or of the umpires awarding a match, or of a side conceding defeat are dealt with below.

WINNING HIT OR EXTRAS

The scoring of the winning run acts as a guillotine. The ball is immediately dead and any subsequent event will not be part of the match. For example, if the side batting last needs one run to win and Wide ball is called, and not revoked, the instant award of a one-run penalty for the Wide means the desired run is scored and the match is won. Even if the wicket-keeper puts the wicket down fairly the striker cannot be stumped or run out. If two runs are needed to win and the batsmen complete two runs, the match is finished and a third run would not be valid, however much the striker might want it to complete his century. If the ball reaches the boundary before the batsmen have completed the winning run, the boundary allowance will count. If the winning run is completed before the ball reaches the boundary, only the runs will count. If the umpire has occasion to award 5 penalty runs for some misdemeanour on this final delivery the Law instructs him to do so when the ball is dead. Although this appears to be 'too late', these runs will in fact count. Although the penalty is not announced until the ball is dead, the misdemeanour must have been committed before it became dead. Paragraph (b) is a reminder that a deletion of runs over-rides the award of runs. If a catch is taken, any runs made before its completion are not to count, so cannot contribute towards a winning score.

WIN BY PENALTY RUNS

This can occur *only* if the side batting last is all out and the award of 5 penalty runs at the very end of the match, as described in the last paragraph, makes the difference between falling short of the target and having enough runs to win. A side is chasing a total of 185 runs and, with 9 wickets down and one ball to go, have reached 183, 2 short of the opposition's total. They need 3 runs to win. The batsmen attempt these runs but one of them is run out on the second run. They will score only 1 run, making their total 184 all out. The result would be a win by 1 run to the fielding side. If, however, 5 penalty runs are awarded to the batting side as a result of a fielding offence on this last delivery, that will bring the batting score to 189 all out. The result is a win by Penalty runs to the batting side.

UMPIRES AWARDING A MATCH

Section 3 makes clear that although no appeal is necessary this is not an arbitrary action by the umpires. First there must be some action by either the fielding side or the batsmen that means play cannot start or cannot continue as it should. Law 31 describes one such situation. Then the umpires together must discover the reason for this action. If play is in progress, this will probably mean leaving the field and going to the pavilion. Time must be called before doing so and the umpires should take possession of the ball. The umpires should agree and note the time, as adjustments to time for close of play may be needed, as instructed in 3(c)(iii).

If it is apparent to the umpires that there is indeed a refusal to play they must warn the captain of the side of the consequences of this refusal. Failure to start or continue after such warning leaves the umpires no option but to award the match to the other side.

If play starts or continues as a result of the warning, or because there was no intentional refusal to play, calculation of the time lost, to implement 3(c)(iii), must be made jointly by the umpires.

CAPTAIN CONCEDING A MATCH

Although it will be extraordinarily rare, the Law allows a captain to decide that it is not worth continuing play and to admit defeat. The umpires will then declare that the other side has won the match.

MISTAKES IN SCORING

It is a serious reflection on the umpires if mistakes in scoring are discovered when they check with the scorers after it is supposed that the match has been concluded. Keeping a tally and checking throughout play as advised above will mean that any discrepancies are soon discovered and can be put right long before the end of the match. It is especially important to keep to this routine as the match draws near to its close. Both sides will need to know how the scores stand.

Section 9 sets out details of how to proceed if nevertheless a mistake is discovered after the players have left the field, thinking the match was over. Action other than informing those concerned is not required *unless the mistake affects the result*. There are two courses of action. If the batting side was all out or if neither time nor overs remain, then clearly no more play is possible – as indeed would be the case in dangerous conditions of ground, weather or light. The umpires must then alter the score to its correct value and tell the captains of the changed result. Otherwise play must continue, until a result is reached, or until time and overs are used up, or until conditions become unreasonable or dangerous. Failing light may well bring play to an end in such a situation. This is one of the very rare situations in which a captain might concede defeat. If it is discovered that the batting side needs one more run to win and still has five wickets in hand, with half an hour to play in good light and dry conditions, the fielding captain just might concede defeat rather than bring his players back on to the field.

If play is resumed, time will have been lost. This loss of time and any associated decrease in the number of overs to be bowled are both to be disregarded. The clock and the over count are to stop at the original call of Time and will not start again until the call of Play for the resumption.

It is much better to maintain vigilance throughout play so that the situation does not arise.

RESULT NOT TO BE CHANGED

There have been reports of an organising committee changing the result of the match. The Law unequivocally states that once the two umpires have agreed the scores and hence the result, it may not thereafter be changed. The organising committee may, in the light of some irregularity or incident of unfair play, award points or whatever for a match without changing the result, particularly where an award of points is involved. This should not be confused with changing the actual result.

Law 22 The over

1. NUMBER OF BALLS

The ball shall be bowled from each end alternately in overs of 6 balls.

2. START OF AN OVER

An over has started when the bowler starts his run up or, if he has no run up, his action for the first delivery of that over.

3. VALIDITY OF BALLS

(a) A ball shall not count as one of the 6 balls of the over unless it is delivered, even though, as in Law 42.15 (Bowler attempting to run out non-striker before delivery) a batsman may be dismissed or some other incident occurs without the ball having been delivered.

(b) A ball delivered by the bowler shall not count as one of the 6 balls of the over

   (i) if it is called dead, or is to be considered dead, before the striker has had an opportunity to play it. See Law 23.6 (Dead Ball; ball counting as one of over).

  (ii) if it is called dead in the circumstances of Law 23.4(b)(vi) (Umpire calling and signalling Dead ball). Note also the special provisions of Law 23.4(b)(v).

 (iii) if it is a No ball. See Law 24 (No ball).

 (iv) if it is a Wide. See Law 25 (Wide ball).

  (v) when 5 penalty runs are awarded to the batting side under any of Laws 2.6 (Player returning without permission), 41.2 (Fielding the ball), 42.4 (Deliberate attempt to distract striker), or 42.5 (Deliberate distraction or obstruction of batsman).

(c) Any deliveries other than those listed in (a) and (b) above shall be known as valid balls. Only valid balls shall count towards the 6 balls of the over.

4. CALL OF OVER

When 6 valid balls have been bowled and when the ball becomes dead, the umpire shall call Over before leaving the wicket. See also Law 23.3 (Call of Over or Time).

5. UMPIRE MISCOUNTING

(a) If the umpire miscounts the number of valid balls, the over as counted by the umpire shall stand.

(b) If, having miscounted, the umpire allows an over to continue after 6 valid balls have been bowled, he may subsequently call Over as the ball becomes dead after any delivery, even if that delivery is not a valid ball.

6. BOWLER CHANGING ENDS

A bowler shall be allowed to change ends as often as desired, provided he does not bowl two overs consecutively, nor bowl parts of each of two consecutive overs, in the same innings.

7. FINISHING AN OVER

(a) Other than at the end of an innings, a bowler shall finish an over in progress unless he is incapacitated or is suspended under any of the Laws.

(b) If for any reason, other than the end of an innings, an over is left uncompleted at the start of an interval or interruption, it shall be completed on resumption of play.

8. BOWLER INCAPACITATED OR SUSPENDED DURING AN OVER

If for any reason a bowler is incapacitated while running up to deliver the first ball of an over, or is incapacitated or suspended during an over, the umpire shall call and signal Dead ball. Another bowler shall complete the over from the same end, provided that he does not bowl two overs consecutively, nor bowl parts of each of two consecutive overs, in that innings.

THE OVER

Unless there is a special regulation or other prior agreement to the contrary, an over is to consist of 6 valid balls. Umpires should study Section 3 to be sure they understand what a valid ball is and they know which balls are valid and which ones are not. Section 3 lists all those deliveries which are not valid balls and so are not to count in the over.

A ball is not delivered unless the bowler completes his delivery action and releases the ball towards the striker. Although in an attempt to run out the non-striker a bowler may throw the ball on to the non-striker's wicket, this is not delivering the ball since he has not even started his delivery stride and delivery action. The two cases cited in 3(b)(i) are those where the striker is distracted, either inadvertently or deliberately, while he is receiving the ball. In these cases, even if he actually tries to play the ball and makes contact, the delivery will not be a valid ball.

In the cases listed in 3(b)(v), the fact that the ball is not to count in the over is specifically stated in each of these Laws.

The over starts when the bowler starts his run up to deliver the first ball. The Law recognises that there are bowlers, though few in number, who do not have a run up. In that case the starting point for an over is when such a bowler begins his delivery action for the first ball.

It is imperative that umpires count the balls in an over correctly, especially in matches where innings are limited to a number of overs. Commercial devices such as 'clickers' are available, but coins, pebbles or other small objects are widely used. Whatever method of counting is employed, it is essential that the umpire adopts the same procedure for every delivery so that it becomes almost automatic. If a No ball or Wide is bowled, or for some other reason a delivery is not a valid ball, the umpire must remember not to count it as one of the over.

The bowler's end umpire is responsible for the call of Over when 6 valid balls have been delivered. Nevertheless as a fail-safe both umpires should count. It is helpful if an unobtrusive signal passes between the umpires when 5 or nowadays, by quite a few umpires, after 4 valid balls have been bowled. Such an arrangement must be clearly understood in agreement between the two umpires before play begins.

UMPIRE MISCOUNTING

If, as suggested, the two umpires work together in checking the number of deliveries, the possibility of miscounting will be minimised. Mistakes do, however, sometimes occur. In that case, no attempt at correction is to be made. The over stands with the wrong number of valid balls. Moreover, if the bowler's end umpire mistakenly lets the over run on – he may perhaps have allowed 8 valid balls to be delivered – and the next delivery is a Wide, when he realises his mistake he should call Over, when the ball is dead for that delivery, since although that next ball is not valid there have already been 6 valid balls before it.

CALL OF OVER

The call of Over does not <u>make</u> the ball dead. The 6th valid ball has to have <u>become</u> dead *before* calling Over. As with all calls it should be made loudly and clearly. While avoiding waste of playing time by undue delay, the umpire must be sure that the ball is dead before making the call. Dead ball is the subject of Law 23.

Although a simple, clear call of Over is all that is required, without embellishing gestures, if one batsman is right-handed and the other left-handed, it can be helpful to the fielders to indicate which batsman will be facing the next delivery.

OVER MUST BE COMPLETED

There are several reasons – injury or suspension of a bowler; taking an interval at the fall of a wicket; interruptions for weather and so on – for an over being interrupted. If play resumes after the break, an innings ending in mid-over is the *only* situation in which the over will not be completed.

The completion must be by the same bowler unless he is incapacitated or suspended. Umpires must note carefully both the current bowler and the previous bowler when any break occurs, to ensure that a replacement bowler did not bowl any balls in the previous over. Moreover, he will not be allowed to bowl any balls, not even as a replacement bowler partway through, in the next over. The same embargo of not bowling even a few balls in two consecutive overs applies to a bowler changing ends. It is the only restriction on his doing so.

Law 23   Dead ball

I. BALL IS DEAD

(a) The ball becomes dead when
  (i) it is finally settled in the hands of the wicket-keeper or of the bowler.
  (ii) a boundary is scored. See Law 19.3 (Scoring a boundary).
  (iii) a batsman is dismissed. The ball will be deemed to be dead from the instant of the incident causing the dismissal.
  (iv) whether played or not it becomes trapped between the bat and person of a batsman or between items of his clothing or equipment.
  (v) whether played or not it lodges in the clothing or equipment of a batsman or the clothing of an umpire.
  (vi) it lodges in a protective helmet worn by a fielder.
  (vii) there is an award of penalty runs under either of Laws 2.6 (Player returning without permission) or 41.2 (Fielding the ball). The ball shall not count as one of the over.
  (viii) there is contravention of Law 41.3 (Protective helmets belonging to the fielding side).
  (ix) Lost ball is called. See Law 20 (Lost ball).
(b) The ball shall be considered to be dead when it is clear to the bowler's end umpire that the fielding side and both batsmen at the wicket have ceased to regard it as in play.

2. BALL FINALLY SETTLED

Whether the ball is finally settled or not is a matter for the umpire alone to decide.

3. CALL OF OVER OR TIME

Neither the call of Over (see Law 22.4), nor the call of Time (see Law 16.2) is to be made until the ball is dead, either under I above or under 4 below.

4. UMPIRE CALLING AND SIGNALLING DEAD BALL

(a) When the ball has become dead under I above, the bowler's end umpire may call and signal Dead ball if it is necessary to inform the players.

(b) Either umpire shall call and signal Dead ball when
- (i) he intervenes in a case of unfair play.
- (ii) a serious injury to a player or umpire occurs.
- (iii) he leaves his normal position for consultation.
- (iv) one or both bails fall from the striker's wicket before the striker has had the opportunity of playing the ball.
- (v) the striker is not ready for the delivery of the ball and, if the ball is delivered, makes no attempt to play it. Provided the umpire is satisfied that the striker had adequate reason for not being ready, the ball shall not count as one of the over.
- (vi) the striker is distracted by any noise or movement or in any other way while he is preparing to receive, or receiving a delivery. This shall apply whether the source of the distraction is within the game or outside it. Note also (vii) below.
  The ball shall not count as one of the over.
- (vii) there is an instance of a deliberate attempt to distract under either of Laws 42.4 (Deliberate attempt to distract striker) or 42.5 (Deliberate distraction or obstruction of batsman). The ball shall not count as one of the over.
- (viii) the bowler drops the ball accidentally before delivery.
- (ix) the ball does not leave the bowler's hand for any reason other than an attempt to run out the non-striker before entering his delivery stride. See Law 42.15 (Bowler attempting to run out non-striker before delivery).
- (x) he is required to do so under any of the Laws not included above.

5. BALL CEASES TO BE DEAD

The ball ceases to be dead – that is, it comes into play – when the bowler starts his run up or, if he has no run up, his bowling action.

6. DEAD BALL; BALL COUNTING AS ONE OF OVER

(a) When a ball which has been delivered is called dead or is to be considered dead then, other than as in (b) below,
- (i) it will not count in the over if the striker has not had an opportunity to play it.
- (ii) it will be a valid ball if the striker has had an opportunity to play it, unless No ball or Wide has been called, except in the circumstances

of 4(b)(vi) above and Laws 2.6 (Fielder returning without permission), 41.2 (Fielding the ball), 42.4 (Deliberate attempt to distract striker) and 42.5 (Deliberate distraction or obstruction of batsman).

(b) In 4(b)(v) above, the ball will not count in the over only if both conditions of not attempting to play the ball and having an adequate reason for not being ready are met. Otherwise the delivery will be a valid ball.

Play is in progress for the whole period from a call of Play until the next call of Time, as explained in Law 15. The ball is not continuously in play – the opposite of being dead – during this period. The ball is brought into play each time a bowler starts his run up (or action, in the absence of a run up) to deliver the ball. It remains in play until all activity from that delivery has ceased, and is then dead until next brought into play for the following delivery. When the ball is dead, even though play is in progress, runs cannot be scored and batsmen cannot be dismissed. It is almost but not quite a total cessation of activity. For example an appeal can be made while the ball is dead and this is not the only possibility.

DEAD BALL

There are three ways that the ball becomes dead.

1 Automatically

Section 1(a) lists incidents in which the ball becomes dead without action by the umpire. Sometimes, however, the players will not be aware that the ball has become dead and it is then sensible for the umpire to call and signal Dead ball. This is specifically permitted in Section 1(a).

(i) The umpire will have to judge when the ball is finally settled. Obvious situations are:

the bowler receiving the ball from a fielder and starting to walk back to his mark

the wicket-keeper taking the ball after it has passed the batsman and tossing it without any urgency to a fielder.

Not all situations are as clear cut as these. Normally, the urgency or otherwise with which the bowler or wicket-keeper acts will be a good guide.

(ii) The instant that a boundary is scored is laid down in Law 19.

(iii) Law 27 defines the difference between being out and being dismissed. If the batsman is out but not dismissed, the ball will remain in play. If he is dismissed, the ball will have been dead from the moment he was out. For example, there is an appeal for LBW. If the appeal is upheld, but not otherwise, the ball will be dead from the moment the ball made contact with the striker's person, even though by the time the umpire has weighed up the evidence and made his decision a second or two has elapsed. Any run attempted during that second or two will not be allowed and the not out batsman should be returned to his original end.

(iv, v, vi)   There is a difference between becoming trapped and lodging. If the ball is trapped – say between bat and pad – it could possibly fall out. In order to decide that it is trapped, the umpire must be sure that there has been a period of time, even if it is only a very short one, during which the ball was held there. Lodging – say in the top of a batsman's pad – means that it will take positive action to free it.

(vii, viii, ix)   Laws 2.6, 41.2, 41.3 each specify when the ball becomes dead. It is immediately on contact. In Law 20 it is at the instant of the fielder's call.

2 To be called dead by an umpire

Law 4(b) lists incidents in which an umpire is to call and signal Dead ball, to make the ball dead. In each case it is to be 'either umpire'. It will be the umpire who first sees the incident.

The reason for calling Dead ball is to prevent further action of any kind by either side. Such further action might be, for example, a fielder attempting to dismiss a batsman.

(i)   Intervening in a case of unfair play is dealt with in Law 42.

(ii)   The umpire must judge whether a perceived injury is serious or not. Many cases are obvious but for those that are not it is better to be cautious and call Dead ball. If the injury turns out to be serious it would be culpable to have had any delay before getting help for the stricken man.

(iii)   If there has been an appeal and the umpire decides that unobtrusive signals are not sufficient to resolve his doubt, he may go to meet his colleague. As his doubt means he has not yet answered the appeal, the ball is not dead. Again any unfair action must be pre-empted; before leaving his position the umpire must call and signal Dead ball.

(iv)   If the striker's wicket is not intact it will disadvantage the fielding side in attempting a dismissal. Because there has been no agreement to play without bails, if the ball strikes the stumps the wicket may not be put down.

(v)   There are two important points about the striker not being ready. If, in spite of drawing back to indicate that he was not ready, he attempts to play the ball, he will lose the protection afforded by this piece of Law. The umpire will often not know why the striker has drawn away but should call and signal Dead ball nevertheless, to prevent an unfair dismissal, in case the withdrawal was justified. If it turns out to be a genuine reason, such as a fly in his eye or a rush of spectator movement behind the bowler's arm, the ball is not to count in the over. If it was not an acceptable reason this recompense will not apply. Exceptionally, the umpires might form the opinion that it was a ruse to waste time or, worse, a deliberate attempt to avoid dismissal. Either of these would be a serious act of unfair play to be dealt with as laid down in Law 42.

(vi)   The striker is considered to be preparing to receive the ball as soon as it comes into play and has not finished receiving it until he has played or played at it or has had the opportunity to play it. Anything that the umpire considers has distracted the striker during this period requires a call and signal of Dead ball. The distraction may be innocent – a sudden yelp from a close fielder stung by a bee. It may even not be connected with the game. On the other hand, it can be a deliberate attempt by a fielder to unsettle the striker. This is a specified act of unfair play, dealt with in Law 42.4. Whatever the cause, the first response is to call and signal Dead ball. Further action will have to follow if the distraction was a deliberate one.

(vii) Laws 42.4 and 42.5 deal with deliberate attempts to distract respectively the striker and, subsequently, either batsman. They are discussed more fully under Law 42. The point to note here is that they are two of the five exceptions to the general principle that a ball called or becoming dead will count in the over if the striker had the opportunity to play it. Section 6 lists all these five exceptions.

(viii) This is self-evident. The ball is not delivered.

(ix) In attempting to run out the non-striker, the bowler may try to put down the non-striker's wicket with the ball in hand, rather than throwing it on to the stumps. Dead ball is not to be called unless the attempt fails as described in Law 42.15. Or perhaps the bowler may stop in his run up, or go through his whole action and then not release the ball. Then Dead ball is to be called. A particular case in Law 35.2 is dealt with more fully there.

(x) Other Laws in which an umpire is required to call and signal Dead ball are listed below. In each case it is stated in the Law whether either umpire is to make the call and signal or whether a particular umpire is to do so.

Law 22.8	Bowler incapacitated or suspended during an over
Law 24.7	Ball coming to rest in front of striker's wicket
Law 26.3	Leg byes not to be awarded
Law 27.7	Batsman leaving his wicket under a misapprehension
Law 34.5	Runs scored from a ball lawfully struck more than once
Law 35.1(b)	Out Hit wicket
Law 40.4	Movement by wicket-keeper
Law 40.5	Restrictions on actions of wicket-keeper
Law 41.7	Movement by fielders
Law 42.9	Time wasting by the fielding side
Law 42.15	Bowler attempting to run out non-striker before delivery
Law 42.16	Batsmen stealing a run

3 Naturally

The activity after the ball is delivered simply comes to a natural close.

Here the umpire must judge that both sides have lost interest in taking further action. It is usually obvious. Judgments similar to those for the ball being 'finally settled' must be made. Once the umpire has decided in his own mind that all action and intent to act are finished, the ball is dead and no further action will be valid. For instance, if a fielder has the ball, the batsmen are in their grounds and the fielder decides to re-tie his shoelace, everyone can assume the ball is dead. Neither the batsmen nor any fielder can bring it back into play.

WHETHER BALL IS TO COUNT OR NOT

It is important that the umpire knows when 6 valid balls have been bowled, so that he does not allow too many or too few deliveries in an over. The final section of this Law states quite clearly when a ball that has become or been made dead is valid and when it is not. The basic determining factor is whether or not the striker has had the opportunity to play the ball. There are, as noted earlier, five exceptions to this principle. They are listed in Section 6. Each is also noted both in its own Law and in the appropriate sections of Laws 23.1 and 23.4. Umpires must know what these exceptions are.

Law 24   No ball

I. MODE OF DELIVERY

(a) **The umpire shall ascertain whether the bowler intends to bowl right-handed or left-handed, over or round the wicket, and shall so inform the striker.**
It is unfair if the bowler fails to notify the umpire of a change in his mode of delivery. In this case the umpire shall call and signal No ball.
(b) **Underarm bowling shall not be permitted except by special agreement before the match.**

2. FAIR DELIVERY – THE ARM

For a delivery to be fair in respect of the arm the ball must not be thrown. See 3 below.
Although it is the primary responsibility of the striker's end umpire to assess the fairness of a delivery in this respect, there is nothing in this Law to debar the bowler's end umpire from calling and signalling No ball if he considers that the ball has been thrown.
(a) **If, in the opinion of either umpire, the ball has been thrown, he shall call and signal No ball and, when the ball is dead, inform the other umpire of the reason for the call.**
The bowler's end umpire shall then
(i) **caution the bowler. This caution shall apply throughout the innings.**
(ii) **inform the captain of the fielding side of the reason for this action.**
(iii) **inform the batsmen at the wicket of what has occurred.**

(b) If, after such caution, either umpire considers that, in that innings, a further delivery by the same bowler is thrown, the procedure set out in (a) above shall be repeated, indicating to the bowler that this is a final warning.

This warning shall also apply throughout the innings.

(c) If either umpire considers that, in that innings, a further delivery by the same bowler is thrown, he shall call and signal No ball and when the ball is dead inform the other umpire of the reason for the call.

The bowler's end umpire shall then

(i) direct the captain of the fielding side to suspend the bowler forthwith. The over shall, if applicable, be completed by another bowler, who shall neither have bowled the previous over or part thereof nor be allowed to bowl any part of the next over.

The bowler thus suspended shall not bowl again in that innings.

(ii) inform the batsmen at the wicket and, as soon as practicable, the captain of the batting side of the occurrence.

(d) The umpires together shall report the occurrence as soon as possible after the match to the Executive of the fielding side and to any Governing Body responsible for the match, who shall take such action as is considered appropriate against the captain and the bowler concerned.

3. DEFINITION OF FAIR DELIVERY – THE ARM

A ball is fairly delivered in respect of the arm if, once the bowler's arm has reached the level of the shoulder in the delivery swing, the elbow joint is not straightened partially or completely from that point until the ball has left the hand. This definition shall not debar a bowler from flexing or rotating the wrist in the delivery swing.

4. BOWLER THROWING TOWARDS STRIKER'S END BEFORE DELIVERY

If the bowler throws the ball towards the striker's end before entering his delivery stride, either umpire shall call and signal No ball. See Law 42.16 (Batsmen stealing a run). However, the procedure stated in 2 above of caution, informing, final warning, action against the bowler and reporting shall not apply.

5. FAIR DELIVERY – THE FEET

For a delivery to be fair in respect of the feet, in the delivery stride

(a) the bowler's back foot must land within and not touching the return crease appertaining to his stated mode of delivery.

(b) the bowler's front foot must land with some part of the foot, whether grounded or raised

(i) on the same side of the imaginary line joining the two middle stumps as the return crease described in (a) above

and (ii) behind the popping crease.

If the bowler's end umpire is not satisfied that all of these three conditions have been met, he shall call and signal No ball.

6. BALL BOUNCING MORE THAN TWICE OR ROLLING ALONG THE GROUND

The umpire shall call and signal No ball if a ball which he considers to have been delivered, without having previously touched bat or person of the striker,

either (i) bounces more than twice

or (ii) rolls along the ground

before it reaches the popping crease.

7. BALL COMING TO REST IN FRONT OF STRIKER'S WICKET

If a ball delivered by the bowler comes to rest in front of the line of the striker's wicket, without having previously touched the bat or person of the striker, the umpire shall call and signal No ball and immediately call and signal Dead ball.

8. CALL OF NO BALL FOR INFRINGEMENT OF OTHER LAWS

In addition to the instances above, No ball is to be called and signalled as required by the following Laws.

Law 40.3 – Position of wicket-keeper

Law 41.5 – Limitation of on-side fielders

Law 41.6 – Fielders not to encroach on pitch

Law 42.6 – Dangerous and unfair bowling

Law 42.7 – Dangerous and unfair bowling – action by the umpire

Law 42.8 – Deliberate bowling of high full pitched balls

9. REVOKING A CALL OF NO BALL

An umpire shall revoke his call of No ball if the ball does not leave the bowler's hand for any reason.

10. NO BALL TO OVER-RIDE WIDE

A call of No ball shall over-ride the call of Wide ball at any time. See Laws 25.1 (Judging a Wide) and 25.3 (Call and signal of Wide ball).

11. BALL NOT DEAD

The ball does not become dead on the call of No ball.

12. PENALTY FOR A NO BALL

A penalty of one run shall be awarded instantly on the call of No ball. Unless the call is revoked, the penalty shall stand even if a batsman is dismissed. It shall be in addition to any other runs scored, any boundary allowance and any other runs awarded for penalties.

13. RUNS RESULTING FROM A NO BALL – HOW SCORED

The one-run penalty shall be scored as a No ball extra. If other penalty runs have been awarded to either side these shall be scored as stated in Law 42.17 (Penalty runs). Any runs completed by the batsmen or any boundary allowance shall be credited to the striker if the ball has been struck by the bat; otherwise they shall also be scored as No ball extras.

Apart from any award of 5 penalty runs, all runs resulting from a No ball, whether as No ball extras or credited to the striker, shall be debited against the bowler.

14. NO BALL NOT TO COUNT

A No ball shall not count as one of the over. See Law 22.3 (Validity of balls).

15. OUT FROM A NO BALL

When No ball has been called, neither batsman shall be out under any of the Laws except 33 (Handled the ball), 34 (Hit the ball twice), 37 (Obstructing the field) or 38 (Run out).

A No ball is a delivery which places the batsman receiving the ball at some disadvantage. The offences which merit a call of No ball are all concerned with the delivery of the ball:

- unfairness by the bowler in the actual delivery
- where the fielders are when the ball is delivered
- how the ball behaves after it is delivered.

UNFAIRNESS BY THE BOWLER IN THE ACTUAL DELIVERY

1 Mode of delivery

When a bowler first comes on to bowl, the umpire is to enquire what his mode of delivery is and to inform the striker. The terms over the wicket and round the wicket are explained in Appendix D. Some bowlers have most of their run up crossing diagonally behind the umpire from one side to the other. What counts is which side he is as he passes the wicket.

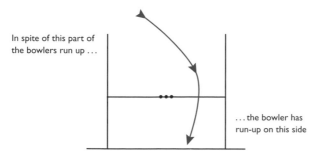

In spite of this part of the bowlers run up . . .

. . . the bowler has run-up on this side

Subsequently it is the bowler's responsibility to tell the umpire if he proposes to change this mode. If a bowler changes without such notification, the umpire is to call and signal No ball as soon as he realises that the bowler is running up on the 'wrong' side.

2 The bowler's feet

Although this is not next in the Law, it is appropriate to consider the bowler's feet in conjunction with his mode of delivery. There is one restriction on the back foot and now two restrictions on the front foot. A new one, introduced in 2010, restricts the area in which the front foot can land, to not only behind the popping crease but also to one side only of the (imaginary) line joining middle stumps. It must be the side on which, according to his stated mode of delivery, he will run up.

These restrictions are set out clearly in Section 5. They are quite independent of each other. For the back foot, position in relation to the popping crease is immaterial. Equally it does not matter if the front foot crosses the return crease. A simple description is that, as each foot <u>lands</u>, the back foot **must not have** *any part grounded* on or beyond the return crease; the front foot **must have** *some part behind* the popping crease *and on the correct side* of the halfway line, even if that part of the foot is raised. Subsequent movement of either foot *after* it has landed is irrelevant.

A No ball. His front foot has no part on the correct side of the 'halfway line'

A fair delivery with respect to the feet. His back foot has landed within the return crease; his front foot has landed with a (raised) part behind the popping crease

A No ball. His front foot has landed with heel on the crease marking. It has no part behind the crease

His back foot has landed fairly. Although overhanging the return crease, it is not touching it

In every case the umpire must see, separately, where the bowler's feet land in his delivery stride. An umpire must be aware that the bowler is running up behind him and be prepared to call and signal No ball immediately if he sees one of the bowler's feet incorrectly placed.

3 The bowler's arm

Whether a bowler bowls the ball, which is fair, or throws it, which is unfair, has been a matter of controversy for years. The difference is in the last part of the delivery swing. Limits are prescribed for this 'last part of the swing'. In crude terms, a bowler's delivery action involves transferring his arm from behind his body to a point in front of his body and then releasing the ball. This transfer is usually, though not necessarily, with his arm close to his head. It must be above shoulder level, to comply with the ban on underarm bowling. The 'last part of the swing' that is crucial to the fairness of the delivery starts when the arm reaches shoulder level behind him, continues as he brings his arm over, and lasts until he releases the ball. During that time his elbow joint must not straighten or partially straighten.

Many bowlers start this part of the swing with a straight elbow and keep it so. Such bowlers present no problem. For other bowlers, however, the arm may be bent during this time. In order for the delivery to be fair, it has to be judged that the arm does not become straight, or less sharply bent at the elbow. It will usually be the striker's end umpire who is better placed to see this, but either umpire is empowered to make the judgment. Should either of them consider that, during the final part of the swing, the bowler's arm is bent at the elbow and, before release of the ball, it becomes straight, or even just somewhat straighter, he will call and signal No ball as soon as possible.

4 A special case
Occasionally, if the striker appears to be well in front of his crease, or even advancing well up the pitch, the bowler will try to run him out and is permitted to do so. If he throws the ball in the general direction of the striker's wicket, the umpire does not have to divine his intention. If the bowler makes such a throw *after* entering his delivery stride there is nothing to distinguish it from any other throw. No ball is to be called with all the consequences of that call. If, however, he throws *before* entering his delivery stride, whilst the call of No ball is still to be made, with its attendant one-run penalty, the procedures laid down in Section 2 are not to be applied.

WHERE THE FIELDERS ARE WHEN THE BALL IS DELIVERED
There are restrictions on the position of the wicket-keeper, on the positions of the fielders on the on (leg) side of the wicket and on the positions of fielders close to the pitch. These are dealt with in Laws 40 and 41. Contraventions of these Laws merit a call and signal of No ball, from the striker's end umpire in the first two cases and the bowler's end umpire in the third.

HOW THE BALL BEHAVES AFTER IT IS DELIVERED
Balls which on pitching rear up so high as to be likely to inflict injury on the striker – 'bouncers' – and those which without pitching reach the popping crease at a dangerous height – 'beamers' – are dealt with in Laws 42.6, 42.7 and 42.8, where they are defined and consequent action discussed in detail.

In addition, although not dangerous, it is considered unfair if,
> before reaching the popping crease, the ball
>> bounces more than twice
> or rolls along the ground
> or, before reaching the line of the striker's wicket, the ball comes to a halt

without in each case having touched the striker's bat or person. Umpires should note this last proviso.

Section 6 sets out the umpire's action for the first two. Section 7 does so for the third. Notice in this third case that the call and signal of No ball is to be followed immediately by a call and signal of Dead ball in any case.

Usually such erratic behaviour by the ball is the result of a mishap by the bowler in the act of delivery. The umpire should consider whether the ball can in fact be counted as having been delivered. This cannot be defined precisely. Certainly if the ball were to travel backwards from the bowler's hand it would not have been delivered. In general, if the ball is launched in a forward direction, rather than a backward or sideways one, it can be considered to have been delivered. It is for the umpire to judge. If he considers that it has not been delivered then, instead of what is prescribed in Section 6 or Section 7, he should call and signal Dead ball to prevent any further action. The ball will not count in the over.

Sadly, in recent times there have been instances where a bowler has deliberately caused the ball to roll along the ground or come to rest prematurely. If the umpire were to form the opinion that this was so, and was confirmed in this view by his colleague, then it would be an act of unfair play. In addition to what is prescribed in Section 6 or Section 7, the umpires should invoke the procedures of Law 42.18. **Although *deliberately* making the ball bounce twice is not contrary to Law, for a bowler to do this often, or at a crucial point in the innings, is unfair. Again, unless a special regulation has prescribed specific action, a call of Dead ball and action under Law 42.18 would be required.**

RECOMPENSE FOR A NO BALL

As stated earlier, a No ball puts the striker at some disadvantage. The Law compensates him in three ways.

- a penalty of one run is awarded to the batting side in addition to any runs accruing in any other way from that delivery. With the exception of Leg byes, these other runs will be recorded just as they would have been if No ball had not been called. The one-run penalty, however, will always be scored as an extra. The scorers will understand this and the umpire need make no modification to his No ball signal on that account. However, as described earlier, he will need to indicate whether the ball touched the bat or not. Leg byes will also be recorded as No ball extras. Scorers will note that all runs accruing from a No ball delivery, with the exception of any 5-run penalty, are to be debited against the bowler.
- the striker himself is immune from dismissal in any of the ways for which the bowler gets credit. The few ways in which he can be out from a No ball are set out in Section 15. Umpires and scorers must be familiar with which ones they are.
- the ball does not count in the over, so (unless the umpire has mistakenly already allowed the over to continue after 6 valid balls have been bowled) another delivery must be made. Both umpires should adjust their counters to take account of this.

FIELD TECHNIQUE

The ball does not become dead on the call of No ball. Both umpires must therefore continue to watch the course of play until the ball is dead. No signalling to the scorers is possible during this time. Although the call and signal of No ball is made as soon as possible after the offence, it is to inform only the players and the other umpire. The signal without the call is repeated to the scorers, with any others that may be needed, when the ball is dead. It of course requires acknowledgement.

Although much of what follows refers to action under other Laws, it is set out here as a description of the umpires' technique every time the ball comes into play, is delivered, received and possibly played by the striker.

1 The striker's end umpire

Before the ball comes into play he should check the positions of the on-side fielders, to see that there are no more than two behind the popping crease. If there are, or if there is any possibility that one of the deep fielders on the on side might stray over the line, he should move to the off side (see Law 3.11). He must not risk the embarrassment of a contravention by a fielder behind him that he cannot see. He will also check the position of the wicket-keeper.

He will then watch the bowler's arm action. Whether he thinks it is fair, or whether he calls and signals No ball because he considers the ball is thrown, he must immediately switch his attention to the striker, the creases and the stumps. If the wicket-keeper is standing close to the wicket he must watch him too. It is fatal to watch the ball's travel through the air. Nor can he watch to see if the wicket-keeper moves from standing back to a close position. He must have his eyes focused ready for the arrival of the ball. Because he is watching that area closely, he will be aware if the wicket-keeper has come close to the stumps from further back. He must be ready to call and signal No ball if he sees a contravention by the fielders or the wicket-keeper. He may need to adjudicate on a stumping or a Run out. He must be ready to assist the other umpire if necessary with information about how the wicket was broken, whether a catch carried and so on. Further stages of his role if the ball is played into the outfield are discussed under Law 38.

2 The bowler's end umpire

As the bowler begins his run up the umpire will check the positions of the fielders close to the pitch. He must then be ready to watch the bowler's feet from when the landing of the back foot starts the delivery stride until the landing of the front foot completes it. It is essential that he has a clear view of the landing of the bowler's feet, which may not always be in the same place. He must control his breathing so that he is completely ready to call No ball at once if he sees either foot land illegally. He will signal as he calls. He may however have to revoke the call if the bowler does not release the ball. See Section 9.

As soon as the umpire has seen the foot placements, whether fair or not, he must watch the ball, picking up its flight as quickly as possible, in order to be able to adjudicate on events at the striker's end. If he moves his head in thus changing his view from the feet to the ball, it will take a little longer for his eyes to focus on the next target. The change must be achieved by merely swivelling his eyes without head movement. It is therefore advisable to stand some way back from the stumps. Each umpire must find for himself the best position.

The umpire must also be clearly aware of the line wicket to wicket, that is, the line joining the two middle stumps. To achieve this he should stand with his head directly in this line and so that he can see both sets of stumps. To accommodate both these needs will require an umpire of average height to be *at least* 4 feet behind the stumps, but a taller umpire will wish to be further back. Each umpire will choose the distance that is comfortable for his stature. The once popular method, of bending over in order to view both sets of stumps, places too much strain on the back to be sensible. Moreover it foreshortens the view of the pitch, which is certainly not desirable for judging distances.

Again his role in subsequent events, until the ball is dead, is discussed under more appropriate Laws. When the ball is dead, the relevant signals are to be made to the scorers, in the order already prescribed. The responsibility for all such communication with the scorers lies with the bowler's end umpire. If his colleague at the striker's end has signalled a No ball, he may have to add others himself, to indicate whether the ball came off the bat, or to award penalties, and so on. Even if he has no signals 'of his own' he is still required to make the final communication to the scorers, when the ball is dead, even for Short run. There the first signal is not made until the ball is dead and may be by the striker's end umpire, if that is the end where the short running occurred. Technically, therefore, it does not require repetition, but the bowler's end umpire is still responsible for informing the scorers as to the number of runs to be recorded and should confirm the signal.

Law 25 Wide ball

1. JUDGING A WIDE

(a) **If the bowler bowls a ball, not being a No ball, the umpire shall adjudge it a Wide if, according to the definition in (b) below, in his opinion the ball passes wide of the striker where he is and which also would have passed wide of him standing in a normal guard position.**

(b) **The ball will be considered as passing wide of the striker unless it is sufficiently within his reach for him to be able to hit it with his bat by means of a normal cricket stroke.**

2. DELIVERY NOT A WIDE

The umpire shall not adjudge a delivery as being a Wide
(a) if the striker, by moving,
   either (i) causes the ball to pass wide of him, as defined in 1(b) above
      or (ii) brings the ball sufficiently within his reach to be able to hit it
         by means of a normal cricket stroke.
(b) if the ball touches the striker's bat or person.

3. CALL AND SIGNAL OF WIDE BALL

(a) If the umpire adjudges a delivery to be a Wide he shall call and signal
   Wide ball as soon as the ball passes the striker's wicket. It shall,
   however, be considered to have been a Wide from the instant of
   delivery, even though it cannot be called Wide until it passes the
   striker's wicket.
(b) The umpire shall revoke the call of Wide ball if there is then any contact
   between the ball and the striker's bat or person.
(c) The umpire shall revoke the call of Wide ball if a delivery is called a No
   ball. See Law 24.10 (No ball to over-ride Wide).

4. BALL NOT DEAD

The ball does not become dead on the call of Wide ball.

5. PENALTY FOR A WIDE

A penalty of one run shall be awarded instantly on the call of Wide ball.
Unless the call is revoked (see 3(b) and (c) above), this penalty shall stand
even if a batsman is dismissed, and shall be in addition to any other runs
scored, any boundary allowance and any other runs awarded for penalties.

6. RUNS RESULTING FROM A WIDE – HOW SCORED

All runs completed by the batsmen or a boundary allowance, together
with the penalty for the Wide, shall be scored as Wide balls. Apart from
any award of 5 penalty runs, all runs resulting from a Wide shall be debited
against the bowler.

7. WIDE NOT TO COUNT

A Wide shall not count as one of the over. See Law 22.3 (Validity of balls).

8. OUT FROM A WIDE

When Wide ball has been called, neither batsman shall be out under any of
the Laws except 33 (Handled the ball), 35 (Hit wicket), 37 (Obstructing the
field), 38 (Run out) or 39 (Stumped).

In order to be fair to the striker, the bowler has to deliver the ball so that the striker can reach it comfortably enough to hit it. It must be emphasised that this is all that the Wide ball Law demands. In the one-day matches of very many competitions, there are other considerations of negative bowling and recently even of a particular distance from the return crease. <u>These do not apply in Law</u>, but understanding of the Wide ball Law has been clouded because players, having seen or played in so many one-day matches, have had their view of Wide coloured by those special regulations.

What is important is the criterion of consistency. Early in an innings a batsman may be cautious about trying to reach a ball. Towards the end, when the side wants to score more quickly, he may be bolder and move to try to hit it. The umpire must maintain exactly the same judgment of what is a Wide in all situations. He must therefore be conscious of what he has considered to be within reach in the early stages, so as to make the same assessment in the later stages.

JUDGING A WIDE

The test is 'is it near enough to the striker for him to hit it?' Merely being within reach is not sufficient. A ball which he could get the toe of his bat to with his arms outstretched at full length is within reach, but he could not hit it in any reasonable sort of way. A ball has to be nearer than that to escape being a Wide. The phrase in the Law 'a normal cricket stroke' does not mean a recognised text-book stroke, such as an on drive or a late cut. It simply requires that the striker could comfortably get his bat to it and hit it 'in a reasonable sort of way'. As an example, a ball over his head could well be within comfortable reach, but hitting it would be more like tennis than cricket. This would therefore qualify as a Wide, and would be one, were it not for the strictures of Law 42 on dangerous bowling, which decree that it is to be a No ball, thus over-riding its Wide status.

Although he could have reached it if he had not moved back a little from a normal guard position, it would only have been on the toe of his bat. A Wide ball

His reach is much less for a low ball

He has failed to hit it only because his bat was at the wrong height. He could have hit it properly. Not a Wide

It must be remembered that, if the striker makes no move towards the ball, he will not be able to reach nearly as far on the leg side as he can on the off side. If, however, he opens up his shoulders by moving his front foot even a modest way towards the leg side, he will have a very much increased reach on that side. A low ball must be nearer to be hittable.

It should be obvious that a tall batsman will be within hittable distance of many more deliveries than a shorter man. Since, by definition, he is not actually going to hit a Wide, the umpire must form a judgment about what he *could* reach comfortably, even though he does not put his bat in the right place.

STRIKER'S POSITION

Where the striker is as the ball passes him is crucial in determining a Wide. The umpire must answer two questions. First, 'Was the ball comfortably within reach when it passed the striker where he actually was?' He may have moved well across to the off, or to the leg side. He may have advanced some way down the pitch. Did the delivery pass him in *that* position sufficiently near to hit in a reasonable sort of way? The second question is '*Would* the ball have been comfortably within reach if the striker had been in **a normal** guard position?' If the answer to <u>either</u> of these questions is 'yes', then the delivery is <u>not</u> a Wide.

The description 'where he actually was' includes not only the piece of ground he was occupying at that instant but the whole of his body alignment. It must be emphasised that a normal guard position is not *necessarily* **this** batsman's guard position. That may be eccentric. Some batsmen take guard standing almost entirely outside the stumps on the leg side. It is not unusual for a batsman to take guard some way down the pitch. The umpire has to judge the ball in relation to an *average* guard position, round about the popping crease and standing so that the bat and pads together largely cover the stumps.

It should also be noted that a ball which passes very wide of the stumps is not necessarily a Wide. It may have passed the striker within comfortable reach and moved away sharply afterwards.

DELIVERY NOT TO BE A WIDE

Three situations are specified in which a delivery is not to be a Wide. The first two relate to movement by the striker.

- If a ball was within comfortable reach, and so not a Wide, the striker *cannot make that delivery a Wide* by moving away from it, to put it out of reach.

He has put this too far away to hit with a normal cricket stroke by moving back from it. Not a Wide

- The striker *can prevent a ball from being a Wide* by moving sufficiently close to it. It will then be comfortably within his reach whether or not it would have been if he had been in a normal guard position.

In addition, any contact between ball and striker will mean that a delivery is not a Wide, whether it would otherwise have qualified or not. Any ball which the striker actually hits is not a Wide. The striker may reach out towards a ball but find it is still not near enough to 'hit in a reasonable sort of way'. He nevertheless may just touch it with the toe of his bat. This will mean it is not a Wide after all.

CALLING AND SIGNALLING WIDE BALL

Although the umpire will be aware during the ball's flight that it is likely to go wide of the striker, he is not to call it so until it passes the wicket, lest something prevents it being a Wide – the striker may touch it, he may move towards it and bring it within reach, the ball may turn on pitching and come in close to the striker. If the ball survives all these hazards, and is indeed Wide, the instruction that it is to be considered to have been a Wide since leaving the bowler's hand is therefore logical and will also remove any doubt as to whether it happened before or after any subsequent events. This instruction is not to be taken as invalidating the statement that No ball is to over-ride Wide.

It is of course possible that a striker may hit the ball after it has passed the wicket, after it has been called Wide. In this case the umpire must revoke his call. It should also be revoked if the other umpire calls and signals No ball. If his call is for encroachment by the wicket-keeper only just before the ball reaches the striker, he may well not articulate it until after the call of Wide ball. Nevertheless, the No ball is to take precedence. This fact is stated in both Laws.

Just as with No ball, the ball does not become dead on the call of Wide. The call and signal as the ball passes the wicket are purely to inform the players and the other umpire. The umpire is to repeat the signal to the scorers when the ball is dead.

RECOMPENSE FOR A WIDE

By definition a Wide is not within comfortable hitting distance of the striker. This does not prevent him from hitting it (thereby annulling it), but means a choice between moving some way from guard position to hit it and not attempting to score off it. He is therefore given recompense similar to that for a No ball. It is, however, less generous.

- a penalty of one run is awarded to the batting side in addition to any runs accruing in any other way from that delivery. All these runs will be extras, since the striker will not have hit the ball. They will, however, with the exception of any 5-run penalty, be debited against the bowler.
- the striker is given some immunity from dismissal, but it is less immunity than for a No ball. In particular he can be out Stumped or Hit wicket and the bowler will be

given credit. The ways in which he can be out from a Wide are set out in Section 8. Umpires and scorers must be familiar with these.

- the ball does not count in the over, so (unless the umpire has mistakenly already allowed the over to continue after 6 valid balls have been bowled) another delivery must be made. Both umpires should adjust their counters to take account of this.

Law 26   Bye and Leg bye

1. BYES

If the ball, delivered by the bowler, not being a No ball or a Wide, passes the striker without touching his bat or person, any runs completed by the batsmen from that delivery, or a boundary allowance, shall be credited as Byes to the batting side.

2. LEG BYES

(a) If a ball delivered by the bowler first strikes the person of the striker, runs shall be scored only if the umpire is satisfied that the striker has either (i) attempted to play the ball with his bat
    or (ii) tried to avoid being hit by the ball.
(b) If the umpire is satisfied that either of these conditions has been met runs shall be scored as follows.
   (I) If there is
       either no subsequent contact with the striker's bat or person,
           or only inadvertent contact with the striker's bat or person
       runs completed by the batsmen or a boundary allowance shall be credited to the striker in the case of subsequent contact with his bat but otherwise to the batting side as in (c) below.
   (ii) If the striker wilfully makes a lawful second strike, Laws 34.3 (Ball lawfully struck more than once) and 34.4 (Runs scored from ball lawfully struck more than once) shall apply.
(c) The runs in (b)(i) above, unless credited to the striker, shall,
   (i) if the delivery is not a No ball, be scored as Leg byes.
   (ii) if No ball has been called, be scored together with the penalty for the No ball, as No ball extras.

3. LEG BYES NOT TO BE AWARDED

If in the circumstance of 2(a) above the umpire considers that neither of the conditions (i) and (ii) therein has been met, then Leg byes shall not be awarded. The batting side shall not be credited with any runs from that delivery apart from the one-run penalty for a No ball if applicable. Moreover, no other penalties arising from that delivery shall be awarded to the batting side. The following procedure shall be adopted.

(a) **If no run is attempted but the ball reaches the boundary, the umpire shall call and signal Dead ball, and disallow the boundary.**

(b) **If runs are attempted and if**

    (i) **neither batsman is dismissed and the ball does not become dead for any other reason, the umpire shall call and signal Dead ball as soon as one run is completed or the ball reaches the boundary. The run or boundary shall be disallowed. The batsmen shall return to their original ends.**

    (ii) **before one run is completed or the ball reaches the boundary, a batsman is dismissed, or the ball becomes dead for any other reason, all the provisions of the Laws will apply, except that no runs and no penalties shall be credited to the batting side, other than the penalty for a No ball if applicable.**

Law 18 specifies that runs are scored when, among other ways, the batsmen cross and make good their ground from end to end. This Law considers two cases when such runs are made without the striker having hit the ball in the first place, namely Byes and Leg byes. These runs are extras, added to the total score but neither credited to the batsman nor debited against the bowler.

BYES

A Bye is simple and straightforward. If there is no contact at all between the ball and the striker's bat or person, the batsmen are entitled to run without restriction. Any runs completed are Byes. No signal is to be made until the ball is dead, although it can be helpful to give an unobtrusive pre-arranged indication to the scorers that a signal will be made when the ball is dead. Then giving the prescribed signal for Bye tells the scorers that the runs they have observed are Byes.

LEG BYES

Runs can be scored, as Leg byes, by the batsmen running after the ball has made contact with the striker's person but not his bat. Here, however, there are important restrictions. The batsmen are *not allowed* to score such runs, *unless the striker has*

        either   attempted to play the ball with his bat

        or   tried to avoid being hit by the ball.

If the ball *first* hits the striker's bat, whether he intended this or not, then no question of Leg byes arises and play will proceed normally. If the ball *first* hits the striker's person, then (setting aside for the moment the possibility of dismissal LBW), the umpire must consider whether, within these restrictions, Leg byes could be allowed or not. Note that subsequent contact with the bat cannot alter a decision that runs are not to be allowed.

STRIKER ATTEMPTING TO PLAY THE BALL

There are two much used phrases which have arisen from earlier versions of the Law and which now represent an entirely mistaken view of it. They are 'illegal deflection' and 'deliberately padding the ball away'.

There is nothing illegal about the ball being deflected off the striker's person. It is running after such a deflection which may be illegal. Whilst an unwise batsman may deliberately push the ball away with his pad, he is equally subject to the prohibition on scoring if he merely lets it hit him, even if he did not intend that to happen. The striker may consider that the ball would pass off stump and lift his bat high to avoid it touching the ball. Then the ball turns sharply and unexpectedly hits him on the pad. There was nothing deliberate about the ball-pad contact, but he is still not allowed to score runs.

Clearly he did not try to hit the ball with his bat. It makes no difference whether he let the ball hit him, did not expect the ball to hit him, or deliberately pushed it away with his pad. He cannot score Leg byes

An attempt by the striker to avoid being hit by the ball is usually obvious. Whether or not he has attempted to hit the ball with his bat may be more difficult to decide. A third, long outdated, incorrect description to add to the two above is 'playing a (genuine) shot'. Playing a shot is not an adequate description of trying to play the ball with his bat. He could sweep his bat through the air in what looks like, say, an off drive, but with every intention of missing the ball. In general, the greater the skill of the batsman the more he will be able to pretend that he is trying to hit the ball while having no intention of doing so. Whilst not being an exhaustive list, the following pointers may be helpful. If the striker

- plays forward defensively, with his bat clearly behind his pad
- makes a flourish of the bat well outside the line of the ball
- puts his leg forward into the line of the ball and then deliberately brings his bat through outside his pad

he is playing a shot but not attempting to hit the ball with his bat. It must not be supposed, however, that all batsmen are trying to deceive. The umpire must use his judgment in every case.

He cannot be genuinely trying to hit the ball. It has reached him and his bat is still tucked behind his pad. He cannot score Leg byes

Was he trying to hit the ball with his bat? Unless the ball had turned sharply, no. He cannot score Leg byes

ACTION FOR THE UMPIRE

If the umpire is satisfied that the striker has genuinely attempted to hit the ball with his bat or, alternatively, has tried to avoid being hit by the ball, then of course no action is required, other than signalling Leg byes to the scorers when the ball is dead and receiving an acknowledgement. If, however, he decides otherwise and Leg byes are not to be allowed, if the batsmen run he must follow the procedure set out in Section 3. Dead ball is not called until either one run has been completed, or the ball goes to the boundary. This 'delay' is in order not to deprive the fielding side of the opportunity of dismissing one of the batsmen if they are running.

The embargo on runs accruing to the batting side is more severe in this Law than in any other. Although it is repeated in Law 34, dealing with hitting the ball twice, and in Law 41 on illegal fielding, it is in exactly the same circumstances. If the conditions for legal Leg byes are not met then no runs whatsoever are allowed to the batting side, except the one-run penalty for a No ball if one is called. That is because the No ball will happen before the batsman receives the ball. Even should the fielding side commit an offence for which 5 penalty runs would normally be awarded, they will not be awarded in this case. The umpire will not signal any penalty runs when the ball is dead, thus effectively not awarding them. He will, however, after repeating the signal for No ball if one has been called, signal Dead ball to the scorers. That will indicate that any runs they may have observed are not to be recorded.

BATSMAN DISMISSED

If the ball's first contact with the striker is on his person, and the umpire is not satisfied that there has been either an attempt to hit the ball with the bat or an attempt to avoid being hit by the ball, the prohibition on running is quite independent of any dismissal. An appeal for LBW may be valid. If the ball is deflected off his person on to his stumps the striker will be bowled. There is in fact no method of dismissal, other than Timed out, to which he could not be subject. There is a belief by some that if the ball touches his bat after the impact on his person, the fact that he is at risk of being caught removes the embargo on scoring runs. This is not so. Whatever is appropriate in Law if he is dismissed, about returning to ends and so on, will apply but the embargo remains.

HOW RUNS ARE TO BE RECORDED

There can be runs <u>only</u> if the umpire is satisfied that the striker either tried to hit the ball with his bat or tried to avoid being hit by the ball. *If runs are allowed*, they will not be Byes, since the ball has struck the person. They will be Leg byes, unless No ball has been called, except in the one case of *inadvertent* contact with the striker's bat after hitting his person. Then the Law permits them to be credited to the striker. If, however, there is later contact with the bat but it is a deliberate but legal second stroke, they will still be Leg byes – again emphasising that they will not be scored at all unless the conditions are satisfied. This is set out more fully under Law 34.

If No ball is called, it will make no difference to the decision as to whether runs are to be allowed or not. As already noted, the one-run penalty will still be awarded even if runs are not allowed. If runs are allowed, however, they will be No ball extras and <u>not</u> Leg byes. As explained in Law 24, the umpire will signal No ball to the scorers when the ball is dead, following it by the Bye signal to tell them that the ball did not come off the bat.

Law 27 Appeals

1. UMPIRE NOT TO GIVE BATSMAN OUT WITHOUT AN APPEAL

Neither umpire shall give a batsman out, even though he may be out under the Laws, unless appealed to by a fielder. This shall not debar a batsman who is out under any of the Laws from leaving his wicket without an appeal having been made. Note, however, the provisions of 7 below.

2. BATSMAN DISMISSED

A batsman is dismissed if
either (a) he is given out by an umpire, on appeal
    or (b) he is out under any of the Laws and leaves his wicket as in 1 above.

3. TIMING OF APPEALS

For an appeal to be valid, it must be made before the bowler begins his run up or, if he has no run up, his bowling action to deliver the next ball, and before Time has been called.

The call of Over does not invalidate an appeal made prior to the start of the following over, provided Time has not been called. See Laws 16.2 (Call of Time) and 22.2 (Start of an over).

4. APPEAL 'HOW'S THAT?'

An appeal 'How's That?' covers all ways of being out.

5. ANSWERING APPEALS

The striker's end umpire shall answer all appeals arising out of any of Laws 35 (Hit wicket), 39 (Stumped) or 38 (Run out) when this occurs at the wicket-keeper's end. The bowler's end umpire shall answer all other appeals.

When an appeal is made, each umpire shall answer on any matter that falls within his jurisdiction.

When a batsman has been given Not out, either umpire may answer an appeal, made in accordance with 3 above, if it is on a further matter and is within his jurisdiction.

6. CONSULTATION BY UMPIRES

Each umpire shall answer appeals on matters within his own jurisdiction. If an umpire is doubtful about any point that the other umpire may have been in a better position to see, he shall consult the latter on this point of fact and shall then give the decision. If, after consultation, there is still doubt remaining, the decision shall be Not out.

7. BATSMAN LEAVING HIS WICKET UNDER A MISAPPREHENSION

An umpire shall intervene if satisfied that a batsman, not having been given out, has left his wicket under a misapprehension that he is out. The umpire intervening shall call and signal Dead ball to prevent any further action by the fielding side and shall recall the batsman.

8. WITHDRAWAL OF AN APPEAL

The captain of the fielding side may withdraw an appeal only if he obtains the consent of the umpire within whose jurisdiction the appeal falls. He must do so before the outgoing batsman has left the field of play. If such consent is given, the umpire concerned shall, if applicable, revoke his decision and recall the batsman.

9. UMPIRE'S DECISION

An umpire may alter his decision provided that such alteration is made promptly. This apart, an umpire's decision, once made, is final.

Section 1 makes it abundantly clear that an umpire is not to give a batsman out without an appeal from the fielding side. For that matter, neither should he pronounce him not out. The batsman however, if he knows he is out, can in effect dismiss himself without an appeal – by leaving his wicket and going off the field.

An appeal 'How's That?' is recommended; it will cover all ways of being out. This does not mean that it is the only way to appeal to the umpire. As long as it is clear beyond all doubt that a fielder is asking the umpire's opinion as to whether or not a batsman is out, small variations such as 'How was that?', 'How was he?' can be construed as appeals. A deaf-mute player will be unable to appeal vocally at all, but can make it absolutely clear that he is requesting the umpire's judgment on a dismissal.

TIMING

Appeals need not be made at the instant of the incident. There are just two restrictions on when an appeal can be made.
- It must be before the ball next comes into play after the incident – when the bowler starts his run up (or action) to deliver the next ball. Even the call of Over does not invalidate this.
- It must be before Time has been called in that session.

An appeal for a possible Run out, or any other dismissal, on the last ball of an over, provided it is not the last over before an interval or interruption, can be made at any time up to the start of the next over. However, appealing before the next over starts after a drinks interval would be too late. Time would have been called at the start of the interval.

BATSMAN OUT; BATSMAN DISMISSED

There is a very clear distinction between a batsman being out and his being dismissed. Being out means that the conditions of the appropriate Law apply. Being dismissed means that an umpire has given him out on appeal, or he has given himself out by walking from his wicket. A batsman who just fails to make good his ground in running when the wicket is put down will be out. If the umpire, with whatever assistance is available, is in doubt and so gives him Not out, then the batsman is not dismissed unless he chooses to walk – unlikely in this situation. The striker may be hit on the pad in circumstances which mean he is out LBW. If, uncharacteristically, no one appeals, he is not dismissed. For this reason none of the Laws on dismissals mentions an appeal. Each Law merely states the conditions in which the batsman is *out*. Whether he is *dismissed* or not depends on an appeal being made and upheld, or on his giving up his wicket by walking. Batsmen will often walk for something obvious like a mid-air catch in mid field. It is virtually certain that they will not do so for an LBW appeal.

No reference to appeals in these Laws does not mean appeals are not required for dismissal by the umpire. Section 1 of this Law will always apply.

UMPIRE'S JURISDICTION

Section 5 allocates each of the methods of dismissal to a particular umpire. Obviously those allocated to the striker's end umpire are those that involve the putting down of the wicket at that end. The Law <u>requires</u> the appropriate umpire to answer an appeal on any matter allocated to him. Every appeal must be answered. Pointedly ignoring an appeal by some gesture such as turning his head away is not acceptable. He must either raise an index finger to give the batsman out, or say Not out.

An appeal is not made **to** an umpire, even though a player may appear to be asking a particular umpire. An appeal is to be assumed to be general. An umpire will answer it if the incident involves, or could involve, a dismissal within his jurisdiction. For example, the striker is hit on the pad; the ball goes through to the keeper, who whips the bails off. If there is an appeal, the bowler's end umpire will consider whether or not the striker was out LBW; the striker's end umpire will consider whether or not he was out Stumped. Two answers will be given. The fact that the bowler's end umpire says Not out (for the LBW) will not negate any judgment of out Stumped by the striker's end umpire. If both umpires give the striker out, the general rule is that the action that happened first will take precedence. In the example above, if both umpires signal Out, then LBW will over-ride Stumped, since the strike on the pad was before the removal of the bails. Where there are such multiple possibilities, it is helpful for the umpire to indicate to the scorers which one is to be recorded. The Laws on Bowled and Caught modify the general rule by stating specifically which is to take precedence.

CONSULTATION

Section 6 makes it clear that an umpire must not hesitate to seek information from his colleague. For example, the bowler's end umpire may see clearly that the ball touched the striker's bat but not see the subsequent travel of the ball because it goes behind the batsman. His colleague at the other end is likely to have seen whether the ball was caught by the keeper or was grounded first. Consultation would remove any doubt as to whether the striker was out Caught or not. Although he has consulted his colleague, it is the bowler's end umpire who must give the decision, since Caught is one of the Laws on which he is to adjudicate.

Consultation on dismissals must be on questions of *fact*, on which the other umpire may have better information, as in the example. If, in a question of dismissal, the appropriate umpire is unsure of some of the facts and his colleague cannot help with them, he is required to give the batsman Not out.

Consultation need not require a conference. In the example, simply an enquiring look would probably be sufficient. If it does require person-to-person conversation, then this must unhesitatingly be undertaken. An umpire who leaves his position for such consultation is to call and signal Dead ball.

LEAVING WICKET UNDER MISAPPREHENSION

Section 7 sets out the procedure should a batsman, mistakenly thinking he is out, walk from his wicket. For instance, if in attempting a run he knows he was well short of his ground when the wicket was broken he will believe he is out, not aware that the wicket was not fairly put down because the ball slipped out of the wicket-keeper's hand just before he broke the wicket. No appeal has been made and <u>no decision has been given</u>. Section 7 would therefore apply. It must be emphasised that Section 7 will apply *only if he has not been given out*. It is not a means whereby one umpire can over-ride a decision by the other one.

WITHDRAWAL OF AN APPEAL

Sometimes a captain may regret an appeal by one of his side, feeling it is not within the spirit of the game. For example, a batsman may have been hit on the ankle by a sharp throw-in and, although not actually injured, he hops about for a minute as the pain subsides. At a point where he is out of his ground, the wicket is broken and a fielder appeals for Run out. The captain may wish to withdraw that appeal. Whatever the reason, he is to follow the procedure set out in Section 8. The salient points are that

- he must seek the permission of the appropriate umpire.

  It is quite possible that the captain will ask the 'wrong' umpire. The latter should simply redirect the plea.

- he must do so before the batsman has left the field of play. In many cases, but not in every one, the request will come before any decision on the appeal has been taken anyway.

  As always, the umpire must use his judgment, but should not refuse without good reason.

- if permission is granted, it is the umpire, not the captain, who is to call the batsman back.

  It may take a little diplomacy to handle an over eager captain on this point as, indeed, on the first one. There is no justification for confrontation.

UMPIRE'S DECISION IS FINAL

This familiar phrase is enshrined as a principle in Section 9. An umpire may realise that he has made a mistake. Perhaps he gave a batsman out Caught, not aware that his colleague had called No ball. Perhaps the mistake is his own. There may be embarrassment but there is no disgrace in admitting it and changing the decision as allowed in this section. It is much better than allowing a miscarriage of justice. He will be the more respected for it than for sticking to a decision he knows to be wrong. The reversal of decision must be made 'promptly' and certainly before any progress at all with the game. Once an umpire has made a decision, and has not altered it, that decision will stand in all circumstances. Special provisions at the highest levels, for challenging umpires' decisions, do not apply in Law.

Law 28 The wicket is down

1. WICKET PUT DOWN

(a) The wicket is put down if a bail is completely removed from the top of the stumps, or a stump is struck out of the ground,

    (i) by the ball,

  or (ii) by the striker's bat if he is holding it or by any part of his bat that he is holding,

  or (iii) notwithstanding the provisions of Law 6.8(a), by the striker's bat in falling if he has let go of it, or by any part of his bat becoming detached,

  or (iv) by the striker's person or by any part of his clothing or equipment becoming detached from his person,

  or (v) by a fielder with his hand or arm, providing that the ball is held in the hand or hands so used, or in the hand of the arm so used. The wicket is also put down if a fielder strikes or pulls a stump out of the ground in the same manner.

(b) The disturbance of a bail, whether temporary or not, shall not constitute its complete removal from the top of the stumps, but if a bail in falling lodges between two of the stumps this shall be regarded as complete removal.

2. ONE BAIL OFF

If one bail is off, it shall be sufficient for the purpose of putting the wicket down to remove the remaining bail or to strike or pull any of the three stumps out of the ground, in any of the ways stated in 1 above.

3. REMAKING WICKET

If a wicket is broken or put down while the ball is in play, it shall not be remade by an umpire until the ball is dead. See Law 23 (Dead ball). Any fielder may, however, while the ball is in play,
   (i) replace a bail or bails on top of the stumps.
  (ii) put back one or more stumps into the ground where the wicket
        originally stood.

4. DISPENSING WITH BAILS

If the umpires have agreed to dispense with bails in accordance with Law 8.5 (Dispensing with bails), it is for the umpire concerned to decide whether or not the wicket has been put down.
  (a) After a decision to play without bails, the wicket has been put down if
       the umpire concerned is satisfied that the wicket has been struck by the
       ball, by the striker's bat, person or items of his clothing or equipment
       as described in 1(a) (ii), (iii) or (iv) above, or by a fielder in the manner
       described in 1(a)(v) above.
  (b) If the wicket has already been broken or put down, (a) above shall apply
       to any stump or stumps still in the ground. Any fielder may replace
       a stump or stumps, in accordance with 3 above, in order to have an
       opportunity of putting the wicket down.

There is a distinction between a wicket being <u>down</u> and its being <u>put down</u>. A wicket is down if it is not a complete wicket as defined in Law 8. The wicket is put down by the act of removing one or more of its constituent stumps and bails. *How* the wicket is put down is crucial in determining whether a batsman is out or not for Bowled, Hit wicket, Run out or Stumped.

Section 1 sets out first what is to be achieved for the wicket to be down and then lists the agencies and methods by which this stage is to be reached, in order for the wicket to have been fairly put down. These agencies and methods are clearly listed in Section 1(a). Umpires should study the list. The words 'break' and 'broken' are sometimes used in relation to removing bails, etc. They do not have the same significance as 'put down'. A bowler may (accidentally) break the wicket by running too close to it as he comes in to bowl. He has not, in the strict sense, put the wicket down.

Section 2 then makes it clear that the starting point for this process does not have to be a complete wicket. A bail may be off already; the other one (or a stump) can be removed. Both bails may be off; a stump can be removed. Putting the wicket down is reducing whatever state it is in to one with fewer bails and/or stumps. Only when all three stumps are out of the ground is it impossible to put a wicket down. Even then, or at any earlier stage, the wicket can be partly re-assembled by a *fielder* replacing stumps or bails to give an opportunity to put the wicket down. It should be noted that

- an umpire should not do any of the re-assembly until the ball is dead
- if fielders replace stumps, as they are permitted to do, they must put them where the wicket originally was.

In talking of the cases where the striker may be responsible for putting down his wicket, it should be noted that this is the only instance in the Laws where items of clothing or equipment, no longer attached to him and therefore no longer part of either his bat or his person, are nevertheless treated as though they were. This is important in considering an appeal for Hit wicket.

COMPLETE REMOVAL

1 A bail

There are instances where a bail has

jumped out of its groove and settled back into the groove

been jerked out of its groove and settled back on top of one stump

fallen between the stumps so that one end is pressed against one stump, the other end sticking up above the neighbouring stump.

Both bails are on top of the wicket – the wicket is not down

Part of the displaced bail is above the top of the stumps – the wicket is not down

One bail is completely below the top of the stumps – the wicket is down

None of these has been completely removed from the top of the stumps. Only when the whole bail, whether on the ground or jammed between two stumps, is below the level of the top of the stumps has it been 'completely removed'. For the purposes of dismissal – deciding perhaps whether the batsmen had crossed or not – a bail has been removed at the moment it leaves its groove. If, however, subsequently it is not completely removed, as in the examples above, then the temporary removal will be considered never to have happened. The umpire, however, is unlikely to be able to make such fine judgment with the naked eye.

2 A stump

A stump is not 'knocked out of the ground' until it is completely free from the ground. Being knocked so severely askew as to be nearly horizontal is not enough.

BALL HELD IN HAND

Although he can throw the ball on to the stumps to put the wicket down, a fielder must have the ball in his hand if he is to do it himself. He can then use the ball he is holding to break the wicket, or he can use his hand – or even his arm right up to the shoulder – but it must be the *hand which is holding the ball, or that same arm.* He can use no other part of his body.

Pulling a stump out of the ground is virtually impossible with the ball held in the same hand, unless it is a very large hand. Usually it will have to be achieved by holding the ball in both hands and pulling up the stump with both hands. Holding the ball in one hand and pulling up the stump with the other is no use. Rather than pulling, the Law permits him to strike a stump out. As noted above, he must knock it clear out of the ground – difficult to do if the stumps are firmly set.

The fielder has struck the wicket with his arm, holding the ball in that hand. He has put the wicket down

If an artificial pitch is being used, it is often not possible to have normal stumps fixed in the ground. Various replacements, such as 'spring-back stumps' are available. They can involve difficulties in judging the breaking of the wicket. Sometimes Special Regulations for the match will instruct umpires on the modifications needed. In any case, the two umpires must agree any necessary details before the start of play.

DISPENSING WITH BAILS

The decision whether to do so or not has been discussed in Law 8. If bails have been dispensed with, the judgment of the wicket being fairly put down is considerably modified. The umpire at that end must judge *not what **might** have happened* if the bails had been there, but what ***has** happened to the stumps*. He must judge whether a **stump or stumps** have been struck by

the ball

the striker's bat or person or items detached from him as set out in Section 1

a fielder with the hand holding the ball, or with the arm of the hand holding the ball.

He does not have to judge how hard the strike was, merely that it has happened. He does not have to consider that from some earlier incident the bails might already have been off, had they been there in the first place. He looks, on each occasion, at what happens to the stumps, even if they are askew, as long as they are in the ground, or at least the one that is struck is in the ground. It must be emphasised that all the above applies *only* if the umpires have **decided** not to have bails. It is not relevant to the situation of the bails coming off accidentally in the course of play, or having been removed in an unsuccessful attempt to secure a dismissal.

Judgment of pulling a stump out of the ground is obviously not affected.

FIELD TECHNIQUE

It was emphasised in Law 18 how important it is for each umpire to have a view of the wicket and the creases while the batsmen are running. The need to watch whether the wicket is fairly put down, especially for a possible Run out, underlines again the importance of this. The essentials are that he must be able to see, with his head stationary, the putting down of the wicket and the position of the batsman in relation to the popping crease at that time. This means he must move as quickly as possible without waiting to assess the situation. He must not get in the way of the fielding of the ball, a particular hazard if this is happening close to the wicket. In that situation, however, it will be obvious where he must go to avoid the fielders. If there is a runner, he must not have the runner behind him and must go to the side his colleague is on. He must not get in the way of the throw-in, lest he disadvantage the fielding side, or get hit himself. With all these difficulties, and in spite of the growing practice at higher levels of the game of the fielder receiving the throw-in standing sideways on between the wicket and the fielder throwing the ball, the traditional advice is probably still the best at lower levels of the game. That advice is to go to the side to which the ball has been hit, avoiding the path of the throw-in, unless the existence of a runner, or of fielding being close to the wicket, demand otherwise. What is important is not so much which side he goes to – there are advantages and disadvantages for either side – but that he should do it very quickly and therefore as a habit without having to think about it. At worst the umpire may have to have a diagonal view of events rather than a side-on one. This could happen in any case.

The striker's end umpire is 'stuck' on one side of the wicket but, as he is already at a good distance from the wicket, he can usually move to one side in sufficient time if he is unsighted by a fielder.

The two things that an umpire must watch for with the utmost vigilance are that
- the fielder actually had the ball in his hand. It is not uncommon for the fielder to take the ball but in the act of moving his hand quickly to put down the wicket, to let go of it. He may be moving his hands towards the stumps in anticipation of receiving the ball but break the wicket before he has actually got it in his hand. This is a special risk for the wicket-keeper.

The wicket-keeper takes a throw in ...

... but drops the ball before breaking the wicket. It is rarely, if ever, as obvious as this!

- it is the hand (or arm of the hand) holding the ball that breaks the wicket. It can happen that a fielder, concentrating on catching the throw-in, knocks against the wicket with some other part of his person.

Law 29 Batsman out of his ground

1. WHEN OUT OF HIS GROUND

(a) A batsman shall be considered to be out of his ground unless his bat or some part of his person is grounded behind the popping crease at that end.

(b) Notwithstanding (a) above, if a running batsman, having grounded some part of his foot behind the popping crease, continues running further towards the wicket at that end and beyond, then any subsequent total loss of contact with the ground of both his person and his bat during his continuing forward momentum shall not be interpreted as being out of his ground.

2. WHICH IS A BATSMAN'S GROUND

(a) If only one batsman is within a ground
  (i) it is his ground
  (ii) it remains his ground even if he is later joined there by the other batsman.

(b) If both batsmen are in the same ground and one of them subsequently leaves it, (a)(i) above applies.

(c) **If there is no batsman in either ground, then each ground belongs to whichever batsman is nearer to it, or, if the batsmen are level, to whichever batsman was nearer to it immediately prior to their drawing level.**

(d) **If a ground belongs to one batsman then, unless there is a striker who has a runner, the other ground belongs to the other batsman, irrespective of his position.**

(e) **When a batsman who has a runner is striker, his ground is always at the wicket-keeper's end. However, (a), (b), (c) and (d) above will still apply, but only to the runner and the non-striker, so that that ground will also belong to either the non-striker or the runner, as the case may be.**

3. POSITION OF NON-STRIKER

The non-striker, when standing at the bowler's end, should be positioned on the opposite side of the wicket to that from which the ball is being delivered, unless a request to do otherwise is granted by the umpire.

A batsman's ground is one of the definitions in Appendix D. To be in it he must have some part of himself or his bat grounded behind the popping crease at that end. 'Making good his ground' is exactly that act of grounding bat or person behind the popping crease. Law 6 makes it clear that he has to be holding the bat. Appendix D

He is not within his ground. He has neither his bat nor any part of his person grounded behind the popping crease and has clearly not yet grounded any part of either foot behind the line. Even if he had grounded his bat and raised it again, it would not qualify as being within his ground in the position shown

His bat is on the crease marking; this is not behind the popping crease. He is not within his ground

shows that he can achieve this by having his hand in contact with some part of the bat. A bat he is not holding has no validity except in Laws 28 and 35, where its role in putting down the wicket is specifically stated.

IS IT *HIS* GROUND?

Whether it is *his* ground or not is set out in Section 2 of this Law. It is a simple matter if each batsman is in a ground. Each is then in *his* ground. It is equally simple if neither is in a ground, while they are running (or even stationary) between the wickets. Each ground belongs to the batsman who is nearer to it than the other batsman is. If the batsmen are actually level, then where they were before drawing level is the deciding factor. If one is in a ground and the other is not, the empty ground belongs to the one who is not in a ground.

The apparent complications in Section 2 arise from cases where there are two batsmen in the same ground and when there is a striker with a runner.

1 Two batsmen in the same ground

- Was batsman A in the ground and batsman B arrived to join him? It is A's ground.
- Did they both run towards the same ground and both arrive there? Who arrived first, even if by only a small margin? If it was batsman A, then it is A's ground. If, however, A sees the predicament and sets out to run to the other end, then he has left B alone in the ground and so it is now B's ground.
- If A and B are both in the same ground, and it is A's ground, then B's ground is at the other end, even though he is not at that end.

2 Striker with a runner

Here the complication is that there are three people to share two grounds. As far as the non-striker and the runner are concerned they are the batsman A and batsman B of the previous paragraph. For them, everything is as stated there. As they cross they change ends, so that the runner, for instance, starts off with his ground at the wicket-keeper's end, but after crossing with the non-striker, his end is at the bowler's end, and so on. The ground at the wicket-keeper's end belongs alternately to the runner and to the non-striker. All the time, however, it also belongs to the striker who has the runner. He never has the ground at the bowler's end even if, in spite of his injury, he actually runs to that end. When he is not the striker he has no end at all. The two grounds are then partitioned between the other two in the normal way.

POSITION OF NON-STRIKER

Section 3 is quite separate from the rest of the Law. It specifies the position of the non-striker as the ball comes into play. It should cause no difficulty. It is accepted practice that, as the Law requires, he stands on the opposite side of the wicket to that on which the bowler is going to run up. It is very rare for a player to ask to stand on the other side. If he did, the umpire would have to consider very carefully whether to allow it. To be clear of the bowler's action and run-off from the pitch, he would have to be some way out on that side. This could make it difficult for the umpire to see his movements, particularly as the bowler runs between them. However, there might be good reason for the change – the fielding positions might mean he had to stand even further out if he remained on the normal side. The umpire must weigh up the *pros* and *cons* carefully. Wherever the non-striker stands he must not obstruct either the bowler delivering the ball, or the striker's view of that delivery, nor must he impede close fielders. On the other hand he must not stand so far from the pitch that the bowler's end umpire cannot see his movements.

Law 30 Bowled

I. OUT BOWLED

(a) **The striker is out Bowled if his wicket is put down by a ball delivered by the bowler, not being a No ball, even if it first touches his bat or person.**

(b) **Notwithstanding (a) above he shall not be out Bowled if before striking the wicket the ball has been in contact with any other player or an umpire. He will, however, be subject to Laws 33 (Handled the ball), 37 (Obstructing the field), 38 (Run out) and 39 (Stumped).**

2. BOWLED TO TAKE PRECEDENCE

The striker is out Bowled if his wicket is put down as in I above, even though a decision against him for any other method of dismissal would be justified.

Bowled is the first of the ten methods of dismissal, arranged alphabetically except for Timed out. It is in most cases so obvious that the majority of batsmen will walk from the wicket without appeal, perfectly understanding that they are out.

The crucial points for a batsman to be out Bowled are:

- the wicket is put down by the ball
- the delivery is not a No ball
- nobody but the striker himself is involved between the bowler's delivering the ball and the ball breaking the wicket.

The phrase 'clean bowled' is not found in the Laws but it gives a good picture of the ball, having left the bowler's hand, striking the stumps and breaking the wicket without touching anything in between, except that usually it will have pitched on the ground.

The striker can equally be bowled, however, if he and the ball make contact before the ball hits the stumps. The ball may touch his bat or be deflected off his person. He may stop it with a defensive stroke, lose sight of it and accidentally kick it on to the stumps. He may attempt a second stroke to defend his wicket but succeed only in hitting the ball on to the stumps. The question of 'completing his stroke' is not relevant. Until the ball has been touched by another player or an umpire, the striker must suffer the consequences of his actions, voluntary or involuntary. If a delivery is not a No ball, and from whatever cause the ball hits the stumps thereby putting down the wicket, he is out Bowled, providing the ball has not touched either another player or an umpire since it left the bowler's hand.

DID THE BALL BREAK THE WICKET?

Occasionally there may be doubt about this. The wicket-keeper may be standing very close, and might himself dislodge the bails, or the ball may rebound from him on to the stumps. Perhaps the bail fell off accidentally. Perhaps there is uncertainty as to whether the striker's person or the ball itself broke the wicket. In all these cases the striker's end umpire should be in a position to help his colleague to determine how the wicket was broken.

BOWLED TO TAKE PRECEDENCE

There maybe other cause for appeal. The striker, having played a ball defensively, uses his bat to tap the ball to a fielder without permission (see Law 34) and accidentally hits it on to his wicket. Before going on to his wicket the ball may hit his pad in such a way that he is out LBW. The ball might touch the edge of his bat before hitting the wicket and then go on to be caught by the wicket-keeper. Section 2 establishes firmly that, providing it is not a No ball, if the ball breaks the wicket when no fielder has been involved, then the striker is out Bowled, whatever other possibilities there are.

Law 31 Timed out

1. OUT TIMED OUT

(a) After the fall of a wicket or the retirement of a batsman, the incoming batsman must, unless Time has been called, be in position to take guard or for his partner to be ready to receive the next ball within 3 minutes of the dismissal or retirement. If this requirement is not met, the incoming batsman will be out, Timed out.

(b) In the event of protracted delay in which no batsman comes to the wicket, the umpires shall adopt the procedure of Law 21.3 (Umpires awarding a match). For the purposes of that Law the start of the action shall be taken as the expiry of the 3 minutes referred to above.

2. BOWLER DOES NOT GET CREDIT

The bowler does not get credit for the wicket.

This Law is designed to minimise the time taken for a new batsman to come in when a wicket has fallen. The first paragraph specifies the state of readiness he must achieve within 3 minutes. This time should be ample. If a batsman does not meet the deadline, he is out and could be dismissed.

ACTION BY UMPIRES

For him to be dismissed there must be an appeal. The umpires cannot adjudicate on the appeal unless they know how long the arrival process had taken. Both should always note the time at which any wicket falls, in case the next batsman is late in arriving. If there is an appeal, the umpires should check times with each other to ascertain whether the 3-minute limit has been exceeded or not. The bowler's end umpire will give the decision accordingly. If that decision is Out, this is the fall of the next wicket, starting a new 3-minute span; the time must again be noted. Except in the extreme case of protracted delay, described below, a batsman cannot be given out until his innings has begun. The umpire must therefore ensure that the next batsman is on the field of play when giving the decision Out. He must wait if necessary until the batsman steps on to the field of play.

PROTRACTED DELAY – AWARDING THE MATCH

If no batsman appears at all, umpires must not allow play to be held up indefinitely. They should consider the possibility that the batting side may be refusing to play. As in Law 21.3 they must investigate the cause of the delay. The ball will have become dead at the fall of the wicket and the umpires will have taken possession of the ball. Now, before leaving the field and going to the pavilion, Time must be called, as the prolonged delay is to be considered as an interruption. This interruption, for the purposes of any possible calculations of time lost is, however, to be taken as the expiry of the 3 minutes.

If no appeal has yet been made it will now be too late. Although a batsman is out he cannot be dismissed. The umpires' sole concern will be whether there has been a refusal to play or not. The procedure for this has been discussed in Law 21. The steps are set out below, as a reminder.

Discover the cause of delay
    If action considered a refusal
        warn captain
        if action persists award match to fielding side
        otherwise play continues
    If action not considered a refusal
        set a time for play to resume
        jointly calculate time lost, from expiry of 3 minutes until resumption. Close of play on that day to be put back by this length of time.
    In either case inform scorers of all details

If an appeal has already been made, it must be answered. In addition to a possible refusal to play, a batsman is out and will therefore be dismissed, whether play continues or not. The umpires will so inform the captain of the batting side. The captain will decide which batsman is out. This information must also be reported to the scorers.

Law 32 Caught

1. OUT CAUGHT

The striker is out Caught if a ball delivered by the bowler, not being a No ball, touches his bat without having previously been in contact with any fielder, and is subsequently held by a fielder as a fair catch before it touches the ground.

2. CAUGHT TO TAKE PRECEDENCE

If the criteria of 1 above are met and the striker is not out Bowled, then he is out Caught, even though a decision against either batsman for another method of dismissal would be justified.

3. A FAIR CATCH

A catch shall be considered to have been fairly made if
(a) throughout the act of making the catch
    (i) any fielder in contact with the ball is within the field of play. See 4 below.
    (ii) the ball is at no time in contact with any object grounded beyond the boundary.
The act of making the catch shall start from the time when the ball in flight comes into contact with some part of a fielder's person other than a protective helmet, and shall end when a fielder obtains complete control both over the ball and over his own movement.
(b) the ball is hugged to the body of the catcher or accidentally lodges in his clothing or, in the case of the wicket-keeper only, in his pads. However, it is not a fair catch if the ball lodges in a protective helmet worn by a fielder. See Law 23 (Dead ball).
(c) the ball does not touch the ground even though the hand holding it does so in effecting the catch.
(d) a fielder catches the ball after it has been lawfully struck more than once by the striker, but only if it has not been grounded since first being struck.
(e) a fielder catches the ball after it has touched an umpire, another fielder or the other batsman.
However, it is not a fair catch if the ball has previously touched a protective helmet worn by a fielder. The ball will then remain in play.
(f) a fielder catches the ball in the air after it has crossed the boundary provided that

(i) he has no part of his person touching or grounded beyond the boundary at any time while he is contact with the ball.

(ii) the ball has not been grounded beyond the boundary. See Law 19.3 (Scoring a boundary).

Note also Law 19.4 (Ball beyond the boundary).

(g) the ball is caught off an obstruction within the boundary provided the obstruction had not been designated a boundary by the umpires before the toss.

4. FIELDER WITHIN THE FIELD OF PLAY

(a) A fielder is not within the field of play if he has any part of his person touching, or grounded beyond, the boundary. See Law 19.3 (Scoring a boundary).

(b) 6 runs shall be scored if a fielder

(i) has any part of his person touching, or grounded beyond, the boundary when he catches the ball.

(ii) catches the ball and subsequently touches the boundary or grounds some part of his person beyond the boundary while carrying the ball but before completing the catch.

See Laws 19.3 (Scoring a boundary) and 19.5 (Runs allowed for boundaries).

5. NO RUNS TO BE SCORED

If the striker is dismissed Caught, runs from that delivery completed by the batsmen before the completion of the catch shall not be scored but any runs for penalties awarded to either side shall stand. Law 18.12 (Batsman returning to wicket he has left) shall apply from the instant of the completion of the catch.

In many cases it will be clear to the striker (and others on the field) that he is out Caught and he will often go without an appeal. Equally, however, it is often very difficult for the umpire to decide. He must have observed all that happens to the ball from immediately after seeing the bowler's front foot land. It is no use waiting for an appeal. It is then too late to gather the information needed. The requirements for the striker to be out Caught are simple.

• The ball must have touched the striker's bat. Law 6 indicates that he must have been holding the bat and that the whole of the glove on a hand holding the bat counts as part of the bat. In the virtually non-existent case of a batsman holding the bat with a bare hand, the hand will count instead of the glove.

• The ball must thereafter not touch the ground or any kind of boundary, including fielders touching or grounded beyond the boundary.

• The catch must be completed by a fielder holding it within the field of play.

Judging these requirements may not always be so simple.

DID THE BALL TOUCH THE BAT?

1 A fine edge

The sooner the umpire picks up the flight of the ball from the bowler's hand, the better chance he has of seeing whether there was very fine contact with the edge of the bat. He must look to see if there was any deflection of the ball as it passed the bat. If he hears a sound, he must know whether it was at the moment the ball passed the bat and whether the ball was then very close to the bat. He must judge whether it was the sound of the ball striking the bat and not, for instance, the bat hitting the striker's boot. Whatever difficulties there may be, he must not guess. He must judge on what he observes about the flight of the ball and the movement of the bat. Sometimes his colleague can help if the contact was on the leg side, hidden from the bowler's end by the striker himself. If he is unsure and the other umpire is unable to help, he must give the striker Not out.

2 Other contacts

All that the Law requires is that the ball touches the bat. It does not matter if the ball touched the striker's person first, or if it did so afterwards. It does not matter whether the contact was intentional or inadvertent. It does not matter if it was part of a legitimate second strike nor, if it was, whether it was the first or the second contact that was with the bat – although in the case of a double strike the ball must not have been grounded between the strikes. If the ball touched the bat and has not been grounded, the striker can be out Caught.

WAS THE BALL GROUNDED AFTER CONTACT WITH THE BAT?

A point at which difficulty may arise is immediately after leaving the bat. If the striker hits the ball when it is near the ground, sharp observation is needed to see whether the ball hits the ground before going further. Such contact is often called a 'bump' (or bumped) ball. The angle of the bat as it strikes the ball, the lower speed of the ball than the strength of the blow would suggest, the ball rising more than expected, are all pointers. The other umpire can often help from his side-on position.

The ball that is grounded just before the fielder catches it is also difficult to discern. Again concentration and the opinion of the other umpire, if available and necessary, can help – and so sometimes can the honesty of the fielder.

DID THE BALL COME INTO CONTACT WITH ANYTHING ELSE?

Another problem is the catch near the boundary. The question of the fielder being within the field of play is discussed later. Additionally, there may occasionally be some object within the field of play, such as a tree, which will have been designated a boundary. If the ball hits it, no catch can follow. Apart from such rarities, the obstacles the ball may encounter on its path, and whether contact invalidates a catch, are set out in the chart below. In each case, the assumption is that the ball has come direct from the striker's bat and has not yet been grounded.

CATCH POSSIBLE?

YES	NO
Strikes fielder's* person, except helmet	Strikes fielder's helmet being worn
Lodges in fielder's clothing	Lodges in fielder's helmet being worn
	Strikes fielder's helmet on ground
Lodges in keeper's* pads	Lodges in either batsman's pads
Strikes either batsman's person	Trapped among items of either batsman's clothing or equipment
Strikes either batsman's helmet	Lodges in either batsman's helmet
Strikes stumps at bowler's end	
Strikes stumps at keeper's end sometimes[†]	Strikes stumps at keeper's end in normal circumstances[†]
Strikes umpire	Lodges in umpire's clothing

*'fielder' always includes wicket-keeper; 'keeper' being specified means only the wicket-keeper.

[†] If the ball strikes the stumps after leaving the striker's bat, he would normally be out Bowled, so that even if the ball were caught, Bowled would take precedence. However, he would not be out Bowled in the rare case of the ball failing to dislodge a bail. Then a catch would be possible.

Note also that the chart specifically excludes the ball touching anything else between leaving the bat and striking the named object. However, if the ball were to touch a fielder between leaving the bat and hitting the stumps at the keeper's end, the striker would not be out Bowled. Again, a catch would be possible and would, if relevant, over-ride Run out or Stumped.

Many of the entries in the 'NO' column are instances of the ball becoming automatically dead. However, the ball does not become dead on striking a helmet worn by a fielder. A catch is ruled out, but the ball remains in play.

It should be noted that if the ball lodges in a fielder's clothing, a catch can be valid. Nevertheless he cannot hold out his cap like a butterfly net, nor hold the body of his sweater away from him to act like a fireman's blanket. The lodging has to be accidental.

DID THE FIELDER CATCH IT FAIRLY?

A fielder does not have to catch the ball in his hands. He might try to catch the ball high up but it slips through his hands. It does not fall to the ground because it lodges in the V made by his forearms and is held against his body. This is an instance of 'hugged to his body'. Instances have been known of a catch being held between a fielder's knees! There is more on the question of valid catches near the boundary after the paragraphs on completing a catch.

DID THE FIELDER *COMPLETE* THE CATCH?

This is a vital issue. The fact that a fielder interrupts the flight of the ball and holds it in his hands does not *necessarily* mean that a catch had been taken. There is no catch until a fielder has completed it. The umpire has to be satisfied that the fielder has
- complete control over the ball
- complete control over his own movement.

1 Control over the ball

He can catch the ball between his knees, but unless he can keep it there, even if he overbalances, he has not completed the catch. A diving catch which is jerked from his hand as he lands on the ground has not been completed. If he can retain the ball it does not matter that his hand is on the ground, as long as the ball has been kept clear of the ground.

2 Control over his movement

A diving catch, taken when he is in the air and nearly horizontal, is again an example. Until he has recovered after hitting the ground, he is not in control of his movement. If he takes a running catch, he will not have completed the catch *until he can stop running*. Sometimes a fielder will continue running from sheer excitement at having taken the catch. Provided the umpire is satisfied that he has control over his running, so that he *could* stop, rather than being unable to, the catch is completed.

WAS THE FIELDER WITHIN THE FIELD OF PLAY?

A fielder is *not* within the field of play if he is either touching the boundary or grounded beyond the boundary. What these two phrases mean was explained in

In Law 32 he is not touching the boundary fence. A fair catch, unless the ball bounced before the fence, when the ball would simply still be in play

He jumped up from inside the boundary. A catch will be valid as long as he lands and completes it inside the boundary

He jumped up from outside the boundary. If he is the first fielder to touch the ball, 6 runs will be scored (and the ball will become dead)

Law 19. Therefore, even if he is standing with both feet inside the boundary line, he can be 'not within the field of play' if he is, for instance, touching the boundary fence. Conversely, it is possible for him to handle the ball, even take a catch, when he is wholly or partly outside the boundary as long as he is either standing inside the field of play, merely leaning over but not touching the boundary, or in the air, since he is not in either of these cases grounded beyond the boundary. There are limitations, however, on the fielder in the latter case. If he is the first fielder to touch the ball he must have jumped up from a point within the field of play. It must be understood, though, that the fielder who starts a catch need not be the fielder who completes it. Strictures about being within, or jumping up from within, the boundary apply only to the fielder who first came into contact with the ball, so starting the catch. Another fielder can then catch the ball even when he is beyond the boundary provided he is not in contact with the ground. There will obviously be no catch unless he lands within the boundary. He still has then to complete the catch. He could, however, instead of catching the ball, legitimately push it back into the field for another fielder to catch or field.

He jumped up from outside the boundary. If the ball has already been touched by a fielder who did not jump up from outside the boundary, he is allowed to parry the ball back like this for someone else to field

If a fielder who is outside the boundary handles the ball the important points are:

- the fielder who first touched the ball must have done so when either grounded inside the boundary or in the air having jumped up from a point within the boundary
- any fielder can continue a catch started by another fielder
- after the initial contact, the original fielder and any subsequent fielders can be in contact with the ball outside the boundary. The only restriction is that a fielder must not simultaneously be in contact with the ball and the ground outside the boundary
- a catch can be completed only by a fielder grounded within the boundary;

and, of course, throughout all this, the ball itself must not have had any contact with the ground, either directly or via some other object!

NO RUNS TO BE SCORED

It may be some time before a catch is completed if it is hit high into the air or is juggled between fielders. The batsmen may run while that is happening. If the catch is not held, the runs will count. If the catch is held, the striker will be out and, if dismissed, the runs will not count. The end to which the non-striker must go is dealt with in Law 18.

CAUGHT TO TAKE PRECEDENCE

It has already been stated in Law 30 that Bowled takes precedence over any other form of dismissal. Caught is next in priority, taking precedence over everything except Bowled. If, for instance, the striker made an illegitimate second strike, this would mean that he was out Hit the ball twice. If however one of these strikes was with the bat and the ball was caught without being grounded at any point, he would be out Caught, even though the second strike came before the catch.

Law 33 Handled the ball

1. OUT HANDLED THE BALL

(a) **Either batsman is out Handled the ball if he wilfully touches the ball while in play with a hand or hands not holding the bat unless he does so with the consent of a fielder.**

(b) **Either batsman is out under this Law if, while the ball is in play, and without the consent of a fielder, he uses his hand or hands not holding the bat to return the ball to any fielder.**

2. NOT OUT HANDLED THE BALL

Notwithstanding 1(a) above, a batsman will not be out under this Law if he handles the ball to avoid injury.

3. RUNS SCORED

If either batsman is dismissed Handled the ball, runs completed by the batsmen before the offence shall be scored, together with any runs for penalties awarded to either side. See Laws 18.6 (Runs awarded for penalties) and 18.9 (Runs scored when a batsman is dismissed).

4. BOWLER DOES NOT GET CREDIT

The bowler does not get credit for the wicket.

'Handling the ball' is shorthand for 'touching the ball either with a hand or with a glove worn on the hand when that hand is not in contact with the bat'. Although not the words used in the Law, the phrase 'free hand' is a useful description of a hand not holding the bat.

The word 'wilful' in the Law is significant. There is no breach of the Law if a batsman has taken his hand off the bat and the ball accidentally touches this free hand. A batsman will be out if he *wilfully* handles the ball except in the following situations:

- The ball is in play and
    either at least one member of the fielding side has given permission for the action
        or the batsman's action was to protect himself from being injured by the ball.
- The ball is dead.

Notice that either batsman can be out Handled the ball. The offence can occur at any time while the ball is in play. Note also that the bowler does not get credit for a dismissal under this Law. This is the first of the Laws on dismissals where this statement is made. Whenever this is so, it means that the dismissal is not affected by a call of No ball. In Laws where it is not stated, then the bowler does get credit for the dismissal.

DEFENDING HIS WICKET

It has been known for a striker to take his hand off the bat and push the ball away from his stumps with this hand, to defend his wicket. If he does so it was clearly a wilful act and he is out Handled the ball. If such action was a second strike in defence of his wicket, he has also breached Law 34, Hit the ball twice, since using a free hand is specifically forbidden in that Law. Nevertheless, if there is an appeal and he is dismissed, it will be as Handled the ball.

RETURNING THE BALL TO A FIELDER

A batsman will sometimes pick up a stationary ball to return it to a fielder. If the ball is dead, no harm is done. The decision that the ball is dead may, however, rest upon the umpire's being satisfied that fielders and batsmen alike have ceased to regard it as in play. If the umpire has not decided the ball was dead and there is an appeal, he would have to give the erring batsman out Handled the ball. This is a change introduced in 2010. Previously, in this situation, the offence was Obstructing the field.

This is a situation where a captain may feel that an innocent act intended to be helpful is not a cause for appeal and, if one of his side appeals, ask to withdraw it. The umpire may wish to ascertain if the appeal is serious, but must not appear to be trying to influence the captain. The batsman is wiser, unless the ball is obviously dead, either to leave the ball where it is, or (usually by an enquiring look as he holds his hand over the ball) to seek permission from a fielder.

RUNS SCORED IF A BATSMAN IS DISMISSED HANDLED THE BALL

A batsman may handle the ball while runs are in progress. He may perhaps do it to prevent a throw-in from striking the wicket. Providing the umpire is satisfied that the batsman's action was not in order to avoid being injured by the throw-in, he will give him out on appeal. The scorers may need advice about the method of dismissal, as indeed would be the case whenever a batsman is dismissed under this Law. The runs scored will be exactly the same as if the dismissal had been Run out. Runs completed before the offence will count; the run in progress will not.

It may be helpful to note that it is a general principle that if any runs at all are to be allowed when a batsman is dismissed, the run in progress will not be included.

Law 34   Hit the ball twice

I. OUT HIT THE BALL TWICE

(a) The striker is out Hit the ball twice if, while the ball is in play, it strikes any part of his person or is struck by his bat and, before the ball has been touched by a fielder, he wilfully strikes it again with his bat or person, other than a hand not holding the bat, except for the sole purpose of guarding his wicket. See 3 below and Laws 33 (Handled the ball) and 37 (Obstructing the field).

(b) For the purpose of this Law 'struck' or 'strike' shall include contact with the person of the striker.

2. NOT OUT HIT THE BALL TWICE

Notwithstanding I(a) above, the striker will not be out under this Law if

 (i) he strikes the ball a second or subsequent time in order to return the ball to any fielder. Note, however, the provisions of Law 37.4 (Returning the ball to a fielder).

(ii) he wilfully strikes the ball after it has touched a fielder. Note, however the provisions of Law 37.1 (Out Obstructing the field).

3. BALL LAWFULLY STRUCK MORE THAN ONCE

Solely in order to guard his wicket and before the ball has been touched by a fielder, the striker may lawfully strike the ball a second or subsequent time with his bat, or with any part of his person other than a hand not holding the bat.

Notwithstanding this provision, he may not prevent the ball from being caught by striking the ball more than once in defence of his wicket. See Law 37.3 (Obstructing a ball from being caught).

4. RUNS SCORED FROM BALL LAWFULLY STRUCK MORE THAN ONCE

When the ball is lawfully struck more than once, as permitted in 3 above, only the first strike is to be considered in determining whether runs are to be permitted and if so how they are to be recorded.

(a) If on the first strike, the umpire is satisfied that

   either (i) the ball first struck the bat

      or (ii) the striker attempted to play the ball with his bat

      or (iii) the striker attempted to avoid being hit by the ball,

   then the batting side shall be credited with any runs for penalties that may be applicable.

(b) Additionally, if the conditions in (a) above are met then, if they result from overthrows and only if they result from overthrows, runs completed by the batsmen or a boundary will be scored. They shall be credited to the striker if the first strike was with the bat. If the first strike was on the person of the striker they shall be recorded as Leg byes or No ball extras as appropriate. See Law 26.2 (Leg byes).

(c) If the conditions in (a) above are met and there is no overthrow until after the batsmen have started to run but before one run is completed,

    (i) only subsequent completed runs or a boundary shall be scored. For the purposes of this clause and (iii) below, the first run shall count as a completed run if and only if the batsmen had not already crossed at the instant of the throw.

    (ii) if in these circumstances the ball goes to the boundary from the throw then, notwithstanding the provisions of Law 19.7 (Overthrow or wilful act of fielder), only the boundary allowance shall be scored.

    (iii) if the ball goes to the boundary as the result of a further overthrow, then runs completed by the batsman after the first throw but before this final throw shall be added to the boundary allowance. The run in progress at the first throw will count as a completed run only if the batsmen had not already crossed at that instant. The run in progress at the final throw shall count as a completed run only if the batsmen had already crossed at that instant. Law 18.12 (Batsman returning to wicket he has left) shall apply as from the instant of the final throw.

(d) If, in the opinion of the umpire, none of the conditions in (a) above are met then, whether there is an overthrow or not, the batting side shall not be credited with any runs from that delivery apart from the penalty for a No ball if applicable. Moreover, no other runs for penalties shall be awarded to the batting side.

5. BALL LAWFULLY STRUCK MORE THAN ONCE – ACTION BY THE UMPIRE

If no runs are to be permitted, either in the circumstances of 4(d) above, or because there has been no overthrow, and

(a) if no run is attempted but the ball reaches the boundary, the umpire shall call and signal Dead ball and disallow the boundary.

(b) if the batsmen run and

    (i) neither batsman is dismissed and the ball does not become dead for any other reason, the umpire shall call and signal Dead ball as soon as one run is completed or the ball reaches the boundary. The run or boundary shall be disallowed. The batsmen shall return to their original ends.

    or (ii) a batsman is dismissed, or if for any other reason the ball becomes dead before one run is completed or the ball reaches the boundary, all the provisions of the Laws will apply except that the award of penalties to the batting side shall be as laid down in 4(a) or 4(d) above, as appropriate.

6. BOWLER DOES NOT GET CREDIT

The bowler does not get credit for the wicket.

The striker is not allowed to make a second attempt to hit the ball, once he has touched it, except in one circumstance – in order to defend his wicket. It is not uncommon for a ball to be hit twice accidentally; 'bat-pad' is a familiar phrase. There is no harm in this. Unless a second strike is wilful it can be ignored. For convenience the text will refer to a second strike but, providing each is to defend his wicket, the striker can make as many as he feels necessary. A second (or third...) strike, however, belongs entirely to the time after the ball has been bowled and before a fielder has touched it. Once a fielder has touched the ball, the striker has no longer any right to hit it for any purpose. See Law 37.

At one time, pushing the ball with his bat to return it to a fielder was categorised as a wilful second strike. The batsman was therefore vulnerable to dismissal Hit the ball twice, if the ball was not dead and the fielding side had not given permission. Now, however, although he is still liable to dismissal, it is under Law 37 Obstructing the field.

The umpire has to make two judgments:
• was the second strike wilful?
• if it was, was it solely in defence of the striker's wicket, or not?
Neither of these is usually difficult to determine, although both are a matter of judgment.

WAS IT A STRIKE?

In Appendix D (pages 280–3) 'strike' is defined as the ball being hit by the bat *unless specifically defined otherwise*. There is just such a specific definition in this Law. In *this* Law, the ball making contact with the striker's person is to count as a strike, just as much as a bat-with-ball contact. Moreover, whereas the first strike is subject to the restrictions discussed under Leg byes in Law 26, the striker is permitted to make a legal second strike, not necessarily with his bat, but with any part of his person *except a hand not in contact with his bat*.

As an example of a lawful second strike, the striker mis-hits the ball, knocking it downwards with the toe of his bat. It fizzes backwards, spinning violently, towards the wicket. He kicks the ball away from his stumps with his back foot. Apart from not being allowed to hit the ball at all once a fielder has touched it, there are just three restrictions on the second strike:
• It must be an attempt to stop the ball from hitting the wicket.
• It must not be with a hand unless the hand is in contact with the bat.
• It must not interfere with a fielder trying to take a catch.
If any of these restrictions is not observed, the striker will be out:
• Hit the ball twice in the first case
• Handled the ball in the second case
• Obstructing the field in the third case.

WAS IT IN DEFENCE OF HIS WICKET?

The Law must be interpreted literally. 'Defending his wicket' is literally trying to prevent the ball hitting the wicket. It is not 'stopping himself being out'. He cannot interfere with an attempted catch, even if he is trying to defend his wicket. He will be out Obstructing the field if he does. On the other hand, should No ball be called, he is not at risk of being bowled, so in that sense his wicket does not need defending. Nevertheless he is still entitled to try to stop the ball hitting his stumps. It would be unreasonable to expect the striker to work out the logic of this in making an almost instinctive move to protect the stumps. Nevertheless the strictures in the next paragraph, about the striker's motives, will apply. Of course, the delivery will not be valid and the one-run penalty for the No ball will apply and will be signalled in addition to anything else when the ball is dead.

A key phrase is 'for the sole purpose of'. The sudden jab to push the ball away from the stumps is clear enough. In contrast, a lusty hit which sends the ball deep into the outfield may be defending the wicket but could not be regarded as *solely* for this purpose. Even if the ball loops up so that the striker has a little more time for consideration, it is usually clear whether his second (or third, or fourth or . . .!) stroke is 'for the sole purpose of guarding his wicket'. However, the umpire must be alert to the possibility that there may be an additional motive. If he considers there is, then the striker will be out.

NO RUNS EXCEPT AS OVERTHROWS

Recompense to the fielding side for the striker being allowed to defend his wicket by a second strike is that the batsmen are not allowed to score runs from the delivery, unless the situation of overthrows arises. Perhaps gully fields the ball after the striker has pushed it away from the stumps. Seeing the striker out of his ground, the fielder throws the ball to attempt a Run out. The ball misses the stumps and goes into the outfield. Not until there has been this overthrow are the batsmen allowed to score runs. The provisions set out in Section 4 look complicated but if read carefully will be seen to be logical.

One difficulty for the umpire is that there are two different circumstances which might prohibit the batsmen from scoring.

- The first strike, which is the all important one, is on the person and such that Leg byes would not be allowed – there is no attempt to play the ball with the bat or to avoid being hit by the ball.
- There may be no overthrow situation after the second strike.

Either of these separately, or both together, will mean that the umpire has to intervene if runs are attempted. These points are set out in the following chart.

FIRST STRIKE	BEFORE OVERTHROW	AFTER OVERTHROW
On the person		
Leg byes	No runs;	Still no runs
would not have been allowed	No penalties*	No penalties*
Leg byes	No runs – but	Batsmen can run
would have been allowed	penalties allowed	Penalties allowed
On the bat	No runs – but	Batsmen can run
	penalties allowed	Penalties allowed

*except one-run penalty if No ball called

RUNS AFTER LAWFUL SECOND STRIKE

The first strike determines the validity of subsequent runs, if an overthrow justifies any being taken. If the batsmen run when runs are not to be allowed, umpires should note that the procedures laid down in Section 5 are the same as those in Law 26, in the case where Leg byes are not to be permitted. If they get as far as 1 run, or the ball reaches the boundary, they must be sent back, Dead ball called and signalled and runs disallowed.

If the <u>only</u> bar to running is lack of an overthrow, and one occurs before the completion of the first run, the batsmen can continue running but only the runs after the overthrow count. The part-run that took place before the overthrow is not legal and will not count. The second part, achieved after the overthrow, will count as a whole run only if it is the larger part of the run. This in turn depends on whether or not the batsmen had already crossed at the instant of the throw.

In the first diagram the batsmen have not yet crossed. The two dotted sections add up to more than the two black sections. The second part of the run is larger than the first part. This run, if completed, will count as a whole run.

In the following diagram the batsmen have crossed. The dotted sections together

are less than the black sections together, so the second part of the run is the smaller part. This run will not count at all.

This seems at odds with the more usual situation, where a run in progress counts only if they have crossed. The reason is that in *those* cases, it is the <u>end</u> of the <u>final run</u> that does not count because the ball has become dead – for hitting a fielder's helmet on the ground, for example. In *this* case it is the <u>start</u> of the <u>first run</u> that does not count, because it is not legitimate until the overthrow.

It should be noted that if the all-important overthrow goes to the boundary, only the boundary allowance will count. This is in line with normal practice, since there are no legitimate runs or part-runs before the instant of the throw. For any subsequent overthrow runs will be scored as usual. It must be noted, however, that in counting how many runs were completed or crossed on before this later throw, the validity of the first run will be exactly as above.

For example, suppose that at the first overthrow they had already crossed, so that the first part of the run does not count. After finishing this initial run, they complete another one and have crossed on a second, when the ball is fielded and thrown and this time goes to the boundary. They will have:

0 on the first run as they had already crossed at the overthrow

1 for the complete run

1 for the part-run, up to the instant of the throw, because they had already crossed.

There will be 2 runs to add to the boundary allowance.

CAUGHT FROM A LAWFUL SECOND STRIKE

The first strike will determine not only whether runs are to be permitted after an overthrow but whether they are runs to the striker or are extras. The striker will be credited with the runs only if the *first* strike was with the bat. Notwithstanding this, if *either* strike is on the bat, then the striker can be out Caught if the ball is not grounded from the first strike until the fielder catches it.

Person-bat-catch, bat-person-catch, bat-bat-catch are all valid catches.

Person-ground-bat-catch is not valid for a catch. Nor is any other sequence if the ball is grounded at any point in the sequence, after the first strike and before the catch is taken and completed.

If a second strike is not lawful, then the striker is out Hit the ball twice. If, however, a valid catch is taken off this double strike, Caught will take precedence.

Law 35   Hit wicket

1. OUT HIT WICKET

(a) The striker is out Hit wicket if, after the bowler has entered his delivery stride and while the ball is in play, his wicket is put down either by the striker's bat or by his person as described in Law 28.1(a)(ii) and (iii) (Wicket put down).

    either (i) in the course of any action taken by him in preparing to receive or in receiving a delivery,

    or (ii) in setting off for his first run immediately after playing or playing at the ball,

    or (iii) if he makes no attempt to play the ball, in setting off for his first run, providing that in the opinion of the umpire this is immediately after he has had the opportunity of playing the ball,

    or (iv) in lawfully making a second or further stroke for the purpose of guarding his wicket within the provisions of Law 34.3 (Ball lawfully struck more than once).

(b) If the striker puts his wicket down in any of the ways described in Law 28.1(a)(ii) and (iii) (Wicket put down) before the bowler has entered his delivery stride, either umpire shall call and signal Dead ball.

2. NOT OUT HIT WICKET

Notwithstanding 1 above, the striker is not out under this Law should his wicket be put down in any of the ways referred to in 1 above if

(a) it occurs after he has completed any action in receiving the delivery, other than in 1(a)(ii), (iii) and (iv) above.

(b) it occurs when he is in the act of running, other than setting off immediately for his first run.

(c) it occurs when he is trying to avoid being run out or stumped.

(d) it occurs when he is trying to avoid a throw-in at any time.

(e) the bowler after entering his delivery stride does not deliver the ball. In this case either umpire shall immediately call and signal Dead ball. See Law 23.3 (Umpire calling and signalling Dead ball).

(f) the delivery is a No ball.

Hit wicket is one of the three methods of dismissal for which the striker's end umpire is responsible. As pointed out under Law 24, it is vital that he turns his attention to the striker, the crease and the stumps as soon as he has seen the bowler's arm action. He must see if the wicket is broken and if so how it was broken. Although not relevant to Hit wicket, he must know whether the striker was in his ground or not at the time it was put down, to judge a possible stumping or Run out.

The essential features for Hit wicket are:

- the bowler must deliver the ball
- the delivery must not be a No ball
- it is the striker himself (including his clothing, equipment etc.), rather than the ball, who puts the wicket down
- when the striker does so, the bowler must have already entered his delivery stride. The end point of the period during which the striker may be out Hit wicket is set out in the detail below.

1 The bowler must deliver the ball. It must not be a No ball

If, because he sees the striker dislodge a bail from his wicket, the bowler stops in his run up, either before or after entering his delivery stride, the umpire must call and signal Dead ball for the non-delivery. Any appeal must be answered Not out.

That the delivery is not to be a No ball is straightforward.

2 How the striker puts down his wicket

It is unlikely that he will knock a stump out of the ground but very possible that he may dislodge a bail, with his 'bat or person'. The striker putting down his own wicket is the only situation in the Laws in which items which are *not* part of his 'bat or person' are included as though they were. Elsewhere in the Laws, mention of the bat implies it is being held. Here it counts even if the striker has let go of it – even if it breaks and he is holding one part and the other part falls. Either part will count. Similarly, in Appendix D, only items of clothing that are attached to him are defined as part of his person. Nevertheless, even though they are not part of his person, a cap, or his glasses or any other detachable items can be agents for putting down his wicket. It is important to realise that such 'abnormal' items count *only in the process of falling from him.*

3 When the striker puts down his wicket

There is a very clear starting point for the period during which the striker is liable to be out Hit wicket. It is when the bowler enters his delivery stride. From that point onwards if any movement the striker makes in preparing to receive the ball, or in receiving the ball, causes his wicket to be put down, he is out Hit wicket. The striker's end umpire will have been watching the bowler's arm action. If when he turns his attention to the stumps and creases at his end, the wicket is already broken, he may have been aware of it happening or may have to rely on his colleague at the bowler's end to tell him whether it happened before the bowler entered his delivery stride, or in that short period between then and release of the ball. A bail may, of course, have come off accidentally, but the bowler's end umpire will have called Dead ball for that.

'Preparing to receive the ball' is any movement of his bat – for example his back-lift – or any movement of his feet – perhaps to get into the line of the ball – before the ball reaches him. 'Receiving the ball' is as much lifting his bat to let the ball through without trying to play it as actually making a stroke to try to hit it. It includes any 'follow-through' swing of the bat after hitting or trying to hit the ball. It also includes any body movement to recover his balance after making his stroke. During all this time, he can be out Hit wicket if he puts the wicket down. Furthermore, he could still be out if he sets out at once for a run and in doing so puts his wicket down. The striker's end umpire will have to judge what 'immediately' is, especially if the striker has not actually played the ball. After that, Hit wicket is no longer a risk – <u>unless</u>, after originally receiving the ball, he makes a second stroke to defend his wicket. This will usually be very soon after the first strike, when he sees his stumps in danger.

STRIKER MAY NOT BE OUT

Section 2 lists the situations in which the striker, even though he has put down his wicket, will nevertheless not be out Hit wicket. Part (a) refers to the various points in time when the striker ceases to be at risk, as described in the previous paragraph. Parts (e) and (f) have also been discussed above. The other points are self-explanatory.

Law 36   Leg before wicket

I. OUT LBW

The striker is out LBW in the circumstances set out below.
  (a) The bowler delivers a ball, not being a No ball
and **(b) the ball, if it is not intercepted full pitch, pitches in line between wicket and wicket or on the off side of the striker's wicket**
and **(c) the ball not having previously touched his bat, the striker intercepts the ball, either full pitch or after pitching, with any part of his person**
and **(d) the point of impact, even if above the level of the bails,**
      either (i) is between wicket and wicket
        or (ii) if the striker has made no genuine attempt to play the ball with his bat, is either between wicket and wicket or outside the line of the off stump.
and **(e) but for the interception, the ball would have hit the wicket.**

2. INTERCEPTION OF THE BALL

(a) In assessing points (c), (d) and (e) in I above, only the first interception is to be considered.
(b) In assessing point (e) in I above, it is to be assumed that the path of the ball before interception would have continued after interception, irrespective of whether the ball might have pitched subsequently or not.

3. OFF SIDE OF WICKET

The off side of the striker's wicket shall be determined by the striker's stance at the moment the ball comes into play for that delivery. See Appendix D.

LBW could be described as a high-profile Law. The esteem, or otherwise, in which an umpire is held will depend very much on his ability, consistency and fairness in judging appeals for LBW.

The requirements to be met for an umpire to uphold an appeal for LBW are clear, although judging them is not always so easy. They are set out in a logical sequence in Section 1. The word 'and' before each of requirements (b), (c), (d) and (e) emphasises that **all these conditions must be met**. The only real variation is provided by:

tried to play the ball with his bat – point of impact **must** be in line between wicket and wicket;

did not try to play the ball with his bat – point of impact **may also** be outside the line of off stump.

The other point, in which there are apparent alternatives, is that the ball may pitch first or may hit the striker's person without having pitched. There is no real variation here. The requirements about where the ball must pitch simply become irrelevant if it doesn't pitch.

BEING PREPARED FOR AN APPEAL

Since all these requirements belong to the behaviour of the ball before it hits the striker, it is obvious that they will have occurred without the umpire knowing beforehand whether there is going to be an appeal. He must therefore be aware *on every delivery*, in addition to all the other things he must be mindful of:

- whether or not the ball is a No ball
- where the ball pitches – if it pitches at all
- what the path of the ball is after it pitched
- whether it misses the striker completely, or first hits his person, or first hits his bat
- if it hits the person first, either after pitching, or full pitch,

    where the striker is in relation to the stumps at that time

    where the ball's path was taking it at that time.

With experience, it will become a matter of almost unconscious habit to observe all these things, and more, every time the ball is bowled. Much of the information will be required for adjudicating on other situations, anyway.

Clearly the most difficult part of the decision is the last item in the list above. Others can, however, sometimes cause problems. It can be difficult to see if the ball hit the bat or not – a very fine edge – and if it did, whether it was before or after it hit the striker's person. It can also be difficult at times to see if the part of the striker that was hit was in line between wicket and wicket. The striker will often move away quickly. The umpire must judge on where the striker was at the moment of impact.

WHERE DID THE BALL PITCH?

Being a round object, the ball pitches on its lowest *point*. It is this point that the umpire must judge. Anywhere, <u>except outside leg stump</u> will keep alive the possibility of LBW. On the line of leg stump will do. Beyond it will not.

WAS THE POINT AT WHICH THE STRIKER WAS HIT IN LINE BETWEEN WICKET AND WICKET?

If the striker is only partly in front of the wicket, this judgment is not too difficult. Nearly always, however, he will be completely hiding the stumps. It is helpful when first going out to the pitch, before there is a batsman in the way, for the umpire to study carefully how the pitch looks and how the 9-inch strip of grass from his wicket to the other one looks. The inexperienced umpire is often surprised to see what a narrow strip it is. There may well be signs, such as a lighter patch of grass, a worn patch on a length, that will help him to build a mental picture of the stumps behind the striker's body. As the game progresses, the bowler's footmarks at the other end will provide more landmarks.

Study the pitch and the far wicket without the players. Notice how the perspective (only marginally exaggerated by the photography) makes that crucial 9 inches look narrower at the other end than at yours. Draw lines in your mind's eye from the outer edges of your stumps to those at the other end

DID THE BALL HIT THE BAT BEFORE HITTING THE PERSON?

Whether the ball did or did not get a fine edge on the bat before hitting the striker is no less difficult than the same judgment for a catch behind. A batsman playing defensively will almost certainly have his bat close to his pad – often behind it, as already discussed in Law 26. Sharp observation is needed to be sure, since a touch on the bat before hitting the person means that an appeal will fail. If the ball struck the pad first, the possibility of LBW remains alive. An umpire who is not sure must not guess, but it is not fair to the bowler and his side if the umpire takes refuge in being unsure. He must train himself to watch with the utmost concentration, to be sure, in as many cases as possible, which was hit first.

Umpires must also remember that it is not only a case of the first strike being on the striker's person rather than his bat, it is only the first impact on the striker which is to be considered at all. If the ball hits his front pad and then goes on to hit the other pad, this second impact is irrelevant.

The ball has ricocheted off his front leg on to his back leg. Only the first strike is to be considered for LBW

WHERE WAS THE BALL'S PATH TAKING IT WHEN IT HIT THE STRIKER?

To answer this question, the umpire must first have a good picture of where the ball was going *before* it hit the striker. It cannot be stated too often how important it is for the umpire to switch his attention from the bowler's feet to the flight of the ball at the earliest possible moment.

His first point of information is the bowler's delivery stride. Was it close to the stumps, as wide out on the return crease as a fair delivery would allow, or somewhere in between? This will give valuable information about the angle of flight from delivery point towards the opposite end.

The actual flight is also informative. Was the ball swinging? How well flighted was it? How fast was it? Although the umpire will know that in general the bowler is quick, medium or slow, every delivery is likely to have some variation of speed. The umpire needs to gauge the pace and flight. Both will affect how the ball will come off the pitch when it hits the ground. If it doesn't pitch, all this information is exactly what the umpire needs to know about where the ball was going when it hits the striker.

When the ball pitches, if it does, it will alter its path, even if only from descending to ascending. First, how quickly did the ball rise? If it rises sharply and at a good pace, it is likely that it would have gone over the top of the stumps. A slower ball probably would not. Very often, however, the ball will also alter course laterally on pitching. The path of the ball as it hits the striker is what will determine whether or not it would have hit his wicket. The umpire must therefore have seen enough of its path after pitching to know what that path is. The fact that he has good information from before pitching means that the way it changes can tell him what he needs to know. If he waited until the ball pitched before taking an interest he would have little hope of being sure what it did thereafter. There must be enough distance of travel, between pitching and hitting the striker, for him to judge the path accurately.

It is not possible to lay down what that distance should be. Satisfactory information about its path will depend on the pace of the ball, its previous flight and on the alertness of observation by the umpire. In general, the faster the delivery, the less time it will take between pitching and impact and therefore the greater the distance required to assess its path. It will become easier with experience. The practised umpire will have accumulated knowledge of the way that moving balls behave, just as a good fielder knows where the ball will be by the time he reaches it. The basic criterion must be 'Did the umpire see enough of the ball's travel after pitching to *know* what its final path was?'

At least, the umpire is relieved of one difficulty. The ball may hit the striker low down, or be dropping rapidly as it hits him. In this case, the umpire is to assume that there would have been no lateral deviation of the path if, being low, the ball would have subsequently hit the ground before reaching the stumps.

WOULD THE BALL HAVE HIT THE WICKET?
It is a temptation for the umpire to read into the behaviour of the ball things which he has not observed, by relying on the way previous balls have behaved. For instance he may *subconsciously* think 'This is an off spin bowler. All his previous balls have turned so this one turned.' Previous balls however did not strike the pad – so this one is likely to be different! The umpire must resolutely ignore previous balls and judge *this* ball on its own merits, strictly on what he has observed about it.

Having decided what its final path before impact is, deciding whether the ball would have hit the wicket is simply a matter of sufficient experience in extending that path in the mind's eye, onward to the stumps. One very important point is how far that extension would have to be. If the striker's pad is only two feet – it is often more – in front of the popping crease when hit, the ball would have had to travel another six feet before reaching the stumps. Umpires must remember that, except in the case of the striker not having tried to hit the ball with his bat, the point of impact on the striker and the point where it would have reached the wicket must **both** *be within the 9-inch strip* between wicket and wicket. This means that the last section of travel must be fairly straight (parallel to the edges of the 9-inch strip). If the striker has played forward, his front leg may be 4 feet in front of the popping crease and so 8 feet in front of the stumps. If he is hit in line with off stump, a ball coming in from the off can move sideways only 1 inch per foot of travel if it is not to miss leg stump. If he is hit in front of middle stump this amount of movement is reduced to half that. The path of a ball which has turned considerably, or that of a swinging ball, will not meet this requirement. The continuation of such paths will be outside leg, probably by a good margin.

It follows that the further forward the striker is when hit, the further the ball would still have had to travel, the straighter the path would have to be if it is to remain within the 9-inch strip until reaching the level of the stumps. The umpire must not assume that every batsman playing forward is immune. It is perfectly possible for him to be out LBW, but the margin for error is small and the umpire must be entirely sure of his observations. The balls with the best chance of remaining within the 9-inch strip are those whose deflection on pitching '*straightens*' them.

The diagrams/pictures on pages 190–4 illustrate some of the main points in judging LBW.

There is very little of this striker in line between wicket and wicket

He is hit in line with middle stump "plumb in front". No guarantee of LBW

He is hit in line with middle stump. Not LBW as the ball pitched outside leg stump

He is hit in line with middle stump. Not LBW as the ball will go over the stumps

He is hit in line with middle stump. Not LBW as the ball touched his bat first. Note the slight deflection

He is hit full pitch in line with the middle stump but not out LBW as the curved path of the swinging ball would miss leg stump

He is hit in line with leg stump

Ball 1 – He is hit in line with leg stump. The ball is going towards leg with at least 5 feet to travel to the wicket. It would miss leg stump.
Ball 2 – The movement towards leg is slight The ball will probably just graze leg stump.
Ball 3 – The ball is going directly towards leg stump and would hit it. Only paths between this and ball 2 could allow LBW for a hit in line with leg stump. Ball 4 – The ball has pitched outside leg stump and so he cannot be out LBW

STRIKER NOT TRYING TO PLAY THE BALL WITH THE BAT

Very little is changed in this situation. Every one of the conditions (a) to (e) must still be met, but (d) is expanded. If the striker is hit in line between wicket and wicket, well and good, but in addition LBW is still possible *even if he is hit outside off stump*. The effect of this is that a turning ball will have more chance than otherwise of securing an LBW dismissal. The last part of the travel can be at a greater angle to the line between wicket and wicket and still satisfy the conditions. The problems facing the umpire in deciding whether he has tried to play the ball with his bat are exactly the same as those discussed under Law 26.

He is hit outside off stump. Was he trying to hit the ball with his bat? Unless the ball had turned sharply, no

He is hit outside off stump. He is not trying to hit the ball with his bat. Would the ball have hit the wicket? Ball 1 – just missing leg stump. Not out. Ball 2 – yes: out if everything else is right. Ball 3 – just missing off stump. Not out

Clearly he did not try to hit the ball with his bat. The ball is heading for the stumps. He will be out

THE OFF SIDE OF THE WICKET

Whatever is the off side of the field when the ball comes into play, remains the off side until the ball is dead, even though the striker himself may change his stance from right handed to left-handed (or vice versa). This clarifies the position for the 'reverse sweep' and the 'switch-hit'. In the latter case, fewer deliveries will be Wides – so fewer one-run penalties will accrue to the batting side. A batsman's reach is greater on his off side than on his leg side. A ball is not a Wide unless it is out of reach from where he is and where he would be in a normal guard position. Although from the umpire's point of view in making any decisions the off side stays the same throughout, from the point of view of the batsman's reach he now has *two* off sides – one a normal guard position, the other the new stance he has switched to. He has two sides with a greater theoretical reach. Apart from LBW, the fact that the off side of the field does not change when the batsman switches his stance is important for consideration of leg side fielders behind the line. Because the off side stays the same, any appeal for LBW that would have been upheld in his original stance would still be upheld. Even though the batsman may *feel* that balls are coming from his leg side, it is in fact still officially the off side.

This is an appropriate point to remind umpires that if a ball pitches outside leg, or if the striker is first hit outside leg, all thoughts of LBW can be abandoned.

Law 37 Obstructing the field

1. OUT OBSTRUCTING THE FIELD

Either batsman is out Obstructing the field if he wilfully obstructs or distracts the fielding side by word or action.

Furthermore, it shall be regarded as obstruction if while the ball is in play either batsman wilfully, and without the consent of a fielder, strikes the ball with his bat or person, other than a hand not holding the bat, after the ball has been touched by a fielder. This shall apply whether or not there is any disadvantage to the fielding side. See 4 below.

2. ACCIDENTAL OBSTRUCTION

It is for either umpire to decide whether any obstruction or distraction is wilful or not. He shall consult the other umpire if he has any doubt.

3. OBSTRUCTING A BALL FROM BEING CAUGHT

The striker is out should wilful obstruction or distraction by either batsman prevent a catch being made.

This shall apply even though the striker causes the obstruction in lawfully guarding his wicket under the provisions of Law 34.3 (Ball lawfully struck more than once).

4. RETURNING THE BALL TO A FIELDER

Either batsman is out Obstructing the field if, without the consent of a fielder and while the ball is in play, he uses his bat or person, other than a hand not holding the bat, to return the ball to any fielder.

5. RUNS SCORED

If either batsman is dismissed Obstructing the field, runs completed by the batsmen before the offence shall be scored, together with any runs for penalties awarded to either side. See Laws 18.6 (Runs awarded for penalties) and 18.9 (Runs scored when a batsman is dismissed).

If, however the obstruction prevents a catch from being made, runs completed by the batsmen before the offence shall not be scored, but any runs for penalties awarded to either side shall stand.

6. BOWLER DOES NOT GET CREDIT

The bowler does not get credit for the wicket.

Two specific cases are noted in the Law. One is of a batsman using his bat to strike the ball in play after it has been touched by a fielder. This includes tapping the ball with his bat to return it to a fielder, without permission, while the ball is in play. If he uses his hand instead of his bat, it is still an offence but he is out Handled the ball in that case. It must be remembered that these are offences *only* if the ball is in play. It is also worth re-stating from time to time that being out is not the same as being dismissed.

The other specific case is of the striker preventing an attempted catch, in the act of legitimately defending his wicket by a second strike.

However, any act by a batsman, designed to reduce the capacity of the fielding side to field the ball or secure a dismissal, is obstructing the field. The word 'designed' is important. It is only when such acts are wilful that they become obstruction. The obstruction can take a number of different forms. Shouting to distract a fielder, or running into his path are obvious ones. There are other more subtle ways. One is a batsman deliberately changing his course to try to block the path of the ball being thrown in for a Run out attempt.

A case was reported not long ago of a running batsman, realising he would not make his ground in time, throwing his bat at the stumps to break the wicket. As he was in the act of running he would not be out Hit wicket. He was, however, out Obstructing the field, as the fielding side would be delayed in putting down the wicket for a Run out by having to replace at least one bail, or pull a stump out with ball in hand.

WAS THE OBSTRUCTION WILFUL?

A batsman when running is intent on making his ground and may possibly collide with a fielder, especially if the fielder is also moving quickly to field the ball. If, following such a collision, there is an appeal, the decision will hinge on whether or not the bowler's end umpire considered the collision was deliberate or accidental. The Law does not require him to consult the other umpire. He may have had a clear view himself of what happened and give his decision. If not, however, his colleague at the striker's end may have had a better view from his side-on position, and should be consulted.

OBSTRUCTING A CATCH

A batsman is certainly guilty of obstructing the field if at any time he deliberately interferes, by a carefully timed shout or in any other way, with a fielder trying to take a catch. It is not restricted to the special case of a second strike to defend his wicket. If a catch is obstructed it does not matter which batsman is guilty, it is the striker who is out – he would have been out if the catch had been taken. For any other obstruction it is the batsman causing it who is out. If No ball had been called, then although a fielder might be trying to catch the ball, it will not be a catch. Distraction by a batsman will still be obstruction, however. The fielder, instead of having the ball in hand, will be delayed while he picks it up after dropping it. In this case, it will be the batsman who caused the distraction who is out, as a catch was not involved.

RUNS SCORED

If a batsman is dismissed under this Law, runs scored follow the general principle that the run in progress does not count, because the batsman is dismissed. All completed runs will count. In any case, a one-run penalty for Wide or No ball will of course stand as usual. However, on the same principle that no runs are scored if the striker is out Caught, if the obstruction prevents a catch, not only will it be the striker who is out, but no runs except penalties will be scored.

This is a case where the scorers may well be in doubt as to the method of dismissal and even as to the number of runs to be recorded. The umpire should make sure they have this information, at the earliest opportunity.

Law 38 Run out

I. OUT RUN OUT

(a) **Either batsman is out Run out, except as in 2 below, if, at any time while the ball is in play,**
> (i) **he is out of his ground**
> and (ii) **his wicket is fairly put down by the action of a fielder.**

(b) **(a) above shall apply even though No ball has been called and whether or not a run is being attempted, except in the circumstances of 2(e) below.**

2. BATSMAN NOT RUN OUT

Notwithstanding 1 above, a batsman is not out Run out if

(a) he has been within his ground and has subsequently left it to avoid injury, when the wicket is put down.
Note also the provisions of Law 29.1(b) (When out of his ground).

(b) the ball has not subsequently been touched by a fielder, after the bowler has entered his delivery stride, before the wicket is put down.

(c) the ball, having been played by the striker, or having come off his person, directly strikes a protective helmet worn by a fielder and without further contact with him or any other fielder rebounds directly on to the wicket. However, the ball remains in play and either batsman may be Run out in the circumstances of 1 above if a wicket is subsequently put down.

(d) he is out Stumped. See Law 39.1(b) (Out Stumped).

(e) No ball has been called
and (i) he is out of his ground not attempting a run
and (ii) the wicket is fairly put down by the wicket-keeper without the intervention of another fielder.

3. WHICH BATSMAN IS OUT

The batsman out in the circumstances of 1 above is the one whose ground is at the end where the wicket is put down. See Laws 2.8 (Transgression of the Laws by a batsman who has a runner) and 29.2 (Which is a batsman's ground).

4. RUNS SCORED

If either batsman is dismissed Run out, the run in progress when the wicket is put down shall not be scored, but runs completed by the batsmen shall stand, together with any runs for penalties awarded to either side. See Laws 18.6 (Runs awarded for penalties) and 18.9 (Runs scored when a batsman is dismissed).

If, however, a striker who has a runner is himself dismissed Run out, runs completed by the runner and the other batsman before the wicket is put down shall not be scored, but any runs for penalties awarded to either side shall stand. See Law 2.8 (Transgression of the Laws by a batsman who has a runner).

5. BOWLER DOES NOT GET CREDIT

The bowler does not get credit for the wicket.

The basic application of this Law is simple. The ball is in play. A batsman is out of *his* ground. The wicket at *his* end is fairly put down by the fielding side. He is out Run out.

HIS GROUND
Which ground belongs to which batsman has been fully discussed under Law 29, including all the complications of two batsmen in the same ground, and of a striker who has a runner. When the wicket is put down, which batsman is out rests on an understanding of which batsman's ground is at that end.

If there is a runner, it is not as complicated as it might seem. It will always be a normal decision based on the positions of the runner and the non-striker only, *except in one situation*. If the striker with a runner is out of his ground (always at the keeper's end) and the wicket is put down at that end, the striker is out regardless of the positions of the other two. Law 2 defines whether he is out Stumped or Run out. This situation is discussed in more detail later.

EXCEPTIONS – WHEN A BATSMAN WILL NOT BE RUN OUT
1 Avoiding injury
A batsman in his ground may fear that a ball being thrown in to the wicket may hit him on the ankle, and jump in the air to avoid being hurt. If his wicket is put down while he is in the air he will not be Run out. Another example is the batsman who is outside his crease but with his bat grounded behind the line. He ducks to avoid a wild throw-in and in the movement his bat comes off the ground. Again he is not liable to be run out. Perhaps he moves out of his ground to avoid a potentially injurious collision with a fielder or umpire. The two points are:
- he must have been within his ground
- he must have left it only to avoid injury.

The first is a matter of fact, the second a matter of judgment. It will usually not be difficult for the umpire to make this judgment.

2 In continuing his running
When a batsman is running very hard to gain his ground, he is unlikely to slow down as he reaches the crease and will continue running in the same direction. The test for running as opposed to walking is that at times both feet are off the ground. It is difficult, not to say a little dangerous, to keep his bat in continuous contact with the ground while running, especially near the creases where there will be footmarks, making the ground uneven. It could happen, therefore, that at some point neither his feet nor his bat are in contact with the ground. He would technically be 'out of this ground'. However, Law 29.1(b), newly introduced in 2010, specifies that this situation is not to be so interpreted. Consequently, if the wicket is put down at that instant, he would not be run out. The two points needed to give him this immunity are that he has
      grounded a foot behind the popping crease before the wicket is put down
and   continued running in the same direction.

In a game without the benefit of cameras, it is unlikely but not impossible that an umpire could discern that he (and his bat) were in the air at the precise moment that the wicket was put down. It does mean, however, that once the umpire has seen some part of the batsman's foot grounded behind the popping crease, he need not worry about what happens if the batsman continues running in the same direction.

3 Ball not touched by a fielder

This covers three situations.

The bowler is entitled to run out the non-striker who has left his ground too soon as long as the attempt is made before entering his delivery stride. Once he has entered his delivery stride the ball must be touched by another fielder before a Run out can be attempted.

When the striker hits the ball, it cannot yet have been touched by a fielder. If the ball then breaks the wicket at the bowler's end, even though the non-striker may be out of his ground he will not be run out if a fielder has still not touched the ball since it left the striker's bat.

A striker cannot be out Bowled if No ball has been called. If the ball breaks his wicket, technically it has been put down by the opposing side. This provision of Law ensures that the failed Bowled will not simply turn into Run out, if the striker is out of his ground, unless a fielder has touched the ball since it left the bowler's hand. He is, of course, not entitled to do so until after the striker has had an opportunity to play the ball.

4 Rebounding off a helmet

If either wicket is put down by a ball which has rebounded from a fielder's helmet, being worn, then the batsman at that end is not liable to be run out, providing that the rebound from the helmet is the only contact (except with the ground) between leaving the striker and hitting the stumps. If, either before or after rebounding from the helmet, the ball touches the fielder wearing the helmet, or any other fielder, or even an umpire or the other batsman, then neither batsman has immunity from being run out. Contact with the ground between impacts is not significant. It should be noted that the provision applies only to *this* breaking of the wicket. If play continues, any further attempt at Run out will be considered normally. It also applies only if the ball has made contact with the striker before hitting the helmet. There is no reason to confer immunity on a batsman if the striker has either not attempted or made only a failed attempt to make contact with the ball.

If the ball rebounds off a fielder's helmet on the ground, it immediately becomes dead on contact and no question of dismissal can arise.

If the ball rebounds from either batsman's helmet, it is still in play and any normal dismissal is possible.

5 Out Stumped

Stumped is a special form of Run out. The interlocking of Run out and Stumped is discussed in the next Law. The proviso in this Law affirms that if the method of dismissal is Stumped, this will over-ride Run out.

6 A special case of not out Stumped

The requirements for being out Stumped are the same as those for being Run out, with some additions. In many cases, therefore, if all the conditions for Stumped are not fulfilled, the lesser charge of Run out will apply. The conditions set out in Section 2(e) are exactly those for out Stumped, with the single exception that No ball has been called. In such circumstances, the verdict of Run out is not valid, even though the basic requirements for Run out apply.

STRIKER WHO HAS A RUNNER

If the batsman who has a runner is not the striker, the question of his being run out rests entirely on whether his runner is run out. If, however he is the striker, then either his runner or he himself may be run out. Although he may not be 'injured' but have been granted a runner by the umpires for some other good reason, it will simplify the explanation if he is referred to as the 'injured striker', rather than as 'the striker who has a runner'.

Law 29 makes it clear that the 'injured striker's' end is always at the keeper's end, never at the bowler's end. The first consequence of this is that if the wicket is put down at the bowler's end he *himself* cannot be run out. The umpire is to decide which of the other two, if either, is out, on the normal basis for two batsmen.

If, however, the wicket is put down at the keeper's end, which belongs both to him and to one of the others, the question could arise as to whether it is the 'injured striker' himself who is out, or the other man. Law 2 and Law 29 together make it clear that if he is out of his ground he will be the one who is out regardless of where his runner and the non-striker are. He will be Stumped if the conditions in Law 39 (Stumped) apply. Otherwise he is Run out, even if No ball has been called. If he is in his ground the decision is again on the normal basis for the other two batsmen. If it is the runner who is out, then automatically, the 'injured striker' is out.

RUNS SCORED

Section 4 sets out the runs scored. Normally, when a batsman is out Run out, completed runs *only* will be scored in addition to penalties. Although the run in progress is not scored, whether or not the batsmen have crossed in this run, before the wicket is put down, will determine not only who is out but the ends to which the not out batsman and his new partner will go. When the striker who has a runner is himself run out, which will be at the wicket-keeper's end, no runs other than penalties are to be scored and the new batsman will go to that end. The details are set out in Law 18.

The chart summarises the above facts about dismissal and runs scored.

STRIKER WHO HAS A RUNNER – RUN OUT?	
Wicket put down at **bowler's** end	
Ignore 'injured striker'; consider positions of other two	
Wicket put down at **keeper's** end	
'injured striker' in his ground	*'injured striker' out of his ground*
Ignore him	He is out
Consider positions of other two	Ignore other two
Completed runs + penalties	Penalties but no runs
Not out batsman goes to *his* end	New batsman goes to *that* end

Of course, if the runner is out, the striker is automatically out by definition, but runs will be scored on the normal basis. If there are two runners, one of them is always to be regarded as an ordinary non-striker.

In order to record the correct number of runs, the scorers will certainly need to know if it was the striker *himself* who was run out, or whether he was out because his runner was.

FIELD TECHNIQUE
It cannot be said too often that, whenever the batsmen are running, the umpires must be in a position to see the wickets and the creases at their respective ends, and to see where the batsmen are. They need:

to see that, if the wicket is put down, it is fairly put down

to know whether or not the batsman was in his ground at that time

to be aware when the batsmen cross during the run

to watch for short running.

The striker's end umpire is already in a good position for this, though he may have to dodge quickly to one side if a fielder moves across his line of vision. If there is a runner, where to stand himself and where to place the runner has been set out under Law 2. It will take time for the bowler's end umpire to reach the ideal position for adjudicating on events at his wicket. He must remain at the wicket until the ball has been hit, in case there are any events at the striker's end on which he must exercise judgment. Then he must move very quickly. He must develop a sense of where the players are, and where they may be running to, to avoid getting in their way as he is moving. He also needs to avoid getting in the path of the throw-in. This has already been discussed in more detail in Law 28.

If the ball is returned to the stumps very quickly, he may not have time to get as far as he would wish. He must get to the best position he can achieve in the time. He must be able to see the stumps, the crease and the running batsman, and must also have his head stationary at the moment when a fine judgment has to be made about the grounding of the bat and the breaking of the wicket. A particular difficulty is the ball hit hard by the striker back to the bowler's end stumps. Getting any distance from the stumps in this case is impossible, but he should be able to get a sideways, or at least a diagonal view of the action. He must see where the non-striker is when the wicket is put down. He must see whether a fielder touched the ball before the wicket was put down.

When there is a Run out attempt at one end, the umpire at the other end will realise this possibility and will watch to see whether or not the batsmen had crossed before the wicket is put down. If the Run out decision is a close one, the problem of crossing is likely to be an easier task.

Law 39 Stumped

I. OUT STUMPED

(a) The striker is out Stumped, except as in 3 below, if
        (i) a ball which is not a No ball is delivered
  and (ii) he is out of his ground, other than as In 3(a) below
  and (iii) he has not attempted a run
when (iv) his wicket is fairly put down by the wicket-keeper without the intervention of another fielder. Note, however, Laws 2.8(c) (Transgression of the Laws by a batsman who has a runner) and 40.3 (Position of wicket-keeper).
(b) The striker is out Stumped if all the conditions of (a) above are satisfied, even though a decision of Run out would be justified.

2. BALL REBOUNDING FROM WICKET-KEEPER'S PERSON

(a) If the wicket is put down by the ball, it shall be regarded as having been put down by the wicket-keeper if the ball
      (i) rebounds on to the stumps from any part of the wicket-keeper's person or equipment other than a protective helmet
or (ii) has been kicked or thrown on to the stumps by the wicket-keeper.
(b) If the ball touches a protective helmet worn by the wicket-keeper, the ball is still in play but the striker shall not be out Stumped. He will, however, be liable to be Run out in these circumstances if there is subsequent contact between the ball and any fielder. Note, however, 3 below.

3. NOT OUT STUMPED

(a) **Notwithstanding I above, the striker will not be out Stumped if he has left his ground to avoid injury, when his wicket is put down.**

(b) **If the striker is not out Stumped he may, except in the circumstances of Law 38.2(e), be out Run out if the conditions of Law 38 (Run out) apply.**

Stumped is a special case of Run out. Only the striker can be stumped; either batsman can be run out. The bowler will get credit for a stumping but not for a Run out. The basic conditions for a Run out are:

- the batsman must be out of his ground
- the wicket at *his* end must be put down fairly by the fielding side while he is out of his ground.

These are also the basic requirements for the striker to be out Stumped, but three more conditions are added to these:

- the delivery must not be a No ball
- the striker must not be attempting a run
- the putting down of the wicket must be by the keeper alone, without any other fielder being involved.

If the first two conditions of the total of five are met, but any of the last three are not, then the decision can revert back, as it were, to Run out. Section 3 spells this out but also lays down a specific ban on one particular situation. It is the same one as in Section 2(e) of Run out. If all the conditions for Stumped are met *except* that No ball is called, then not only will the striker not be out Stumped, he will not be out Run out either.

This is one of the ways of dismissal within the jurisdiction of the striker's end umpire.

WICKET PUT DOWN BY THE WICKET-KEEPER ALONE

Section 2 clarifies what counts as being 'put down by the wicket-keeper'. For a stumping to be possible, 'put down by the wicket-keeper' is not enough. He must be the *only* fielder in contact with the ball before the breaking of the wicket. Intervention of another fielder need not be intentional. If the ball rebounds off the slip fielder's boot, then slip has 'intervened' and stumping is not possible – though Run out might be.

It should be noted that if the ball rebounds from the wicket-keeper's helmet, either accidentally or otherwise, then the striker is not liable to be stumped. Furthermore he cannot be run out either, unless the ball touches a fielder after contact with the helmet and before breaking the wicket. That fielder can be the keeper as much as any other fielder.

BATSMAN NOT ATTEMPTING A RUN

It is precisely because he has moved forward to play the ball that a striker may be at risk of being stumped. If he misses the ball and it goes through towards the wicket-keeper standing up, he will be aware of his danger and be only too anxious to return to his ground immediately. It will therefore not be difficult to distinguish between movement made to play the ball and an attempt to run. It should be noted that if he has left his ground to avoid injury, that will protect him from being stumped. Since only the wicket-keeper can be involved, it will be rare for the ball to come from a direction where the striker might be injured, but it can happen.

It has already been explained that if there is a striker with a runner – an 'injured striker' – the bowler's end can *never* be his end. His end is *always* the wicket-keeper's end. It is not uncommon for an 'injured striker' to set off instinctively as if for a run. Even if he crosses with the non-striker, however, and reaches the other end, a run will not be scored. He will not have 'made good **his** ground from end to end' – the bowler's end cannot be his (new) end. Consequently, even though, as frequently happens, an 'injured striker' sets off from his crease, it is not to be regarded as attempting a run. This means that the question of 'attempting a run' cannot arise, even if he moves forward. He has handed over to his runner the right to score runs and cannot do so himself. This is why Law 2 makes special provision for his being liable to be run out or stumped, simply by being out of his (only) ground. The details are set out in Law 2 Section 8.

The detail of the 'injured striker' being himself Run out was discussed under Law 38. The only difference from Run out is that, for an 'injured striker' to be Stumped (apart from not being a No ball), the putting down of the wicket is to be by the keeper alone.

FIELD TECHNIQUE

In judging a stumping, watching for the wicket being fairly put down and seeing whether or not the striker was at that time in his ground are exactly the same as for Run out. As noted under Law 28, the wicket-keeper may break the wicket just before he actually has the ball in his hands, or may drop the ball before his hands reach the stumps. The striker's end umpire must be sure the wicket was fairly put down and that the bails came off before the striker was grounded behind the line. At times, the two actions will be very close, making it difficult to be sure which came first. Complete concentration is essential. However, until the batsmen start to run, he does not have to worry about the batsmen crossing, nor about short running. Instead he must see that only the wicket-keeper was involved in putting down the wicket and judge whether or not the striker was attempting a run. Most of the four pieces of information will come from his normal action for every delivery – the close scrutiny of the creases, the stumps and the positions of the wicket-keeper, striker and nearby fielders. As stated before, as soon as he has seen the ball leave the bowler's hand, the striker's end umpire must switch his attention to the creases and stumps at his own end. He must be aware on every delivery that there may be an attempted stumping. Even if the keeper is standing back, he may kick or throw the ball on to the stumps or the ball may rebound – as long as it is not off the keeper's helmet. If the keeper is standing close, the umpire must watch to see that he does not come in front of the wicket too soon – snatching the ball too early, in the hopes of a stumping – and be ready to call and signal No ball if he does.

Another of his duties, watching for too many fielders behind the popping crease on the leg side at the instant of delivery, will also contribute, since a contravention will mean a call of No ball and the destruction of a stumping chance.

Law 40 The wicket-keeper

1. PROTECTIVE EQUIPMENT

The wicket-keeper is the only fielder permitted to wear gloves and external leg guards. If he does so these are to be regarded as part of his person for the purposes of Law 41.2 (Fielding the ball). If by his actions and positioning it is apparent to the umpires that he will not be able to discharge his duties as a wicket-keeper, he shall forfeit this right and also the right to be recognised as a wicket-keeper for the purposes of Laws 32.3 (A fair catch), 39 (Stumped), 41.1 (Protective equipment), 41.5 (Limitation of on-side fielders) and 41.6 (Fielders not to encroach on pitch).

2. GLOVES

If, as permitted under 1 above, the wicket-keeper wears gloves, they shall have no webbing between the fingers except joining index finger and thumb, where webbing may be inserted as a means of support. If used, the webbing shall be
(a) a single piece of non-stretch material which, although it may have facing material attached, shall have no reinforcements or tucks.
(b) such that the top edge of the webbing
    (i) does not protrude beyond the straight line joining the top of the index finger to the top of the thumb.
    (ii) is taut when a hand wearing the glove has the thumb fully extended.
See Appendix C.

3. POSITION OF WICKET-KEEPER

The wicket-keeper shall remain wholly behind the wicket at the striker's end from the moment the ball comes into play until
    (a) a ball delivered by the bowler
      either (i) touches the bat or person of the striker
        or (ii) passes the wicket at the striker's end
or (b) the striker attempts a run.

In the event of the wicket-keeper contravening this Law, the striker's end umpire shall call and signal **No ball** as soon as possible after the delivery of the ball.

4. MOVEMENT BY WICKET-KEEPER

It is unfair if the wicket-keeper standing back makes a significant movement towards the wicket after the ball comes into play and before it reaches the striker. In the event of such unfair movement by the wicket-keeper, either umpire shall call and signal **Dead ball**.

It will not be considered a significant movement if the wicket-keeper moves a few paces forward for a slower delivery.

5. RESTRICTION ON ACTIONS OF WICKET-KEEPER

If, in the opinion of either umpire, the wicket-keeper interferes with the striker's right to play the ball and to guard his wicket, Law 23.4(b)(vi) (Umpire calling and signalling **Dead ball**) shall apply.

If, however, either umpire considers that the interference by the wicket-keeper was wilful, then Law 42.4 (Deliberate attempt to distract striker) shall also apply.

6. INTERFERENCE WITH WICKET-KEEPER BY STRIKER

If, in playing at the ball or in the legitimate defence of his wicket, the striker interferes with the wicket-keeper, he shall not be out except as provided for in Law 37.3 (Obstructing a ball from being caught).

EXTERNAL PROTECTIVE EQUIPMENT

The wicket-keeper is a fielder. Any reference to fielders in the Laws will include him unless specifically stated otherwise. He is, however, a special fielder. He alone is allowed to wear external pads and gloves. These count as part of his person where relevant. Although not defined, the normal duties of the keeper are well understood. He is expected to stand behind the wicket, in a line along which the ball is likely to travel if the striker misses it or deflects it only slightly. He must be far enough back to have time to see the ball, but not so far as to miss the chance of a catch or a stumping. If the umpires consider he is not in such a position – perhaps he is behind the stumps but virtually on the boundary – perhaps he is in a slip or fine leg position – then *he is not a wicket-keeper* and loses the privilege of wearing protective equipment. If nevertheless he does wear it, then contact between the ball and any such item is illegal fielding, to be dealt with as in Law 41.2. This does not mean that he cannot leave his 'keeper's position' to field the ball. Provided on every delivery he stands in a suitable 'keeper's position' while the ball is being delivered and the striker is receiving it, he can thereafter move away freely to field the ball, without forfeiting his right to pads and gloves.

Note that very particular requirements are laid down about his gloves, stated in Section 2 and illustrated in Appendix C. Although these restrictions caused some problems when first introduced in 2000, they have become generally accepted by manufacturers. Players are now not likely to transgress. If nevertheless a keeper does wear illegal gloves, there are specified procedures at the highest levels. At more humble levels, the umpire must use his judgment. It could be unsafe for a keeper not to wear gloves, but a legal pair may not be available. The incident should certainly be reported, to prevent the same player 'getting away' with illegal gloves at match after match.

POSITION OF WICKET-KEEPER

Apart from where he must be, in general terms, to earn his status as a keeper, Section 3 of this Law adds a specific restriction on his position. Behind the wicket is defined in Appendix D. It is clear that he must not have *any* part of his person – tips of his fingers, peak of his cap, etc. – further forward than the back of the stumps. He is confined from the moment the bowler starts his run up. The three events, any one of which will release him from this 'prison', are set out in this section of Law. A keeper seeing a chance of a stumping will often push his hands too far forward, at the last minute, in his anxiety to take the ball. The striker's end umpire will be watching for this. The keeper is allowed to come in front for a catch, since the ball will have touched the striker's bat. Again the striker's end umpire must watch that the keeper does not anticipate the catch and come in front before the ball has touched the bat. No ball is to be called and signalled for any transgression.

The wicket-keeper is not wholly behind the stumps while the ball is being delivered – a No ball

This will be legal only if the ball touched the striker or his bat, or a run was attempted, before the keeper came in front. Otherwise No ball is to be called and signalled by the striker's end umpire

MOVEMENT BY WICKET-KEEPER

As well as confining the keeper behind the stumps during the specified period, the Law forbids him to make any significant movement between the ball coming into play and the ball reaching the striker. If he realises that the delivery is a slower one he can move forward a little. If he is standing back and comes up close, to a stumping position, he is in breach of the Law and Dead ball is to be called. Either umpire may see this movement. Whichever one does must make the call and signal. There is no harm done if both umpires do!

STRIKER'S RIGHT TO PLAY THE BALL

The striker is entitled to play the ball without interference from the fielding side. This enables him to make a late cut, or to follow the ball round on the leg side and hit it after it has passed the line of his wicket. He cannot run into the outfield to try to hit the ball but is entitled to move a pace or so to either side to put himself in a better position to play the ball. This, however, should be regarded as the extent of his right to play the ball. If the wicket-keeper interferes with this, it is likely to be accidental and the call of Dead ball and the ball not counting in the over is the only action required. The umpires must, however, judge whether the action was deliberate. If either umpire so decides then this is a case of obstruction or distraction of the striker. Action will be as set out in Law 42.4.

STRIKER INTERFERING WITH WICKET-KEEPER

The striker has an absolute right to play the ball and to defend his wicket, even with a second stroke, subject to the two provisos:

> he must be <u>either</u> *genuinely* trying to playing the ball <u>or</u> *solely* defending his wicket

and he must not obstruct a catch by any fielder, not only one by the keeper.

As long as these two requirements are met, no action is to be taken if the striker interferes with the wicket-keeper's attempt to gather the ball. He may play a very late cut when the wicket-keeper is already in the process of taking the ball. Provided he is genuinely playing the ball, he is allowed to do so without penalty, although he will be out Obstructing the field if the 'interference' baulks a catch. The same is true of a second strike, provided it is genuinely and solely in defence of his stumps.

In the case of a second strike, however, should either umpire form the opinion that defending his wicket was not the striker's sole motive, if the action interferes with the wicket-keeper then, rather than being out Hit the ball twice, he will be out Obstructing the field.

Law 41 The fielder

1. PROTECTIVE EQUIPMENT

No fielder other than the wicket-keeper shall be permitted to wear gloves or external leg guards. In addition, protection for the hand or fingers may be worn only with the consent of the umpires.

2. FIELDING THE BALL

A fielder may field the ball with any part of his person, but if, while the ball is in play, he wilfully fields it otherwise,

(a) the ball shall immediately become dead

and (b) the umpire shall

(i) award 5 penalty runs to the batting side.

(ii) The penalty for a No ball or a Wide shall stand. Additionally, runs completed by the batsmen shall be credited to the batting side, together with the run in progress if the batsmen had already crossed at the instant of the offence.

(iii) inform the other umpire and the captain of the fielding side of the reason for this action.

(iv) inform the batsmen and, as soon as practicable, the captain of the batting side of what has occurred.

(c) The ball shall not count as one of the over.

(d) The umpires together shall report the occurrence as soon as possible after the match to the Executive of the fielding side and to any

Governing Body responsible for the match, who shall take such action as is considered appropriate against the captain and the player or players concerned.

3. PROTECTIVE HELMETS BELONGING TO THE FIELDING SIDE

Protective helmets, when not in use by fielders, should, if above the surface, be placed only on the ground behind the wicket-keeper and in line with both sets of stumps. If a protective helmet belonging to the fielding side is on the ground within the field of play, and the ball while in play strikes it, the ball shall become dead, and 5 penalty runs shall then be awarded to the batting side, in addition to the penalty for a No ball or a Wide, if applicable.

Additionally runs completed by the batsmen before the ball strikes the protective helmet shall be scored, together with the run in progress if the batsmen had already crossed at the instant of the ball striking the protective helmet. See Law 18.10 (Runs scored when the ball becomes dead other than at the fall of a wicket).

4. PENALTY RUNS NOT TO BE AWARDED

Notwithstanding 2 and 3 above, if from the delivery by the bowler, the ball first struck the person of the striker and, if in the opinion of the umpire, the striker
neither (i) attempted to play the ball with his bat
 nor (ii) tried to avoid being hit by the ball,
then no award of 5 penalty runs shall be made and no other runs or penalties shall be credited to the batting side except the penalty for a No ball, if applicable.

If runs are attempted, the umpire should follow the procedure laid down in Law 26.3 (Leg byes not to be awarded).

5. LIMITATION OF ON-SIDE FIELDERS

At the instant of the bowler's delivery there shall not be more than two fielders, other than the wicket-keeper, behind the popping crease on the on side. A fielder will be considered to be behind the popping crease unless the whole of his person whether grounded or in the air is in front of this line. In the event of infringement of this Law by any fielder, the striker's end umpire shall call and signal No ball.

6. FIELDERS NOT TO ENCROACH ON PITCH

While the ball is in play and until the ball has made contact with the striker's bat or person, or has passed the striker's bat, no fielder, other than the bowler, may have any part of his person grounded on or extended over the pitch.

In the event of infringement of this Law by any fielder other than the wicket-keeper, the bowler's end umpire shall call and signal No ball as soon as possible after delivery of the ball. Note, however, Law 40.3 (Position of wicket-keeper).

7. MOVEMENT BY FIELDERS

Any significant movement by any fielder after the ball comes into play, and before the ball reaches the striker, is unfair. In the event of such unfair movement, either umpire shall call and signal Dead ball. Note also the provisions of Law 42.4 (Deliberate attempt to distract striker).

8. DEFINITION OF SIGNIFICANT MOVEMENT

(a) For close fielders anything other than minor adjustments to stance or position in relation to the striker is significant.

(b) In the outfield, fielders are permitted to move towards the striker or the striker's wicket, provided that 5 above is not contravened. Anything other than slight movement off line or away from the striker is to be considered significant.

(c) For restrictions on movement by the wicket-keeper see Law 40.4 (Movement by wicket-keeper).

EXTERNAL PROTECTIVE EQUIPMENT

The only visible protective equipment that a fielder, other than the wicket-keeper, is allowed to wear is a protective helmet. Appendix D spells out that this term includes face guards. If he genuinely needs protection for a damaged hand or fingers, permission to wear it must be obtained from the umpires, who will ensure that it is neither excessive nor unreasonable.

FIELDING THE BALL

Fielding the ball is not necessarily stopping it and grasping it. It is contact with the ball in a deliberate attempt to stop it. A fielder is allowed to do this with any part of his person, as defined in Appendix D. Wilfully 'fielding it otherwise' is deliberately using something that is not a part of his person to field it. The classic (but extremely rare) example is using a cap he has taken off to field the ball. Equally it could be contact with an illegal item of visible protective clothing. There have been rare cases of a fielder fielding the ball while holding a glove discarded by the keeper. Equally, cases have been known of the ball *accidentally* falling into a fielder's open-necked shirt, and even into one if his pockets. Such incidents are not unlawful, because they are not wilful acts.

There is a difference between illegal fielding, defined in this Law, and the transgression in Law 2 of a fielder coming on without permission. There the contact with the ball does not have to be deliberate though it almost always is. The offence is merely coming on to the field without permission and touching the ball, even accidentally. The penalty is nevertheless the same in both Laws. The ball immediately becomes dead and does not count in the over. Five penalty runs are awarded to the batting side, together with runs completed or crossed at the instant of the illegal contact and any penalty for a No ball or Wide. The matter is to be reported.

HELMETS ON THE GROUND

It has long been accepted that whilst an umpire will hold a bowler's cap or sweater during his over, umpires do not carry helmets. Fielders are allowed to put them on the ground behind the wicket-keeper. Umpires should check that they are reasonably in line with the stumps and far enough back. The penalties set out in Section 3, however, apply to a fielder's helmet on the ground *anywhere* within the field of play. Perhaps a helmet fell off. That is no excuse. It will still earn the penalty if the ball in play, whether on its journey out into the field or on a throw-in, hits it. This applies only to helmets. If some other item of a fielder's person, such as a cap, or a pair of glasses, falls off accidentally, no action need be taken if the ball in play hits it. However, although not specifically stated in the Law, the umpire should take the same action as for a helmet on the ground if the ball in play hits, for example, a sweater knowingly discarded by a fielder, or a cap he has deliberately taken off. Moreover if the fielder deliberately *uses* such an item to try to stop the ball, contact with the ball in this case is illegal fielding as defined under Section 2 and the full penalty stated in Section 2 must be imposed, including a report. It should be noted that there is no report to be made under Section 3 – the only instance in the Laws where the award of 5 penalty runs is not followed by a report after the match. This is because putting the helmet on the ground is not in itself an unfair act, whereas trying to field the ball by manoeuvring it or, for example, by pulling out his sweater to form a pouch, is deliberately unfair.

PENALTIES NOT ALLOWED

The penalty for a No ball or a Wide will always stand. Section 4 refers only to the 5-run penalties for illegal fielding or contact with a fielder's helmet (etc.) on the ground. The situation described here is *exactly* that in Law 26 where not only are the batsmen prohibited from scoring Leg byes, but other penalties that might have accrued are withheld too.

LIMITATION ON THE POSITION OF FIELDERS

1 Behind the popping crease

The restriction in Section 5, to two fielders here, <u>on the on side</u>, is absolute. A third fielder with his hand overhanging the dividing line contravenes the Law. Sometimes, however, the wicket-keeper will stand on the leg side to get a better view of the flight of the ball. If so, he does not count as one of the two.

The time when the embargo is in force is at the instant of delivery. Apart from having a number of other things to watch, the main difficulty for the striker's end umpire is the fielder walking in towards the wicket, who may start in a legitimate position before the ball is delivered but, as he walks in, crosses the popping crease – which, of course, extends to the boundary. A situation in which this could happen is when there are already two behind the popping crease as the bowler runs up, and a fielder at square leg in front of it but close to it. It is essential that the umpire can observe that square leg fielder, which he can't do if the man is behind him. He must cross to the off side so that he can see this fielder. For any contravention, the striker's end umpire must call and signal No ball.

2 Encroaching on the pitch

The other restriction on fielders' positions is in Section 6. Here the embargo is in force, not just at an instant in time, but over a longer period, set out in detail in the Law. The bowler will run on the pitch, within strict limits, in his follow-through. No other fielder is allowed on the pitch throughout the stated period. Again, just as for fielders behind the popping crease, 'on the pitch' includes not only feet grounded on the pitch, but any part of a fielder's person overhanging it. The penalty for contravention is again a call and signal of No ball but in this case by the bowler's end umpire. Although it may appear that the wicket-keeper is excluded from the embargo, this is only because if he offends, as he will do if, for example, he has any part of his hands in front of the stumps too soon, then action is to be taken as laid down in Law 40 (The wicket-keeper) rather than under this Law.

Even though his hand is in the air, the fielder is encroaching on the pitch while the ball is being delivered – a No ball

MOVEMENT BY FIELDERS

The striker is entitled to know where the fielders are. Therefore, once the bowler starts his run up, when the striker will be concentrating on that, it is unfair if a fielder moves to a significantly different position. Significant movement is defined in Section 8. A call and signal of Dead ball must be made immediately by whichever umpire sees any such movement. In Law 40, a similar restriction is set on movement by the wicket-keeper. There, however, it is primarily distance from the wicket that is envisaged. The keeper is a fielder and will also be subject to the wider restriction in this Law. He cannot, while the bowler is running up, rush round to, for example, a short fine leg position, even if he is only the second fielder behind the popping crease on the leg side.

FIELD TECHNIQUE

All the things that have been said previously, about where umpires must focus their attention while the ball is being delivered by the bowler and received by the striker, will apply. An additional point for this Law is that it is quite possible that the players will continue play, not realising that the ball has become dead automatically in a case of illegal fielding, or even of the ball hitting a helmet on the ground. In such a situation, the bowler's end umpire may need to take up the option offered in Law 23.4(a), of nevertheless calling and signalling Dead ball. It will not be necessary to repeat this to the scorers, as it is an 'extra' signal to inform the players. It may well be helpful, however, to tell the scorers the number of runs to be recorded. It is possible that they will not be able to tell whether the batsmen had crossed or not before the instant of the throw.

Law 42 Fair and unfair play

I. FAIR AND UNFAIR PLAY – RESPONSIBILITY OF CAPTAINS

The responsibility lies with the captains for ensuring that play is conducted within the spirit and traditions of the game, as described in The Preamble – The Spirit of Cricket, as well as within the Laws.

2. FAIR AND UNFAIR PLAY – RESPONSIBILITY OF UMPIRES

The umpires shall be the sole judges of fair and unfair play. If either umpire considers an action, not covered by the Laws, to be unfair he shall intervene without appeal and, if the ball is in play, call and signal Dead ball and implement the procedure as set out in 18 below. Otherwise umpires shall not interfere with the progress of play without appeal except as required to do so by the Laws.

3. THE MATCH BALL – CHANGING ITS CONDITION

(a) Any fielder may
   (i) polish the ball provided that no artificial substance is used and that such polishing wastes no time.
   (ii) remove mud from the ball under the supervision of the umpire.
   (iii) dry a wet ball on a piece of cloth.
(b) It is unfair for anyone to rub the ball on the ground for any reason, to interfere with any of the seams or the surface of the ball, to use any implement, or to take any other action whatsoever which is likely to alter the condition of the ball, except as permitted in (a) above.
(c) The umpires shall make frequent and irregular inspections of the ball.
(d) If the umpires together agree that the deterioration in the condition of the ball is greater than is consistent with the use it has received, they shall consider that there has been a contravention of this Law. They shall
   (i) change the ball forthwith. It shall be for the umpires to decide on the replacement ball. It shall, in their opinion, have had wear comparable to that which the previous ball had received immediately prior to the contravention.
   Additionally the bowler's end umpire shall
   (ii) award 5 penalty runs to the batting side.
   (iii) inform the batsmen that the ball has been changed.
   (iv) inform the captain of the fielding side that the reason for the action was the unfair interference with the ball.
   (v) inform the captain of the batting side as soon as practicable of what has occurred.
   (vi) together with the other umpire report the occurrence as soon as possible after the match to the Executive of the fielding side and to any Governing Body responsible for the match, who shall take such action as is considered appropriate against the captain and team concerned.
(e) If the umpires together agree that there has been any further instance in that innings of greater deterioration in the condition of the ball than is consistent with the use it has received, they shall
   (i) repeat the procedure in (d)(i), (ii) and (iii) above.
   Additionally the bowler's end umpire shall
   (ii) inform the captain of the fielding side of the reason for the action taken and direct him to suspend the bowler forthwith who delivered the immediately preceding ball. The bowler thus suspended shall not be allowed to bowl again in that innings. If applicable, the over shall be completed by another bowler, who shall neither have bowled any part of the previous over, nor be allowed to bowl any part of the next over.
   (iii) inform the captain of the batting side as soon as practicable of what has occurred.

(iv) together with the other umpire report the further occurrence as soon as possible after the match to the Executive of the fielding side and to any Governing Body responsible for the match, who shall take such action as is considered appropriate against the captain and team concerned.

4. DELIBERATE ATTEMPT TO DISTRACT STRIKER

It is unfair for any fielder deliberately to attempt to distract the striker while he is preparing to receive or receiving a delivery.

(a) If either umpire considers that any action by a fielder is such an attempt, at the first instance he shall immediately call and signal Dead ball and inform the other umpire of the reason for the call. The bowler's end umpire shall

    (i) warn the captain of the fielding side that the action is unfair and indicate that this is a first and final warning.

    (ii) inform the batsmen of what has occurred.

Neither batsman shall be dismissed from that delivery. The ball shall not count as one of the over.

(b) If there is any further such deliberate attempt by any fielder in that innings, the procedures, other than warning, as set out in (a) above shall apply. Additionally, the bowler's end umpire shall

    (i) award 5 penalty runs to the batting side.

    (ii) inform the captain of the fielding side and, as soon as practicable, the captain of the batting side of the reason for the action.

    (iii) together with the other umpire report the occurrence as soon as possible after the match to the Executive of the fielding side and to any Governing Body responsible for the match, who shall take such action as is considered appropriate against the captain and the player or players concerned.

5. DELIBERATE DISTRACTION OR OBSTRUCTION OF BATSMAN

In addition to 4 above, it is unfair for any fielder wilfully to attempt, by word or action, to distract or obstruct either batsman after the striker has received the ball.

(a) It is for either one of the umpires to decide whether any distraction or obstruction is wilful or not.

(b) If either umpire considers that a fielder has caused or attempted to cause such a distraction or obstruction, he shall immediately call and signal Dead ball and inform the other umpire of the reason for the call.

(c) Neither batsman shall be dismissed from that delivery.

Additionally

(d) The bowler's end umpire shall

    (i) award 5 penalty runs to the batting side.

    (ii) inform the captain of the fielding side of the reason for this action and as soon as practicable inform the captain of the batting side.

(e) The ball shall not count as one of the over.

(f) Runs completed by the batsmen before the offence shall be scored, together with any runs for penalties awarded to either side. Additionally, the run in progress shall be scored whether or not the batsmen had already crossed at the instant of the offence.

(g) The batsmen at the wicket shall decide which of them is to face the next delivery.

(h) The umpires together shall report the occurrence as soon as possible after the match to the Executive of the fielding side and to any Governing Body responsible for the match, who shall take such action as is considered appropriate against the captain and player or players concerned.

6. DANGEROUS AND UNFAIR BOWLING

(a) Bowling of fast short pitched balls

    (i) The bowling of fast short pitched balls is dangerous and unfair if the bowler's end umpire considers that by their repetition and taking into account their length, height and direction they are likely to inflict physical injury on the striker irrespective of the protective equipment he may be wearing. The relative skill of the striker shall be taken into consideration.

    (ii) Any delivery which, after pitching, passes or would have passed over head height of the striker standing upright at the popping crease, although not threatening physical injury, shall be included with bowling under (i) above, both when the umpire is considering whether the bowling of fast short pitched balls has become dangerous and unfair and after he has so decided. The umpire shall call and signal No ball for each such delivery.

(b) Bowling of high full pitched balls

    (i) Any delivery, other than a slow paced one, which passes or would have passed on the full above waist height of the striker standing upright at the popping crease is to be deemed dangerous and unfair, whether or not it is likely to inflict physical injury on the striker.

    (ii) A slow delivery which passes or would have passed on the full above shoulder height of the striker standing upright at the popping crease is to be deemed dangerous and unfair, whether or not it is likely to inflict physical injury on the striker.

7. DANGEROUS AND UNFAIR BOWLING – ACTION BY THE UMPIRE

(a) As soon as the bowler's end umpire decides under 6(a) above that the bowling of fast short pitched balls has become dangerous and unfair, or, except as in 8 below, there is an instance of dangerous and unfair bowling as defined in 6(b) above, he shall call and signal No ball. When the ball is dead, he shall caution the bowler, inform the other umpire, the captain of the fielding side and the batsmen of what has occurred. This caution shall apply throughout the innings.

(b) If there is any further instance of dangerous and unfair bowling by the same bowler in that innings, the umpire shall repeat the above procedure and indicate to the bowler that this is a final warning. This warning shall also apply throughout the innings.

(c) Should there be any further repetition by the same bowler in that innings, the umpire shall call and signal No ball and

   (i) when the ball is dead direct the captain to suspend the bowler forthwith and inform the other umpire of the reason for this action. The bowler thus suspended shall not be allowed to bowl again in that innings.

   If applicable, the over shall be completed by another bowler, who shall neither have bowled any part of the previous over, nor be allowed to bowl any part of the next over.

Additionally he shall

  (ii) report the occurrence to the batsmen and, as soon as practicable, to the captain of the batting side.

 (iii) together with the other umpire report the occurrence as soon as possible after the match to the Executive of the fielding side and to any Governing Body responsible for the match, who shall take such action as is considered appropriate against the captain and bowler concerned.

8. DELIBERATE BOWLING OF HIGH FULL PITCHED BALLS

If the umpire considers that a bowler deliberately bowled a high full pitched ball, deemed to be dangerous and unfair as defined in 6(b) above, then the caution and warning prescribed in 7 above shall be dispensed with. The umpire shall

(a) (i) call and signal No ball.

  (ii) when the ball is dead direct the captain of the fielding side to suspend the bowler forthwith.

   The bowler thus suspended shall not be allowed to bowl again in that innings.

   If applicable, the over shall be completed by another bowler, who shall neither have bowled any part of the previous over, nor be allowed to bowl any part of the next over.

 (iii) inform the other umpire of the reason for this action.

(b) report the occurrence to the batsmen and, as soon as practicable, to the captain of the batting side.

(c) together with the other umpire report the occurrence as soon as possible after the match to the Executive of the fielding side and to any Governing Body responsible for the match, who shall take such action as is considered appropriate against the captain and bowler concerned.

9. TIME WASTING BY THE FIELDING SIDE

It is unfair for any fielder to waste time.

(a) If either umpire considers that the progress of an over is unnecessarily slow, or time is being wasted in any other way, by the captain of the fielding side or by any other fielder, at the first instance the umpire concerned shall

    (i) if the ball is in play, call and signal Dead ball.

    (ii) inform the other umpire of what has occurred.

(b) The bowler's end umpire shall then

    (i) warn the captain of the fielding side, indicating that this is a first and final warning.

    (ii) inform the batsmen of what has occurred.

(c) If either umpire considers that there is any further waste of time in that innings by any fielder, he shall

    (i) if the ball is in play, call and signal Dead ball.

    (ii) inform the other umpire of what has occurred.

The bowler's end umpire shall

    (iii) either, if the waste of time is not during an over, award 5 penalty runs to the batting side and inform the captain of the fielding side of the reason for this action

    or, if the waste of time is during the course of an over, direct the captain of the fielding side to suspend the bowler forthwith. The bowler thus suspended shall not be allowed to bowl again in that innings.

If applicable, the over shall be completed by another bowler, who shall neither have bowled any part of the previous over, nor be allowed to bowl any part of the next over.

    (iv) inform the batsmen and, as soon as is practicable, the captain of the batting side of what has occurred.

    (v) together with the other umpire report the occurrence as soon as possible after the match to the Executive of the fielding side and to any Governing Body responsible for the match, who shall take such action as is considered appropriate against the captain and team concerned.

10. BATSMAN WASTING TIME

It is unfair for a batsman to waste time. In normal circumstances, the striker should always be ready to take strike when the bowler is ready to start his run up.

(a) Should either batsman waste time by failing to meet this requirement, or in any other way, the following procedure shall be adopted. At the first instance, either before the bowler starts his run up or when the ball becomes dead, as appropriate, the umpire shall

(i) warn both batsmen and indicate that this is a first and final warning. This warning shall apply throughout the innings. The umpire shall so inform each incoming batsman.

(ii) inform the other umpire of what has occurred.

(iii) inform the captain of the fielding side and, as soon as practicable, the captain of the batting side of what has occurred.

(b) If there is any further time wasting by any batsman in that innings, the umpire shall, at the appropriate time while the ball is dead

(i) award 5 penalty runs to the fielding side.

(ii) inform the other umpire of the reason for this action.

(iii) inform the other batsman, the captain of the fielding side and, as soon as practicable, the captain of the batting side of what has occurred.

(iv) together with the other umpire report the occurrence as soon as possible after the match to the Executive of the batting side and to any Governing Body responsible for the match, who shall take such action as is considered appropriate against the captain and player or players and, if appropriate, team concerned.

11. DAMAGING THE PITCH – AREA TO BE PROTECTED

(a) It is incumbent on all players to avoid unnecessary damage to the pitch. A player will be deemed to be causing avoidable damage if either umpire considers that his presence on the pitch is without reasonable cause. It is unfair to cause deliberate damage to the pitch.

(b) An area of the pitch, to be referred to as 'the protected area', is defined as that area contained within a rectangle bounded at each end by imaginary lines parallel to the popping creases and 5 ft/1.52 m front of each, and on the sides by imaginary lines, one each side of the imaginary line joining the centres of the two middle stumps, each parallel to it and 1 ft/30.48 cm from it.

12. BOWLER RUNNING ON PROTECTED AREA AFTER DELIVERING THE BALL

(a) A bowler will contravene this Law if he runs on to the protected area, either after delivering the ball or, if he fails to release the ball, after the completion of his delivery swing and delivery stride. See 11 above, Law 23.4(viii) (Umpire calling and signalling Dead ball) and Appendix D.

(b) If, as defined in (a) above, the bowler contravenes this Law, at the first instance and when the ball is dead, the umpire shall

(i) caution the bowler and inform the other umpire of what has occurred.
This caution shall apply throughout the innings.

(ii) inform the captain of the fielding side and the batsmen of what has occurred.

(c) If, in that innings, the same bowler again contravenes this Law, the umpire shall repeat the above procedure indicating that this is a final warning. This warning shall also apply throughout the innings.

(d) If in that innings the same bowler contravenes this Law a third time, the umpire shall,

   (i) when the ball is dead, direct the captain of the fielding side to suspend the bowler forthwith.
   The bowler thus suspended shall not be allowed to bowl again in that innings.
   If applicable, the over shall be completed by another bowler, who shall neither have bowled any part of the previous over, nor be allowed to bowl any part of the next over.

  (ii) inform the other umpire of the reason for this action.

 (iii) inform the batsmen and, as soon as practicable, the captain of the batting side of what has occurred.

 (iv) together with the other umpire report the occurrence as soon as possible after the match to the Executive of the fielding side and to any Governing Body responsible for the match, who shall take such action as is considered appropriate against the captain and bowler concerned.

13. FIELDER DAMAGING THE PITCH

(a) If any fielder causes avoidable damage to the pitch, other than as in 12(a) above, at the first instance the umpire seeing the contravention shall, when the ball is dead, inform the other umpire. The bowler's end umpire shall then

   (i) caution the captain of the fielding side and indicate that this is a first and final warning. This warning shall apply throughout the innings.

  (ii) inform the batsmen of what has occurred.

(b) If, in that innings, there is any further instance of avoidable damage to the pitch, by any fielder, the umpire seeing the contravention shall, when the ball is dead, inform the other umpire. The bowler's end umpire shall then

   (i) award 5 penalty runs to the batting side.

  Additionally he shall

  (ii) inform the fielding captain of the reason for this action.

 (iii) inform the batsmen and, as soon as practicable, the captain of the batting side of what has occurred.

 (iv) together with the other umpire report the occurrence as soon as possible after the match to the Executive of the fielding side and to any Governing Body responsible for the match, who shall take such action as is considered appropriate against the captain and player or players concerned.

14. BATSMAN DAMAGING THE PITCH

(a) If either batsman causes avoidable damage to the pitch, at the first instance the umpire seeing the contravention shall, when the ball is dead, inform the other umpire of the occurrence. The bowler's end umpire shall then

    (i) warn both batsmen that the practice is unfair and indicate that this is a first and final warning. This warning shall apply throughout the innings. The umpire shall so inform each incoming batsman.

    (ii) inform the captain of the fielding side and, as soon as practicable, the captain of the batting side of what has occurred.

(b) If there is any further instance of avoidable damage to the pitch by any batsman in that innings, the umpire seeing the contravention shall, when the ball is dead, inform the other umpire of the occurrence. The bowler's end umpire shall then

    (i) disallow all runs to the batting side from that delivery other than the penalty for a No ball or a Wide, if applicable.

    (ii) additionally, award 5 penalty runs to the fielding side.

    (iii) return the batsmen to their original ends.

    (iv) inform the captain of the fielding side and, as soon as practicable, the captain of the batting side of what has occurred.

(c) The umpires together shall report the occurrence as soon as possible after the match to the Executive of the batting side and to any Governing Body for the match who shall take such action as is considered appropriate against the captain and player or players concerned.

15. BOWLER ATTEMPTING TO RUN OUT NON-STRIKER BEFORE DELIVERY

The bowler is permitted, before entering his delivery stride, to attempt to run out the non-striker. Whether the attempt is successful or not, the ball shall not count as one of the over.

If the bowler fails in an attempt to run out the non-striker, the umpire shall call and signal Dead ball as soon possible.

16. BATSMAN STEALING A RUN

It is unfair for the batsmen to attempt to steal a run during the bowler's run up. Unless the bowler attempts to run out either batsman – see 15 above and Law 24.4 (Bowler throwing towards striker's end before delivery) – the umpire shall

    (i) call and signal Dead ball as soon as the batsmen cross in such an attempt.

    (ii) inform the other umpire of the reason for this action.

    (iii) return the batsmen to their original ends.

    (iv) award 5 penalty runs to the fielding side.

    (v) inform the batsmen, the captain of the fielding side and, as soon as practicable, the captain of the batting side, of the reason for this action.

(vi) together with the other umpire report the occurrence as soon as possible after the match to the Executive of the batting side and to any Governing Body responsible for the match, who shall take such action as is considered appropriate against the captain and players concerned.

17. PENALTY RUNS

(a) When penalty runs are awarded to either side, when the ball is dead the umpire shall signal the penalty runs to the scorers. See Law 3.14 (Signals).

(b) Notwithstanding the provisions, of Law 21.6 (Winning hit or extras), penalty runs shall be awarded in each case where the Laws require the award.

Note, however, that the restrictions on awarding penalty runs, in Laws 26.3 (Leg byes not to be awarded), 34.4 (Runs scored from ball lawfully struck more than once) and Law 41.4 (Penalty runs not to be awarded), will apply.

(c) When 5 penalty runs are awarded to the batting side under any of Laws 2.6 (Player returning without permission), 41.2 (Fielding the ball), or 41.3 (Protective helmets belonging to the fielding side) or under 3, 4, 5, 9 or 13 above, then

  (i) they shall be scored as penalty extras and shall be in addition to any other penalties.

  (ii) they are awarded when the ball is dead and shall not be regarded as runs scored from either the immediately preceding delivery or the immediately following delivery, and shall be in addition to any runs from those deliveries.

  (iii) the batsmen shall not change ends solely by reason of the 5-run penalty.

(d) When 5 penalty runs are awarded to the fielding side, under Law 18.5(b) (Deliberate Short runs), or under 10, 14 or 16 above, they shall be added as penalty extras to that side's total of runs in its most recently completed innings. If the fielding side has not completed an innings, the 5 penalty runs shall be added to the score in its next innings.

18. PLAYERS' CONDUCT

If there is any breach of the Spirit of the Game

either in the case of an unfair action not covered by the Laws, under 2 above,

  or by a player

    either failing to comply with the instructions of an umpire

      or criticising an umpire's decisions by word or action

      or showing dissent

      or generally behaving in a manner which might bring the game into disrepute,

the umpire concerned shall immediately report the matter to the other umpire.

The umpires together shall
 (i) **inform the player's captain of the occurrence, instructing the latter to take action.**
 (ii) **warn him of the gravity of the offence, and tell him it will be reported to higher authority.**
 (iii) **report the occurrence as soon as possible after the match to the Executive of the player's team and to any Governing Body responsible for the match, who shall take such action as is considered appropriate against the captain and player or players and, if appropriate, team concerned.**

INTRODUCTION

The heading of this Law makes it clear that it is all about fairness and unfairness. For many years, it has contained statements about what is fair and what is not. The 2000 Edition of the Laws for the first time embodied, as a Preamble, a wide-ranging and general statement about the Spirit of Cricket and the traditions of the game. Since then, not only the actual statements but the concept behind them have been recognised worldwide as a yardstick by which the behaviour of the players is to be measured. Whilst following the detail of particular situations set out in the Laws, the umpires must also judge all the players' actions by this yardstick. In particular, Section 2 of this Law instructs the umpires to intervene if they consider any action, not covered by the Laws, is unfair. The Spirit of Cricket will guide them in coming to such a conclusion. Section 18 of this Law spells out some examples of breaches of the Spirit of Cricket. Applying its principles should not be limited to these two sections of Law. Umpires and players should be conscious of those principles throughout.

There are several instances of 'unfairness' throughout the Laws. To name but two, the batsmen attempting Leg byes when the striker has not fulfilled the conditions for these to be allowed, and the wicket-keeper moving significantly during the bowler's run up. These, however, are dealt with by 'on the spot penalties'. There are just four cases in Laws 1 to 41 in which more severe penalties, including a report to Higher Authority, are to be imposed. These are in Laws 2.6 (Fielder returning without permission) – where the actual offence is touching the ball after thus coming on – 18.5 (Deliberate Short runs), 24.2 (Fair delivery – the arm) and 41.2 (Fielding the ball). Law 42 covers eleven other unfair actions and additionally, in Section 2, makes provision for those not specifically covered in any Law. At first sight these eleven, indeed all fifteen, present a bewildering mass of detail for action by umpires. From 2010, however, they all conform to the same basic pattern, which should enable umpires to master the detail more easily.

THE PROCEDURES FOR APPLYING PENALTIES

Law 42.18 is an exception to most of what follows. It is an important Law dealing with dissent and other breaches of the Spirit of Cricket. The procedure to be followed is largely different from that in the other fourteen instances of unfair play. It should be assumed that the points below do not include Law 42.18, which will be discussed separately.

In the other Laws, there are individual variations – how many warnings are to be issued, whether 5 penalty runs are to be awarded or the bowler is to be taken off and so on – but the general pattern, except in Law 42.18, is always as follows:

- If the first step is to call and signal either No ball or Dead ball, the umpire to do this will be named and will be the one best placed to see the action, although in some cases both umpires will be equally qualified. Remember that 'the umpire' always means the bowler's end umpire.
- He will inform the other umpire.
- All action is then taken by the bowler's end umpire. The only exception, other than 42.18, is ball tampering (42.3) where part of the action is to be by both umpires together.
- In addition to informing the other umpire immediately, the following are always to be informed:

     The fielding captain;

     The batsmen at the wicket;

     The batting captain.
- The umpires together report the incident as soon as possible after the match to the Executive of the offending side and the Governing Body responsible for the match. The first of these will be the club committee or equivalent; the second will be the League or other body that has set up the competition of which the match is part.

Notice that if the players are so misguided as to repeat the offence after all due warnings have been given and final action taken, that final action will be repeated for every further contravention.

Section 17 of the Law sets out general points about the signalling, awarding and recording of penalty runs. They apply in all cases, including the 'not unfair' case of the ball hitting the helmet. Section 17 also allows for penalty runs to be awarded when the final ball of the match has become dead – the basis on which a win by penalty runs (Law 21) can occur. It must, however, have arisen from the final delivery. If the umpires, walking off when the match is concluded, realise that the ball has sustained unfair damage, they cannot then award 5 penalty runs retrospectively. If, however, on the last delivery a batsman, one warning having already been issued, caused avoidable damage to the pitch, it would be in order to award the 5 penalty runs when the ball is dead, since that is when such awards are to be made in any case.

Note also from this Section that, although the penalty is an odd number of runs, the batsmen do not change ends merely on that account. For example, suppose that the batsmen have nearly completed two runs when the ball is thrown in and hits a fielder's helmet on the ground. The ball becomes dead. The batsmen having crossed on the second run count as having run 2. The penalty makes the score 7 in total, an odd number. Nevertheless because of the 2 runs, they will be at the same ends as when the ball was delivered and will stay there.

Umpires must study the procedures to become familiar with the particular points of each one. They might find it helpful to document for themselves each Law under the headings

Call – No ball / Dead ball / neither

Which umpire – Bowler's end / Striker's end / the one involved / either

Offence by – Bowler / other fielder / batsman

Warnings – 2 / 1 / 0

Penalty at each repetition – Some have increasing penalty at each stage; others have no penalty till the warnings have all been given.

Ball to count in over – Yes / No

INFORMING PLAYERS

Any of those named who have already been involved by, for instance, having been given a warning, will not need telling separately, of course.

The fielding captain and batsmen are to be told at every occurrence of the offence.

This is not true of the batting captain. For an offence by a fielder, there is no need to inform the captain of the batting side until warnings have expired and final action is to be taken. He is to be told at every occurrence only if the offence is by a batsman. Play must never be held up, however, in order to inform him. He may, of course, be one of the batsmen currently at the wicket and can be told immediately. Otherwise the umpire must take the first opportunity of a break in play to inform him. In the case of a batsman transgressing, there may therefore be a gap in time before the captain can be told that a warning has been issued to the batting side. When the batting captain is to be informed, the umpire is to also inform each incoming batsman even after the warning has been issued to the captain, to ensure that all understand that a warning is in force.

WARNINGS

If either a batsman or the bowler contravenes the Law, he is the one to be warned. If a fielder other than the bowler commits an offence, it is his captain who is to be warned.

- The purely bowling offences of No balls for throwing, running on the protected area in the follow-through, dangerous and unfair bowling are the only ones for which two warnings are issued. The final penalty is always suspension of the bowler. Umpires must ensure that they know which of the other offences by the fielding side carry a 5-run penalty and which lead to the suspension of the bowler.

The offences committed by batsmen are deliberate short running, time wasting, causing avoidable damage to the pitch and attempting to steal a run during the bowler's run up. These lead to cancellation of runs where appropriate – which does not apply to time wasting – and eventually to a 5-run penalty.

In every case, once a warning is issued it will remain in force for the remainder of the innings.

BALL NOT COUNTING IN THE OVER

Not all offences relate to a particular delivery of the ball. For these, the question of the validity of a delivery does not arise. In some of the others, No ball is to be called, hence the delivery is not valid in any case. For the rest, there is a general principle, based on the logic of the situation. If the fielding side offends, thus possibly restricting the number of runs that the batsmen might have scored, then the delivery will not be a valid ball. This does not apply to the ball hitting the helmet, since this is not a direct unfair action by the fielding side. There the general principle enunciated in Law 23.6 applies; the delivery is a valid ball. Notice, however, that although a fielder causing unnecessary damage to the pitch could possibly be put into this category, a further opportunity to exploit the damage caused is not in the batsmen's interest and the ball will count in the over.

Except for time wasting, where a particular delivery is not pertinent, when it is a batsman who has breached the Law, it would be inequitable to reward him with a further chance to score. It will be a valid ball, counting in the over in all cases.

The chart summarises the cases for fielders:

FIELDER'S OFFENCES

Law	Offence	Ball valid
2.6	Returning without permission*	NO
24.2	Throwing	No ball called
41.2	Illegal fielding	NO
42.3	Ball tampering	Not applicable
42.4	Distracting striker	NO
42.5	Obstructing batsman	NO
42.9	Time wasting	Not applicable
42.13	Pitch damage	Yes. See note above

*Remember, it is not returning illegally that is the offence. It is then coming into contact with the ball.

DETAILS OF THE OFFENCES

Before looking at these, it should be noted that the statement in Section 1 is extremely important. If there is any difficulty with the conduct of the game, the umpires will act through the captain of the side, rather than intervene to rebuke or discipline a player directly. The only direct contact with an individual player is warning a batsman for an offence, or warning a bowler for one of the purely bowler offences.

The eleven offences in this Law fall under the headings:
- Changing the condition of the ball
- Deliberate distraction of a batsman
- Dangerous and/or unfair bowling
- Time wasting
- Damaging the pitch
- Unfair running by the batsmen
- Unacceptable behaviour in ways not listed above; breaches of the Spirit of Cricket.

CHANGING THE CONDITION OF THE BALL

Wear and tear is inevitable as the ball continually strikes the ground, is hit by the bat and runs across the outfield. This wear must not be artificially assisted by any of the players. The Law makes it very clear in Section 3(a) what they are allowed to do, and in Section 3(b) what they are not allowed to do. Cleaning and drying the ball in wet or muddy conditions is permitted, but the umpire is to watch the process to ensure that nothing but the cleaning and drying is done. A cloth – which can include a player's shirt and trousers, etc. – is the *only* agency permitted for drying. Neither using sawdust nor rubbing on the ground, even wiping gently on wet grass, is allowed. The well-equipped umpire will take a suitable cloth out to the pitch with him.

Polishing the ball by rubbing on the shirt, etc. is a time-honoured ritual. It must be done without the assistance of any artificial substance such as hair cream or lip salve, and must not waste time.

In Section 3(b) a number of unfair ball-treatments are listed. Lest the players think that avoiding the items in the short list is sufficient, there is the catch-all embargo *or any other action whatsoever that is likely to alter the condition of the ball.*

Preventive action required of the umpire is to make frequent and irregular inspections. Both frequency and irregularity are important, so that the players feel that the ball is under constant surveillance. Further opportunities for inspection are provided by the umpire taking the ball at each wicket-fall and each cessation of play as required by Law 5. The telltale signs to look for are:
- the stitching of the seam still prominent after considerable use
- disturbance of the corners where the quarters meet the seam
- one side of the ball much rougher than the other, even allowing for the players having polished only one side

• the bowler appearing suspiciously different, holding the ball out of sight in front of him, apparently in both hands, and looking down at it as he walks back to his mark. The striker's end umpire will be the one to see this.

If either umpire has any suspicion that the ball is being mistreated, he should consult his colleague. Together they will look at the ball and see what change there has been since the last inspection. If they agree that this is more than is consistent with the use the ball has had in that time, they will conclude that the fielding side has made unfair changes and will institute the procedure laid down in the rest of Section 3.

DELIBERATE DISTRACTION OF A BATSMAN

The regrettable practice of chatter (or more aggressive utterances), the continual last-minute movement of fielders and other such distractions could be designed to unsettle the striker. Any distraction while the striker is preparing to receive or receiving a delivery is to bring an instant call and signal of Dead ball, as set out in Law 23. If the umpire considers that such behaviour by a fielder is a deliberate attempt to distract the striker, Section 4 sets out the procedure that he must follow.

There may be subsequent attempts at distraction or obstruction. As discussed under Law 37, the umpire must decide whether or not a physical collision between a batsman and a fielder is accidental. If the umpire considers, with his colleague if necessary, that it was wilful, it is not usually difficult to identify the perpetrator. If an attempt at obstruction or distraction is not physical but, perhaps, by a sudden shout, it is more obvious that it was wilful and will be clear who was responsible. For a deliberate attempt by a fielder to obstruct or distract a batsman, after the striker has completed receiving the ball, the penalties set out in Section 5 are six-fold. Neither batsman can be dismissed. This Law is unique in that the run in progress will count, even if the batsmen have not crossed. The delivery is not a valid ball, so the batting side get a further chance to score runs. Five penalty runs are awarded against the fielding side. The two batsmen choose which of them will face the next delivery; this is something the umpire should check that they know. There will be a report after the match. Since the umpire is to call and signal Dead ball as soon as the attempt is made, it is not necessary to gauge how successful the attempt might have been. It is making the attempt that breaches the Law.

DANGEROUS AND UNFAIR BOWLING

The two types of delivery – the fast short pitched ball that rises sharply off the pitch, and the ball that without pitching reaches the striker at a dangerous height – are collected together under the one heading of dangerous and unfair bowling. The terms 'bouncer' and 'beamer' respectively for these are firmly established in cricket's jargon. They are not used in the Law but are useful descriptions.

It must be emphasised that regulations in some high-level matches, allowing a certain number of bouncers in an over, do not apply except in those particular matches. Nevertheless, the Law does allow for some bouncers to be bowled before the penalty procedure is started, though any beamer will instantly trigger that procedure.

1 Bouncers

The umpire does not have to read the bowler's intention. What he has to decide is the likelihood that the delivery could inflict injury on the striker. He must ignore the effect of protective clothing. A ball at the striker's head is not to be considered harmless because the striker is wearing a helmet. The umpire must decide 'that is a dangerous ball', not 'how well protected the striker is'. In making his assessment, the umpire must take into account:

- length – was it short pitched? He can easily observe this fact.
- height – did it pass the striker knee high, waist high, head high? The dangerous levels apply only to the striker *standing* **upright at the crease**. The striker may not be in this position. The umpire will have to judge from the flight of the ball what the situation would have been, had the striker been so positioned. If the ball would have hit the striker, upright at the crease, at upper rib level, at neck/shoulder level or on the head, it is 'high' in this context.
- direction – was it travelling towards the striker's body? This is also an observable fact.
- repetition – are such deliveries being made frequently? Although a competent batsman will probably be able to deal with some bouncers, receiving them continually is likely to unsettle him and wear down his resistance through frustration. It will also make a nonsense of the game.
- the skill of the striker – a really skilled batsman can score freely off such balls and will enjoy doing so. A capable but less skilful batsman will be able to preserve himself from injury but be unable to score off them. Increasing frustration may eventually put him at risk. An inexperienced batsman will be in real danger. The umpire will have to categorise the batsmen, whom he may not have seen before, by the way they react. Just because a batsman is low in the order does not necessarily mean he is incompetent. He may or may not be.

There is a special point about the bouncer passing over the striker's head. Clearly it is not likely to injure him. Nevertheless, the Law recognises it as part of the attack upon his self-confidence and as contributing to his increasing frustration at not being able to score. The bowler is therefore not to be allowed to think that by interlarding dangerous bouncers with a number of these over-head-height bouncers, he can escape penalty. Although such a ball comes within the definition of Wide, it is to be called a No ball. A No ball call gives the striker protection from dismissal from this unfair and dangerous delivery. Moreover, if the striker touches it, even inadvertently in trying to avoid it, a Wide would be annulled, thereby cancelling the one-run penalty and replacement delivery. Each one will form part of the repetition sequence, not in the sense that it is to be counted as a dangerous bouncer, but on the basis of another contribution to the striker's growing frustration and increasing alarm for his own safety.

When the umpire comes to the point that these potentially dangerous bouncers, and over-head-height bouncers, are too often repeated, he will start and follow through the procedure in Section 7. He should probably reach that point after the first bouncer bowled to a batsman who is so inexperienced – perhaps a young player – that it is immediately obvious he is quite unable to cope with it and is therefore in danger from the start. For the really skilful striker, scoring feely from them, the bowler himself will soon realise that bowling bouncers is counterproductive and will cease doing so of his own accord. Between these two extremes, for an ordinarily competent or a fairly inexperienced batsman, the umpire must judge when the repetition is taking its toll of the striker, or when it is simply of itself becoming excessive.

Notice that 'the sequence' is for a particular bowler against the same batsman. Consequently the umpires must keep track of that particular bowler-batsman pair, if the bowler changes ends. He will carry his record of bouncers *to that batsman*, dangerous or over-head-height, with him. The warning procedure, once started, is inexorable. This will be discussed further after the following points on beamers.

2 Beamers

There is no question of repetition or likelihood of injury for the umpire to consider in deciding whether a beamer is unfair. Every beamer is to be considered dangerous and unfair. His only difficult observation will be the height at which it would have passed the striker standing upright at the crease. His only assessment is whether or not the ball counts as slow. This latter judgment must be within the context of the game. It is a matter of how much time the batsman has to deal with that delivery. The less capable he is, the more time he needs. However, the judgment should not be made for each batsman. A general level of competence in that game should be the criterion. One guide, but not a sure one, is whether or not the wicket-keeper is standing up. He may be outstandingly good and able to deal with much faster balls than most of the players. He may be foolhardy. A mistaken belief is held by some that a slower ball delivered by a fast bowler should count as slow. This is not so. Once the umpire has decided the pace at which, in that game, he will judge a delivery as slow, it is absolute. It is the pace of the ball itself that counts, not how it compares with other balls from that bowler. It should also be recognised that slow is not 'not fast'. Balls that are not slow may be medium slow, medium, medium fast, or fast.

The ball that is difficult to judge for height is one that is dropping as it reaches the striker. If he tries to play it well in front of his body, it will be difficult to know how far it would have dropped by the time it reached the popping crease. An enquiring look to your colleague, answered by a little mime from him can be extremely helpful.

The first time that an umpire identifies any delivery as within the definition of beamer (or slow beamer), the warning process starts – or continues if it has already begun. Although the umpire has to decide that 'enough is enough' for bouncers before instituting warnings, *any* beamer will start the process or continue it if it has already begun. A bowler will earn a warning if:

- he bowls a dangerous bouncer or over-head-height bouncer to any batsman for whom he has already been warned
- when the umpire decides, for a different batsman, that the bowling has become dangerous and unfair and issues a first warning with respect to that batsman
- he bowls a beamer to *any* batsman

Once a bowler has been warned, the process continues inexorably. If he is given another warning in any of the three situations above, it will be *his* second warning, even if it is the first for that batsman.

Some umpires feel that it is wrong that only the height of the ball is significant for beamers. One that is well wide of the striker is clearly not of itself dangerous. Nevertheless, since all beamers are banned, it betokens a lack of control by the bowler which does carry considerable potential for danger. One 'accident', or even two, of the ball slipping out of the bowler's hand will not end his career. He gets two warnings. If it keeps happening, he is not in full control of the ball and there is a potential danger that an uncontrolled ball will injure the batsman.

Finally, if the umpire considers that a beamer was not an accident, but deliberately bowled, any warnings not as yet issued are dispensed with. The captain must immediately remove the bowler from the attack, for the rest of the innings.

TIME WASTING

1 By fielders

This is usually a corporate activity. It is difficult to detect because the contributory factors – conference between captain and bowler – fine adjustments of the field – the ball being returned to the bowler in a number of steps rather than in one big throw, and so on – are all legitimate. The umpire has to judge when they are being taken too far. It does not matter whether the slowness is a deliberate ploy to slow down play in the hope of influencing the outcome of the game, or not. What matters is whether the particular activity is necessary and if so whether the time spent on it is more than is reasonable.

There are certain obvious points. A bowler with a long run up who waits until the ball is returned to him before starting the walk back to his mark is wasting time; another fielder could be gathering the ball while the bowler is walking back. A captain who arranges that the same man is at deep fine leg at both ends is wasting time. On the other hand, if a right-handed and a left-handed batsman are in at the same time, running a lot of singles, so that the sight-screen has to be moved virtually every ball, then slow progress is inevitable. As an aside, in such a situation the umpires should try to have someone stationed by the screen so that moving it can be done with minimum delay. The umpire has to judge the situation and would be wise to obtain the agreement of his colleague before embarking on the punitive measures for time wasting laid down in Section 9. Notice the specific instance of time wasting in practising on the field. (See Law 17).

2 By batsmen

Of course, the batsman is entitled to check his guard and look round to see where the fielders are. It is reasonable for him to prod down a small divot on the pitch. If the field is being re-set, a mid-pitch (not actually *on* the pitch!) discussion with the other batsman about strategy may be valid. The umpire has to judge when these things are being taken too far. Again, a check that his colleague takes a similar view is wise. Since many of the activities by which a batsman can waste time will happen before the ball comes into play, Section 10 makes provision for the umpire to award the penalty runs before the delivery, if that is appropriate. The ball must of course be dead. This explains the use of the phrase '*while* the ball is dead', instead of the standard '*when* the ball is dead'.

DAMAGE TO THE PITCH

It is not always realised that merely walking gently and calmly on the pitch will cause damage. Of course, in that case it will be slight, but such slight damage will build up over time. The umpires are therefore to consider that a player is causing avoidable damage simply if he is there unnecessarily. They do not have to wait for damage to be visible. 'Avoidable' and 'unnecessary' are important words. Of course, fielders have to be on the pitch if that is where the ball has to be fielded. The striker will actually stand on the pitch as he waits to receive a delivery and will certainly move on it in playing the ball. If he then runs he cannot *immediately* get off the pitch from the point at which he played the ball. All this is **un**avoidable damage. What is not allowed is fielders and batsmen being on the pitch without reasonable cause.

There are three cases of damage to the pitch.

1 Bowler running on to the protected area

Section 11 defines the protected area. Section 12 specifies that the bowler is not to run on this in following through after delivering the ball. The offence here is not in itself damaging the pitch, although that will be a consequence, it is running on the protected area in the follow-through. The umpire, however, must not divert his attention away from the flight of the ball to watch the bowler's follow-through. He will become aware of the bowler's position if it is not far enough out, since it will then be close to his own line of vision, watching the ball. The bowler may actually get in the way of that line of vision.

This is one of the 'purely bowler' offences mentioned earlier. Two warnings are issued, to the bowler in person rather than the fielding captain. The final penalty is not penalty runs but suspension from bowling for the rest of the innings.

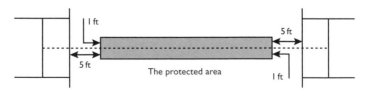

1 ft

5 ft

5 ft

The protected area

1 ft

2 By fielders

Here it is not merely the protected area but the whole pitch that the fielders must not damage beyond what is unavoidable for necessary fielding action. Section 13 sets out the details. An umpire – it can be either umpire who sees the action – will have to exercise considerable judgment in deciding whether a fierce turning on the heel is done in a genuine attempt to field a difficult ball or has been unnecessarily exaggerated in the hope of scarring the pitch.

There is a mistaken belief by some players that if they have to cross from one side to the other at the change of over, they will avoid damaging the pitch by jumping over it. Alas, this is not so. If a fielder is near one end, then he should walk round behind the stumps. If he is not near either end, it is probably better to walk gently across than to take the time walking all the way round, and certainly better than trying to jump. There he would do more damage by landing from a jump, since it will inevitably be short of the 10 feet needed to clear the pitch. Crossing in these circumstances could be described as 'reasonable cause'.

Remember that the bowler is also a fielder and will also come under the provisions of this section of Law. He could also be guilty, as a fielder, of damaging the pitch, certainly after his follow-through, but also during it, if either umpire considers he is deliberately exaggerating his foot movements. It would be wise in this case for the umpire to check that his colleague shared the same view.

3 By batsmen

As explained above, the striker cannot avoid standing and moving on the part of the pitch in the vicinity of his crease. He must, however, get off the pitch as quickly as possible if he is attempting a run. Sadly, there have been instances of tail-end batsmen deliberately ignoring the need to run off, and even making unnecessarily fierce movements in playing at the ball, to roughen the pitch in the hope of assisting their own bowlers in the next innings. The non-striker has no need to be on the pitch at all.

The question of wilfulness does not arise. The batsmen should not be on the pitch except as described above. If damage is wilful, then umpires should make their report after the match a more serious one than they would have done in the case of thoughtless action.

There is a tendency by the striker to run diagonally across the pitch in order to be in the normal position for a non-striker at the end of the run. He is guilty under Law 42.14 of causing unnecessary damage to the pitch. Moreover, if the umpire forms the opinion that it was done *deliberately*, possibly to impede fielding by the bowler or, worse, to come between the ball and either a fielder or the wicket itself, this would additionally be a case of obstructing the field. See Law 37.

Although originally batsmen damaging the pitch merited two warnings, the procedure now laid down in Section 14 allows one warning only. The warning lasts throughout the innings and will apply to any batsman. Although the batting captain is to be told at the first offence, since it is a batsman who has transgressed, there may not be a suitable opportunity to tell him for some time. Even if he has been informed, there is no guarantee that he has told his batsmen, though he probably will have done. The umpire is therefore to tell each incoming batsman, even after the batting captain has been informed.

UNFAIR RUNNING BY BATSMEN

1 Non-striker leaving his ground

Although it is quite a different situation and there is no procedure towards any penalty, we can consider the non-striker who leaves his ground too soon under the heading of 'unfair running by the batsmen'. There is no definition in Law of 'too soon'. It must also be emphasised that in leaving his ground 'too soon' he has committed no specific offence, although if the batsmen run he has gained some advantage. There is no statement anywhere in the Laws that requires any batsman, that is

> the striker
> or a striker with a runner
> or the non-striker
> or a runner

to be within his ground at any particular time. The Law compensates the fielding side for any advantage that the batsman may get from not being within his ground, by making him liable to being run out. The bowler is entitled, right up to the moment he enters his delivery stride, to attempt to run out the non-striker. Consequently, unless the non-striker remains within his ground until that moment, he risks being dismissed Run out. The umpire will have little warning that a Run out is to be attempted and will certainly not be able to move round to square with the wicket and crease. He must do what he can to get an accurate view of the episode.

It may be felt that it is giving the non-striker an advantage to make the landing of the back foot in the delivery stride the cut-off point. It is, however, the only practical one. The umpire must watch the landing of both the bowler's feet from thereon and then pick up the flight of the ball. The difference in time between that first landing and the release of the ball is extremely small. Moreover, the umpire cannot actually see the point of release, since he is watching first the feet and then the flight of the ball at that time.

There are those who feel that a bowler should not actually make the attempt on the first transgression, but should give a warning by stopping and indicating that he could have run the non-striker out. This is a traditional courtesy, but is not obligatory.

If he does attempt a Run out, which he may do either with the ball in his hand, or by throwing the ball at the stumps, and the attempt succeeds, then of course the non-striker is out. Should it fail, the prescribed call and signal of Dead ball will ensure that no runs can accrue to the batting side, nor can there be further action by the fielding side. It will be helpful to the scorers to tell them, as soon as practicable, what has happened.

2 Batsmen stealing a run

Although the ball is in play as soon as the bowler starts his run up, the batsmen are not permitted to attempt runs until the ball is delivered. It should not be confused with the previous situation. It is not a case of one batsman leaving his ground too soon. To be trying to steal a run, both batsmen must be trying to cross and make good their ground from end to end. Section 16 sets out the procedure. It should be noted that the requirement that the umpire must wait until the batsmen have crossed ensures that:

both batsmen are involved, confirming that a run is being attempted;

the bowler has not taken up the option of trying to run out either batsman. If he had done so, action under Section 16 would not be required.

Contraventions of this Law are virtually unknown.

UNACCEPTABLE BEHAVIOUR IN WAYS NOT LISTED IN THE LAWS

Section 2 empowers either umpire to call Dead ball, and thus halt play, if he sees any act which he considers unfair, even though it is not one of the misdemeanours specifically stated in the Laws. The procedure thereafter is that in Section 18. This sets out a very specific list of what constitutes unacceptable behaviour:

* anything meriting a Dead ball call under Section 2
* failing to comply with the instructions of an umpire – for example, refusing to leave the wicket when given out
* criticising the umpire's decision by word or action – for example, making aggressive remarks when an appeal is turned down
* showing dissent – for example, making an overtly petulant gesture such as knocking down the stumps with the bat after being given out, or even standing and glaring at the umpire before leaving the wicket
* generally behaving in a manner which might bring the game into disrepute.

The second, third and fourth are specific breaches of the Spirit of Cricket as laid down in the Preamble. The last is to ensure that any outrageous action is not condoned simply because it has not been listed and is not something to merit intervention under Section 2.

Many of these situations involve a *contretemps* between a player and an umpire. For example, a player may be criticising the umpire in no uncertain terms, using obscene language. For that umpire to impose a direct penalty on the player will only exacerbate the situation. The Law recognises that it is unsuitable for an umpire thus to be awarding a penalty 'on his own behalf' so to speak. This is why the procedure is different from all the others. This does not mean that it is to be treated more leniently. On the contrary, it is to be viewed with the utmost gravity and the seriousness of the umpires' report should reflect this.

INTRODUCTION

Scorers are the unseen participants in every game but Law 4 requires their presence. Moreover, their role is just as important as that of the players and the umpires. Without them, how could we ascertain the result as required under Law 21? Without the information recorded by the scorers, how could we identify the batsman who scored the most runs, or the bowler who took the most wickets? A competent scorer is an important member of a cricket club – who else watches and records every ball in every match played by a team and, hence, writes both the history of the club and a record of the players' achievements as they occur? A well-kept scoring record provides a wealth of information, for players, club officials, league secretaries, the media, selection committees and coaches. They all want, or need, to know the statistics of the match.

It is the information recorded by the scorers that permits coaches and selectors to review the strengths and weaknesses of the players. In earlier times, scorers notched their sticks while sitting within the boundary of the playing area. Each tenth run was cut deeper to match the fingers of their hands and an even deeper notch was cut when twice that was scored. This is thought by many to be the origins of the noun 'score'. As the game progressed, the sticks were laid side by side to assess progress and to see if a result was imminent.

Since then, various other methods have been used – the box system, described by Charles Box in 1877, the lineal system developed by Bill Ferguson in 1905 and later refined by Bill Frindall and others, and now computerisation. To cover the fact that the scorer may not record events on paper, the general term 'scoring record' is now used. This edition does not attempt to explain computerised scoring and will use the box type scoring record in all examples.

Law 4.1 is clear. Two scorers shall be appointed to record the details of the match. Ideally, each team has a scorer who knows and can easily recognise the players in the team from his position beyond the boundary. Identification can be difficult, particularly if players are wearing similar caps, hats or helmets. To assist in the identification of players, scorers should meet with the teams prior to the toss and make notes. These could include both batting and fielding, for example left- or right-handed, fast or slow bowler, clothing, etc. The two scorers must develop a rapport, each respecting the other's abilities and offering help when required. For the duration of the game, their concentration must always be absolute.

Scorers are encouraged to communicate constantly with each other about what is happening on the field of play, thus ensuring nothing is missed and that their records agree.

If only one scorer is available, special care must be taken to record events accurately. No scorer can be expected to complete his duties efficiently and accurately without support. If he finds himself in such circumstances, he may need to let the umpires know he needs a little time to discover the names of players, or balance his scoring record. A mutually acceptable signal can be agreed with the umpires before the match to allow this to happen with a minimum of disruption to the flow of the game. Umpires should be aware of the situation and, as part of the team of officials, should assist whenever possible. In the absence of names, descriptions of players can be entered in pencil and updated later.

The prime responsibility of the scorers is to Law 4. To achieve this, the scorers' principal duties are to make entries in the scoring record that accurately reflect the activity on the field of play and to ensure that the scoreboard operator knows and displays the same score on the scoreboard as is in the scoring record.

DUTIES

Law 4 sets out five principal duties of scorers: Record, Check, Agree, Accept and Acknowledge. These are usually considered as four, as follows:

Record

The most obvious duty of scorers is to record the events of the match in the scoring record.

The Laws state that the scorers shall record all runs scored, all wickets taken, and, where appropriate, the number of overs bowled. In practice most scorers consider this the minimum amount of information and record much more. A standard system of symbols has evolved over time for this purpose and some scorers have added their own additional symbols.

Check

Regular and frequent checking is essential to ensure that the scoring record balances and that it agrees with the record of the other scorer.

At the end of each over the scorer must agree the events of that over with his colleague. This can be done simply by using words like 'Ten off the over, Smith [the bowler] two for twenty-three, score seventy-five for six off twenty-eight overs.' This will reduce the risk of error in the cumulative score.

Checks should also be carried out:
- at the fall of a wicket
- during intervals
- during interruptions
- at the end of an innings
- at the close of each day's play
- at the end of a match
- at any other convenient time.

The checks should ensure that the runs recorded in both the batting and bowling sections agree with the runs crossed off on the cumulative run tally and that the balls bowled and received balance.

There are two checks to balance the runs scored:
- Runs scored by batsmen + Bowling extras (Wide balls and No balls) = Runs scored off all bowlers
- Runs scored off all bowlers + Fielding extras (Byes, Leg byes and penalty extras) = Total runs (Cumulative run tally)

There is one check to balance the balls bowled:
- Balls received by all batsmen + Balls not received by batsmen = Number of Balls Bowled

Balls not received are:
- Wide balls
- those stopping before reaching the striker and called No ball.

Errors such as crediting runs to the wrong batsman or crediting the batsman with runs which should be extras are important but less so than the constant verification of the cumulative team total. It is the team total from which the result will be determined and not the individual performances.

The Law directs that, at least at every interval other than for drinks, and at the conclusion of the match, the scorers and umpires shall agree the runs scored, wickets taken, and where appropriate the number of overs bowled.

Accept

The scorers must accept the signals that the umpire makes even if they have good reason for believing that a mistake has been made. Discussion should take place at the earliest opportunity about any such events.

If the scorer is uncertain about any incident, perhaps over a method of dismissal, such as Caught or LBW, then he should make a note and ask at the first available opportunity. This would usually be at the next interval or interruption, or at the conclusion of the match. If the uncertainty needs an immediate response, for example the side batting needs ten runs to win and you are unsure how many overthrows the umpire allowed on the last ball, find out immediately.

Acknowledge

Always acknowledge clearly and promptly – the umpire should not allow play to continue until he is certain that the scorer has seen and understood each and every signal.

Signals to the scorer will be made when the ball is dead. Some signals, for example No Ball, are first made when the ball is in play. This is for the benefit of the players and will be repeated when the ball is dead. The first signal should not be acknowledged, as the umpire will still be watching the action on the field. There may be more than one signal for a ball depending on the sequence of events. The Laws require that each signal should be given and acknowledged separately. For example, when signalling

Boundary four Byes, umpires will signal Byes, receive the acknowledgement, then signal Boundary 4 and wait for that to be acknowledged.

EQUIPMENT

There are a number of items of equipment that scorers must have to enable them to record the score. The list given below is the basic equipment required, however scorers might wish to add to this:

- **Scoring record**: this may take the form of a scorebook, scoresheet or computer. Even when using computers scorers may prefer to keep a written record in addition to that stored on the computer.
- **Pens/pencils/pencil sharpener**: pens should be smudge proof and water resistant with fine tips, the best being 0.3–0.5 mm. If scoring in colour, make sure the colours selected can be photocopied without loss of quality.
- **Eraser and correcting material**
- **Watch or clock**: synchronised with the official timepiece. It is important to remember that it is the elapsed times that are important to statisticians.
- **MCC Laws of Cricket**: a copy of the Laws is a useful reference should an unusual event occur.
- **Experimental Laws**: (if any) from time to time the MCC introduce experimental Laws and scorers must be aware of any that may impact on the entries in the scoring record.
- **Competition Regulations**: every competition, be it league or cup, will have its own set of regulations, many of which detail the method of determining the result or points awarded. These take precedence over the Laws of Cricket and the scorer should always be aware of them.
- **Tom Smith's Cricket Umpiring and Scoring**
- **White/reflective signaller**: ensure that this is clearly visible to the umpires against the background of the scorebox. Some scoreboxes may be equipped with a light for signalling, in which case make sure it works before play begins and after each interval.
- **Notepaper**: useful for recording information that aids scoring, such as descriptions of players, or for recording incidents that need clarification from the umpires.
- **Ruler**
- **Calculator**
- **Binoculars**: useful when trying to identify players.

BEFORE THE MATCH

Most scorers are affiliated to a team or club and as such will be familiar with the league grounds and regulations and of the individual team members. If appointed to an unfamiliar competition or to a match at an unfamiliar ground then this changes.

Appointed scorers should:

- find out where the ground is and how they will get there
- obtain a copy of the competition regulations
- check all points relating to scoring
- check how the result is to be determined – for example, if a match ends with the scores tied will the result be determined by fewest wickets lost, by comparing the scores after a certain number of overs or by some other method as defined in the playing regulations for the competition?

On the match day the scorer has a number of duties to perform, some laid down in Law, others evolving from good practice and experience.

It is the duty of the scorer to be available and ready at the official start time. There are several pre-match duties and the scorer should arrive in time to complete these. The umpires are directed by Law to arrive at least 45 minutes before the start of play, however there is no such stipulation for scorers. As some of the pre-match duties involve agreements with the umpires it makes sense for the scorers to arrive at the same time as the umpires.

A home scorer should aim to arrive earlier and ensure the scoring position is clean and tidy, with tables and chairs. Personal comfort must always be given proper consideration when scoring. If the location, weather or seating causes discomfort there may be lapses in concentration. If scoring indoors, ensure adequate ventilation and shade from the sun; if scoring outdoors, ensure adequate protection from the weather. Welcome the visiting colleague and acquaint them with the amenities.

Scorers arriving late will often find themselves rushing to fulfil their duties, causing them to overlook some important matters.

Both scorers together should meet the umpires before the toss to discuss and confirm:

- the master timepiece to be used during a match by the umpires. Umpires' and scorers' watches would be synchronised with this timepiece
- the back-up timepiece should the master fail
- the boundary markings and the runs scored should the ball reach the boundary
- whether or not any obstacle, permanent or temporary, within the field of play is to be regarded as a boundary
- where the scorers will be stationed
- method of acknowledgement for all umpires' signals
- the hours of play, the timing and duration of any intervals and if and when any drinks breaks should be taken
- how the scorers will be informed of changes, for example, if lunch is taken early if there is an interruption
- the provision for new balls, if applicable, and where on the scoreboard to record the overs bowled with the new ball

- any special regulations that may apply, particularly if the match has any restrictions of time, the innings is restricted to a maximum number of overs or bowlers are restricted in the number of overs they may bowl
- any local customs which will be applied
- how and who will operate the scoreboard
- how and when the score will be updated on the scoreboard
- how and when the overs bowled will be updated on the scoreboard
- how and when the overs bowled during the last hour are to be displayed (the recommendation is always that the number of completed overs is displayed starting at 0 and working up to the prescribed number).

In local competitions, this meeting may be a formality as everyone involved is usually familiar with the published playing conditions. However, if appointed to score in unfamiliar competitions the pre-match meeting is particularly important.

The scorers must also know:
- the team winning the toss and which team is to bat first.
- the names of the nominated players. Both captains should, ideally, supply two copies of the team sheet, one for the umpires and one for the scorers. If only one copy is supplied the umpires should make it available to allow the scorers to copy the names.
- the names of the umpires.
- it is also useful to consider the likely batting and bowling orders with descriptions of the bowlers and their actions particularly if the players are not known to either scorer. If there is any doubt the information should be entered in pencil and changed later.

Umpires normally take the field five minutes before the start of play and scorers should be in position and ready to start by then.

It should be noted that there is no requirement in the Laws for scorers to maintain the scoreboard. The updating of the scoreboard should never be permitted to distract scorers from their principal duty, to record the progress of the match. If this happens, scorers should ask others to perform the task.

Scoring alone

The absence of a second scorer places additional and unfair burdens on a sole scorer. Occasionally a team may arrive at a match without a scorer, possibly without a scoring record of any kind, totally ignoring the requirement stated in Law 4 that two scorers must be appointed for each match.

As the umpires are responsible for all Law-related matters, the sole scorer should bring this to their attention during the pre-match conference. The umpires should then make any necessary arrangements to assist the scorer, for example by directing the batting captain to have a player stationed alongside the official scorer at all times.

If possible the sole official scorer should supply a spare scoring record to the player/scorer to enable a record to be kept for that team. A solo scorer should not attempt to keep two scoring records simultaneously.

Scoring symbols

When completing the record, numerals are used for runs credited to the batsmen while dots are used to denote runs not credited to the batsman. A system of symbols has evolved and the table below shows them.

Action	Fair Ball	No Ball	Wide Ball
No runs scored	●	N/A	N/A
Striker scores runs	**1 2 3** etc.	N/A	N/A
Umpire signals No ball or Wide ball and no other runs are scored	N/A	○	+
Umpire signals No ball and striker scores runs	N/A	①②③ etc.	N/A
Batsmen run without striker hitting ball and umpire signals No ball and Bye or Wide ball	N/A	⊙ (··) (∴) etc.	·+ ·+· ∴+ etc.
Umpire signals Leg byes	▽· ▽·· ▽∴ etc.	N/A	N/A
Umpire signals Byes	△· △·· △∴ etc.	N/A	N/A
Wicket falls for which bowler gets credit (no runs can be scored other than penalties)	W	N/A	W+
Wicket falls for which bowler does not get credit (runs may be scored by the batsman or as No balls or Wide balls)	● 1 etc.	①②③ ⊙ (··) (∴) etc. ○	·+ ·+· ∴+ etc. +

An underline '_' can be used in conjunction with any of the symbols or numerals if the batsmen finish up at the 'wrong' end. For example:

- The batsmen run 3 but Short run is called
  the batsmen have changed ends
  only 2 runs are scored and this suggests that they are back at their original ends
  the entry would be 2 indicating that they have changed ends
- If the striker is out Caught when running and they have crossed to change ends
  the entry will be w.

COMPLETING A BOX SCORING RECORD

Any person experienced in cricket scoring should be able to pick up a scoring record and, while reading through the entries, state what happened on every delivery. To assist this, an accepted convention of entries and symbols has evolved over time, though scorers may use alternatives. Included herein are the recognised and recommended international methods. By adopting these conventions another scorer can take over during an innings and, except for different handwriting, the change should be unnoticed. Consistent entries by scorers, using the same methodology, ensures the regular checking of the scoring record, required during the match, is made easier.

Many scorers use colours in the scoring record, which if used correctly and neatly can make it easier to read and to follow. The recommended method is to use one colour for each bowler and to make all entries during the overs of that bowler in that colour. It is not recommended to use different colours for different events, for example 6 in red and 4 in green, as this can slow down the scoring process as the scorer searches for a pen.

Some entries can be made before play commences; most are made during play; some are made after play finishes. This section sets out to describe the standard entries in as near chronological order as possible.

BEFORE PLAY IS CALLED

Before the start of an innings the header can be completed. If scoring in colour, it is recommended that these entries are in black. Scoring records have space for different combinations of entry, however the basic information should always be present:

- Home team
- Date(s)
- Scorers' names
- Side winning the toss
- Away team
- Batting side
- Type of match
- Weather
- Venue
- Umpires' names
- Start time
- Pitch condition.

Before the final innings of the match the scorer should, in the cumulative run tally, identify the target score. This should be done in pencil to allow a change to be made if penalties are awarded to the fielding side.

If the batting side has already fielded, they may have been awarded penalty extras while fielding and these runs must be entered as their starting score. The example below shows three awards, totalling 15 runs, being entered in the appropriate sections of the scoring record.

Cumulative Run Tally										End of Over				Pen	
	1	2	3	4	5	6	7	8	9	Ov	Runs	W	B	B	F
48	1	2	3	4	5	6	7	8	9	0	15				
20	1	2	3	4	5	6	7	8	9	1					
30	1	2	3	4	5	6	7	8	9	2					

Batting Sheet

Fielding	Byes		
Extras	Leg Byes		
	Penalties prev inn	15	this inn

The first row of the **end of over** section has an over number of zero. This is used to record any penalty runs awarded to the side currently batting while fielding in the previous innings. In this example the side batting has been awarded 15 penalty runs and so start their innings with 15 runs. The runs must also be crossed off on the **cumulative run tally** as three separate entries of 5 runs rather than one of 15. To make the identification of penalty extras easier some scorers use a double rather than a single line in the tally when crossing them off. Either is acceptable providing consistency is maintained. The runs should also be recorded in the batting sheet under **penalty extras – previous innings**.

As the first batsman takes guard his name is entered in black, as batsman 1, together with the name of the non-striker as batsman 2. The time of the start of their innings is the time when the umpire first calls Play.

As the opening bowler takes possession of the bowler's marker and paces out his run up, his name is entered as bowler 1.

DURING PLAY

Whenever the bowler delivers the ball an entry should be made in both the batting and bowling sections and in the cumulative run tally when runs are scored. The scorer should always complete the entries in the same order to minimise the risk of errors. The recommended order is:

- Bowling
- Batting – this includes any extras
- Cumulative run tally.

This order is not compulsory – it is for each scorer to adopt his own order, as may be dictated by the layout of the scoring record.

At any time during, or after a match, the margins or note area should be used to record details of incidents that cannot be recorded elsewhere:

• the time a fielder leaves the field	D Smith left field 2.35
• the time he returns	D Smith returned 3.10
• the names of any substitutes and runners	F Jones substitute for D Smith 2.35 to 3.10
• the times and balls of milestones, e.g. a batsman or the score reaching 100 runs	100 runs; 135 mins, 245 balls
• incidents where the entries may not be as expected, for example a fairly delivered ball which, because of fielding transgressions, does not count as one of the over	5th Over, 3rd Ball – fielded by D Smith who returned without permission. Ball does not count as one of over.

Cumulative run tally

During play a running total of the score is kept by filling in this section. It consists of a grid of numbers crossed off as runs are scored. When doing so, cross off single runs **diagonally**, two or more runs with a **continuous stroke**. Never cross off the runs individually.

Where a single score continues from one line to the next extend the stroke into the margins at the end of the first line and before the start of the next line to indicate the continuation.

Note that this recommended method permits the entries to be converted back – in this example – to the scoring sequence 1, 1, 3, 6.

Identifying runs scored as extras in the tally can aid the reading of the scoring record. The same basic symbols as used in the other sections can be used. For example, continuing the sequence above, 3 No balls were scored next. The circle is used to denote this. Similarly the Wide, Bye and Leg bye symbols or abbreviations could also be used.

Batting section

The batting section of the scoring record is used to record all runs scored, whether they are credited to a batsman or recorded as extras. It also shows the details of a batsman's dismissal.

For each batsman the section contains:

- **Number**: the pre-printed numbers 1 to 11 for the batting order.
- **Name**: the batsman's name should be entered as he commences his innings, i.e. the opening batsmen as numbers 1 and 2 and the others as their innings start.
- **Time in/out**: the time each batsman starts and concludes his innings.
- **Minutes**: the length of the innings of the batsman. This excludes all intervals and interruptions.
- **Details of balls faced**: in this line a symbol is added for every ball faced and these should correspond to the symbols used in the bowling analysis. Note that the Wide symbol is used to show the batsman on strike when the ball was bowled.
- **Balls**: the number of balls received by each batsman. A Wide is not counted as a ball received (faced) as the batsman is unable to hit it. A No ball is a ball received. However, if a ball delivered by the bowler comes to rest in front of the stumps without the striker having made contact, the umpire will call and signal No ball, followed immediately by Dead ball (Law 24.7). Although recorded as a No ball, this will not count as a ball received by the striker.
- **How out**: the method by which the batsman was dismissed, if applicable.
- **Bowler**: the name of the bowler gaining credit for the dismissal, if applicable.
- **Fielder's** name credited with the dismissal where applicable.
- **Score**: the number of runs scored by that batsman.

As an innings proceeds, a batsman may face a large number of deliveries. A batsman batting for 50 overs and facing the bowling for one third of that time would face 100 deliveries. This will result in a large number of symbols and numerals to be added and balanced at the conclusion of his innings. Scorers have developed a number of ways of keeping count of balls faced. One method of keeping track of the running totals of a batsman's score and balls faced is that after every ten balls faced:

- an oblique slash is made in a batsman's line. At the end of the innings or when balancing, the number of strokes are counted, multiplied by ten and any additional deliveries added
- alongside this slash the batsman's progressive score is entered. This allows the balancing of runs to be easily completed.

Another method is to do this at the end of each over and record the number of runs as well as the number of balls faced.

The example below shows 21 balls faced. The Wide is recorded to show that the batsman was the striker when it was bowled but it is not a ball received.

1	R	$\ldots 1\,2\,4\,.\,1\,1\,2/^{11}\ldots.+6\,1\,..\,1\,4/^{23}\,3$
	FENTON	

1	R	$\ldots 1/^{1}_{4}\,2\,4\,.\,1\,1/^{9}_{9}\,2\,\ldots.+6/^{17}_{15}\,1\,..\,1\,4\,3/^{26}_{21}$
	FENTON	

The scorer will find it helps him to quickly balance the score if he notes in the scoring record margin the cumulative runs and cumulative deliveries faced by all the dismissed and/or retired batsmen. When a wicket falls simply update that cumulative total, agree with colleague and then put a line through or erase the old entry. Using this method he has only to add on the details for the two not out batsmen to give him total batsmen's runs and total deliveries faced.

The extras section contains space to record:

- **Bowling extras**: runs scored as No balls or Wides are debited against the bowler
- **Fielding extras**: runs scored as Byes, Leg byes or penalty runs awarded – these are not debited against the bowler.

It is never correct to credit the same runs to both the striker and extras; they are either one or the other.

Bowling Extras	No Balls				
	Wides				
Fielding Extras	Byes				
	Leg Byes				
	Penalties	prev inn		this inn	

Bowling section

During play two parts of the bowling section are used; the **analysis**, where each ball is recorded, and the **vertical columns**, where each occurrence of a No ball or a Wide is recorded.

ANALYSIS

One box is used for each over bowled by a bowler. The order in which the balls are entered may vary according to the scoring record layout or the preference of the scorer but must never be changed during a match. If the order is changed the history of the innings is lost.

A standard six-ball over can be recorded in the order 1 to 6 shown in A and B. Space must be left to permit the recording of extra deliveries, as shown in C and D. Throughout this book the order shown in A and C are used.

A		B		
1	4	1	2	3
2	5			
3	6	4	5	6

C			D		
1	7	4	1	2	3
2	8	5	7	8	9
3	9	6	4	5	6

If less than, or more than, six balls are delivered in an over for whatever reason:

- each delivery must be recorded
- the over as counted and called is a completed over
- if there are more or less than six balls it can still be a maiden over
- never add an extra dot to make up a full over or leave out a delivery. It is the responsibility of the scorer to record accurately the progress of the match.

A **maiden** over is one where no runs are conceded by the bowler, i.e. the striker has not scored any runs and there have been no bowling extras (No balls or Wides). It may include fielding extras (Byes, Leg byes or penalty runs).

Whenever a maiden over occurs, the dots are joined together to form the letter M. If a wicket is taken during a maiden over it becomes a wicket maiden and the letter W is formed. Any symbols entered (wicket, Byes and Leg byes) should not be crossed over by the M or W used, but the line should be broken as shown. Thus it becomes possible to see on which delivery any event occurred.

VERTICAL COLUMNS

These columns are used to record the number of Wides and No balls bowled by each bowler and the only valid entry is 1. Do not use this section to record the runs scored; the extras section in the batting sheet serves that purpose.

The totals obtained from this example show that the bowler has bowled 3 Wides and 2 No balls. This information is used when calculating the number of balls bowled and received.

Number of	
Wides	No Balls
111	11
3	2

If scoring in colour the runs debited to relevant extras can readily be identified in all sections.

Completion of an over

At the end of each over there are a number of entries to be made and checks to be carried out.

ANALYSIS

Beneath each scoring box, there is a smaller box. This is used to keep a running total of:

- the number of runs conceded by the bowler
- the number of wickets for which the bowler gets credit.

1		2	
2	1	1	w
1	.	2	.
.	.	1	4
4 - 0		12 - 1	

Here 4 runs were scored in the first over and 8 in the second giving a running total of 12 runs. The bowler gained credit for a wicket in the second over. These figures may be reversed to show wickets then runs, for example 0–4 and 1–12, but the scorer should use the same method throughout.

It is often useful to show the match over number in the 'smaller' box as an aid to balancing, tracking back, completing a fuller description of events.

This section contains columns and rows numbered from zero. The pre-printed number denotes the over and the other columns are completed either at the start of, during or end of an over:

- **Runs**: enter the total score recorded at the end of that over – this is a cumulative entry.
- **Wickets**: if a wicket falls during the over enter the total number of wickets lost at the end of that over – this is a cumulative entry.
- **Bowler**: enter his number taken from the bowling analysis, at the start of that over. Should there be a bowling change mid-over, add a margin note.
- **Penalty runs awarded to the batting side**: always enter 1 for each infringement as it occurs, never 5 which is misleading.
- **Penalty runs awarded to the fielding side**: enter a 1 for each infringement as it occurs, never 5 which is misleading.
- **Time**: there may also be space to record the time the over started.

Penalty runs awarded after the call of Over or Time should always be entered in the next over even if there is no play in that over unless it is the last over of an innings.

Information can be extracted from this section, showing for example:

- at the end of the 4th over the score was 27
- bowler 3 had just taken the 2nd wicket to fall
- 5 runs were scored in the 1st over
- bowler 2 has been replaced with bowler 3 for the 4th over
- during the 4th over 5 penalty runs were awarded to the batting side
- during the 2nd over 5 penalty runs were awarded to the fielding side.

End of Over				Pen	
Ov	Runs	W	B	B	F
0	15				
1	20		1		
2	20	1	2		1
3	22		1		
4	27	2	3	1	
5					

Note that, as with the vertical columns, penalty runs are always shown as 1 to denote that an award has been made. These are then multiplied by 5 when recorded in extras and on the tally and, in the case of fielding penalties, when carried forward or back to their next batting innings.

Change of bowler

During an innings a bowler may be changed for one of four reasons:

- the captain makes a bowling change
- a bowler becomes ill or injured and unable to continue
- the umpire orders the suspension of a bowler for transgression of a Law
- a bowler is called away from the game, perhaps by work or an urgent domestic matter.

Each bowling change, whether enforced or not, must be recorded, if necessary with appropriate margin notes.

END OF SPELL

Bowler 1, White, has ended a spell of bowling as shown by the black vertical line after his last over. Scorers using colours, one for each bowler, are recommended to use the colour to be used for the replacement bowler as this makes it easier to follow the progress of the innings.

Bowler		1	2	3	4	5
1	J WHITE		1 w	. . .	4	
			2 .	. +	. .	
			. .	1 .	. .	
			0 – 0	3 – 1	5 – 1	9 – 1

A vertical broken line with the number of the replacement bowler shown can also be used to show end of spells.

ILLNESS OR INJURY TO BOWLER

Bowler 2, Brown, has been injured after 3 balls of his over and bowler 3, Green, has been called upon to complete the over. Brown is shown as having completed his spell. Note the positioning of the 3 balls that Green bowls. Brown would be recorded as bowling 2.3 overs and Green 0.3 overs. Such a part over cannot be deemed to be a maiden over. If a bowler is called away, the entries would be shown in the same way.

Bowler		1	2	3	4	5
2	M BROWN	1 w	. 1	.		
		2 1	. 2	.		
		. 4	3 4	1		
		8 – 1	18 – 1	19 – 1		
3	P GREEN	w				
		.				
		.				
		0 – 1				

BOWLER REMOVED BY UMPIRE

Umpires have the authority to prevent a bowler bowling again in that innings. Here bowler 4, Black, has transgressed the Law on the 3rd ball of his 2nd over and has been removed. The end of spell is shown by the vertical line. A thick horizontal line through the remainder of the boxes shows that he cannot bowl again in that innings. Here, another bowler must complete the over – the entries for Grey's 1st over show how the entries would be recorded.

Bowler	1	2	3	4	5
4 S BLACK	1 . . 1 . . 2 - 0	M 2 - 0	1 6 4 13 - 0		
5 T GREY	1 1 4 6 - 0				

There is no provision for recording the suspension of a bowler in the scoring record. Should this occur, it is unlikely the scorers will become aware of the reasons until the next interval, when a note should be made in the margin.

Fall of wickets

When a batsman is dismissed several entries must be made:

- runs may be scored as a No ball penalty, a Wide ball penalty, runs credited to the striker, Byes, or Leg byes and should be recorded in the appropriate section of the scoring record.

Batsman	Time In/Out	Mins Balls	Innings of NORTHBROOK CC	4/6	How Out	Bowler	Score
1 T STOKES	2:00 2:24	24 20	+ . . 2 . . . . 2 /⁺3 1 . . 4 . . . . w //	1 -	BOWLED	T BROWN	12
2 W.BALL	2:00		1 . 2 . 4				

- if the bowler gets credit for the dismissal enter **w** as the symbol in the batting section and the bowler analysis.
- enter two slashes // after the last ball the batsman faced to show that he has been dismissed, some scorers use a double chevron >> to make it clearly different from a ball count / – if a batsman retires for any reason, enter a single slash, or single chevron > / with a symbol to indicate the retirement. At the time of the retirement it is not known whether the batsman's innings will be resumed.
- enter the time of the dismissal in the batting section.
- enter the method of dismissal in the How out column.
- if the bowler is credited for the dismissal enter his name in the bowler's column, otherwise leave the column blank.
- enter the number of runs he scored in the score column.
- enter (as time permits) the number of minutes of his innings in the top box of the Mins Balls column.
- enter (as time permits) the number of balls he faced in the bottom box of the Mins Balls column – Wides are not balls faced.

- complete the fall of wicket section to show the score and the number of the batsman dismissed. There may also be space to record the number of runs scored since the last wicket fell and the details of the partnership.

Wicket	1	2
Score	31	
Bat Out	2	
Partnership	31	

- enter the name of the incoming batsman and the time he crossed the boundary on to the field of play.

Where the bowler does not get the credit for the dismissal the method should be written in the How out column, not across both columns.

4/8	How Out	Bowler	Score	
	RUN	OUT		✘
	RUN OUT			✔

If the striker is dismissed Stumped, the name of the wicket-keeper is entered.

If a catch has been taken enter the name of the fielder taking the catch. If the catcher is a substitute fielder, enter Caught Sub. As he is not a member of the nominated side, his name is not officially recorded. However, his name may be recorded in brackets.

How Out
Stumped Jones
Caught Smith
Caught Sub

Where a nominated fielder effects a dismissal his name is recorded in the appropriate section. However, a convention is developing permitting the recording of additional information, such as the name of the fielder who effects a Run out. Scorers may wish to record this information within brackets, if time permits, as an aid to players and coaches.

How Out
Run Out (Smith)

Retirement of batsman

A batsman is permitted to retire at any time during his innings (see Law 2.9). Depending on the reason for his retirement, as given to the umpire, he may be permitted to resume his innings. As it is unlikely that the scorers will know whether or not he is likely to return, a note should be made at the time of the retirement in the batting section of the scoring record in **pencil** against his name. If he returns, pencil notes can be erased. If he does not return, the correct entry can be determined from the umpires and entered permanently. If he is recorded Retired – out (under Law 2.9(b), then it counts as one of the team's dismissals. This will be relevant for stating the margin of victory (if it is by wickets) and also for the batsman's own statistics.

How Out	Bowler	Score
Retired, 3-47		

Margin notes should also be used to explain the reason for the retirement as illness, injury or personal reason. Never record personal details although it may be useful to record the incident, such as 'blow to the head' or 'slipped and injured hamstring'.

An entry should be made in the **fall of wickets** section:

- 3 wickets had previously fallen
- the 4th wicket box is split and the retirement shown in the left side
- batsman 4 retires with the score on 49
- the right side will be used when the 4th wicket falls in any other fashion.
- Retirement entries are necessary to calculate stands.

				Fall of Wickets	
Wicket	1	2	3	4	5
Score	2	22	29	49	
Bat Out	2	3	1	4	
Partnership	2	20	7	20	

Last hour

The Laws define a last hour during which a **minimum** of 20 overs must be bowled. This is the last hour on the final day of a match.

- the bowler's end umpire signals the start of the last hour to the scorers using the official signal – acknowledge this signal
- show the overs bowled prior to the last hour by drawing a thick line after those overs already bowled. Label this line Last Hour

	Bowler	1	2	3
1	J WHITE	1 1 2 w 4 . 8 - 1	. . . 1 . . 9 - 1	
2	T BROWN	. 1 1 1 2 4 9 - 0		
3				

- include any unused lines in the analysis as it is possible that a new bowler may bowl during the last hour.

  The end of overs section should also be ruled off to show the start of the last hour:
- draw a line under the last over bowled
- note the time in the margin.

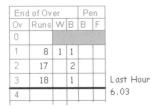

End of Over				Pen		
Ov	Runs	W	B	B	F	
0						
1	8	1	1			
2	17	2				
3	18	1				Last Hour
4						6.03

Ask the scoreboard attendants to maintain a count of the overs on the scoreboard as agreed with the umpires at the pre-match conference. The scoreboard should record the number of overs bowled starting at 1 up to 20 (or more, as time may permit more than the minimum 20 overs to be bowled).

Interruption in play

If there is an interruption in play for ground, weather or light this must be recorded in either the margin, or the notes or the section provided in some scoring records specifically for recording all interruptions:

- time the interruption started
- time the interruption ended
- total time lost
- any overs lost – the scoreboard should be adjusted as necessary
- reason/s for the interruption.

Notes
Rain 12.15 after 3rd ball of 21st over.
Play resumed 12.40
Play lost: 25 mins, 8 overs

Checking with umpires

The Laws of Cricket direct that at every interval (other than the drinks interval) and during every interruption in play, when the players leave the field, the scorers and umpires must agree:

- runs scored
- wickets fallen
- number of overs bowled (where appropriate).

It is during this checking that any other matter requiring clarification can be discussed and entered. The scorers must always have this information recorded on notepaper to hand for the umpires. They should never have to return to the scorebox to get it.

AFTER TIME CALLED

At the call of Time the umpires will remove the bails. This has no significance as it is the time of the call that identifies the end of the session of play and must be recorded. However this act is a visual signal to the scorers that play has ended. Should the umpire then remove the stumps this may be an indication that:

- play has ceased for the day, or
- the match has concluded, or
- the match is abandoned, or
- weather conditions require the suspension of play and the placing of covers.

At the end of an innings the players and umpires leave the field but there are still entries and calculations to be made in the scoring record, as listed below.

Batting sheet

- Any not out batsman (there can only ever be one or two) should have 'Not Out' entered in the method of dismissal.
- Any batsman who has retired should be recorded 'Retired, not out' or 'Retired out' as appropriate. The umpires will advise the correct entry.

How Out	Bowler
NOT OUT	
RETIRED, OUT	
RETIRED, NOT OUT	
⎫	
⎬ DID NOT BAT	
⎭	

- The names of the remaining batsmen should be entered and may be bracketed together with the single entry 'Did Not Bat', which may be abbreviated to 'DNB', against their names.
- Identify the captain by an asterisk *, and the wicket-keeper by a dagger †. Historically, the symbols were used the other way around, and still are at Lord's.
- Enter the runs scored by the batsmen [111].
- Enter the runs scored as No balls [5] and Wides [2] and total to give bowling extras [7]
- Enter the runs scored as Byes [4], Leg byes [1] and awarded as penalties [15] to give total fielding extras [20].
- Add together the batsmen totals [111], bowling extras [7] and fielding extras [20] to the give the provisional score for the innings [138].

				Batsmen Totals	111		
Bowling Extras	No Balls	3 1 1			5	7	
	Wides	1 1			2		
Fielding Extras	Byes	4			4	20	
	Leg Byes	1			1		
	Penalties	prev inn	15	this inn	15		
			PROVISIONAL SCORE FOR INNINGS		138	for 9 wickets	
			Penalties awarded in following innings		10		
			Final Score for Innings		148	for 9 wickets	

- This should agree with the cumulative run tally. If there is an error, complete the bowling section before attempting to locate the error.
- Add up the number of balls received by each batsman and enter the total.
- Enter the number of wickets that have fallen.
- If the batting captain declared show this against the wickets fallen (dec).
- If a captain forfeits an innings, that should be recorded at the top of the batting sheet used for the next innings. There is little point in using up a full sheet for the words 'Innings forfeited'.

Penalties awarded in following innings

This box is used to record penalty extras awarded while fielding **in the next innings**.

If the batting side are not fielding again in the match:

- leave this box blank
- transfer the total, and wickets to the final score row
- this should agree with the final score in the batting section.

If the batting side will field again:

- leave this box blank
- after they have fielded enter the total of any penalty runs into this box [10]
- complete the final score for innings [148]
- this should agree with the final score in the batting section.

Bowling summary

Complete the **summary** for each bowler:

	Bowler		ANALYSIS			Number of		Balls	Overs	Mdns	Runs	Wkts	Ave
			1	7	8	Wides	No Balls	Bowled					
1	J WHITE	+.2	2	2 .		1	1	44	7	1	25	1	25
		. .		1 .									
				2 .									
		3		25 - 1		1	1						
2	T BROWN	. .	4	4 w	W 2			46	7.4	0	44	5	8.8
		. 4		4 .	4								
					6								
		4		32 - 4	44 - 5								

- **Overs**: the number of overs bowled. For a part over, the number of balls are shown. T. Brown has bowled 7 overs 4 balls which is shown as 7.4 (this should not be a decimal: 7.5 is not 7 overs and 3 balls, it is 7 overs and 5 balls).
- **Maidens**: the number of maiden overs bowled taken from the analysis.
- **Runs**: the number of runs conceded by the bowler and taken from the running total.
- **Wickets**: the number of wickets for which the bowler gained credit, taken from the running total.
- **Average**: calculated by dividing the runs by the wickets – normally shown to two decimal places (round up, to be consistent with mathematics). If no wickets have been taken there can be no average and this is shown by a dash – not zero.

- **Balls bowled**: add the number of Wides and No balls delivered by each bowler. The number of balls bowled can then be calculated as:
- (complete overs) x 6 + (number of Wides) + (number of No balls)
- Make adjustments for short (5 balls or less) or long (7 balls or more) overs.
- Add up the balls bowled and enter the total [152]. Enter the number of Wide balls bowled [2] and deduct this to give the number of balls received [150]. This should agree with the total calculated in the batting section – Wide deliveries are not balls faced or received by the striker. If necessary, allowance will have to be made for a ball called and signalled No ball followed by Dead ball, but not received by the striker (Law 24.7).
- Add the overs bowled and enter the total [24.4].
- Add the maiden overs and enter the total [2].
- Add the runs scored from the bowlers [118] and add to the fielding extras [20] to give a total of 138. This total should agree with the tally and the batting section.
- Add the wickets credited to bowlers [9]. Enter number of wickets for which bowlers do not gain credit [0], add together to give the total wickets fallen.

| Number of | | Balls | Overs | Mdns | Runs | Wkts | Ave | |
Wides	No Balls	Bowled						
1	1							
		44	7	1	25	1	25.0	
1	1							
		46	7.4	0	44	5	8.8	
0	0							
2	3	152	24.4	2	118	9		BOWLING TOTALS
less Wides		2			20	0		Extras & other dismissals
Balls Received		150			138	9		PROVISIONAL SCORE
					10			Penalties in following innings
					148	9		FINAL SCORE

End of over

Enter the runs and wickets into the **end of over section** identifying any partial overs. This innings finished after 4 balls of the 25th over.

Result

The result of the match should be completed if the innings just concluded was the last. The scores, wickets, overs (where appropriate) and result should be agreed with the umpires. Invite the umpires to initial the final scoring record to confirm their acceptance of the result.

| End of Over | | | | Pen | |
Ov	Runs	W	B	B	F
0	15				
1	20		1		
2	20	1	2		1
3	22		1		
4	27	2	2	1	
24	134	9	4		
25	138		2		4 balls
26					

Attention is drawn to Law 21 and its accompanying commentary.

Recording penalty extras

Penalty extras introduce a method by which transgressions by players of either side on the field of play can be punished. The fielding side can be awarded runs, introducing the question, How would runs scored when fielding be added to that side's score?

When awarded to the batting side, penalty runs are:

- added into their current innings as fielding extras
- always recorded as penalty extras in both the row provided and in the End of Over section
- never credited to a batsman
- never debited against the bowler.

When awarded to the fielding side they must be added to the runs scored when that side bats. The rule is:

- If the side has already batted the runs are added on to the provisional score of their previous innings. The batting side now requires more runs to win than when they started their innings.
- If the side has not batted the runs are added on to the starting score of their next batting innings. They will commence their innings with runs on the board effectively decreasing the number of runs they need to score to win while batting.

There are three possible scenarios, a one-innings match, a two-innings match and a two-innings match where a side follows on.

1. ONE-INNINGS MATCH

1st innings	Side A bat	Side B field
	Penalty extras awarded to Side A are added to their batting total at the time of the award.	Penalty extras awarded to Side B are recorded at the time of the award and the total runs are used as the starting score of their batting innings.

2nd innings	Side A field	Side B bat
	Penalty extras awarded to Side A are recorded at the time of the award and, at the end of the innings, the total runs are added to the provisional score of their batting innings.	Penalty extras awarded to Side B are added to their batting total at time of the award.

2. TWO-INNINGS MATCH

1st innings	Side A bat	Side B field
	Penalty extras awarded to Side A are added to their batting total at the time of the award.	Penalty extras awarded to Side B are recorded at the time of the award and the total runs are used as the starting score of their first batting innings.
2nd innings	Side A field	Side B bat
	Penalty extras awarded to Side A are recorded at the time of the award and, at the end of the innings, the total runs are added to the provisional score of their first batting innings.	Penalty extras awarded to Side B are added to their batting total at time of the award.
3rd innings	Side A bat	Side B field
	Penalty extras awarded to Side A are added to their batting total at the time of the award.	Penalty extras awarded to Side B are recorded at the time of the award and, at the end of the innings, the total runs are added to the provisional score of their first batting innings.
4th innings	Side A field	Side B bat
	Penalty extras awarded to Side A are recorded at the time of the award and, at the end of the innings, the total runs are added to the provisional score of their second batting innings.	Penalty extras awarded to Side B are added to their batting total at the time of the award.

3. TWO-INNINGS MATCH WITH FOLLOW-ON

1st innings	Side A bat	Side B field
	Penalty extras awarded to Side A are added to their batting total at the time of the award.	Penalty extras awarded to Side B are recorded at the time of the award and the total runs are used as the starting score of their first batting innings.
2nd innings	Side A field	Side B bat
	Penalty extras awarded to Side A are recorded at the time of the award and, at the end of the innings, the total runs are added to the provisional score of their first batting innings.	Penalty extras awarded to Side B are added to their batting total at the time of the award.
3rd innings	Side A field	Side B bat
	Penalty extras awarded to Side A are recorded at the time of the award and, at the end of the innings, the total runs are added to the provisional score of their first batting innings.	Penalty extras awarded to Side B are added to their batting total at the time of the award.
4th innings	Side A bat	Side B field
	Penalty extras awarded to Side A are added to their batting total at the time of the award.	Penalty extras awarded to Side B are recorded at the time of the award and, at the end of the innings, the total runs are added to the provisional score of their second batting innings.

Awards of penalties are recorded as they happen in the Penalty section of the End of Over section.

End of Over				Pen	
Ov	Runs	W	B	B	F
0	15				
1	20		1		
2	20	1	2		1
3	22		1		
4	27	2	2	1	

The number of occurrences of the awarding of penalty runs rather than the actual number of penalty runs are recorded. In the example here an award has been made to the fielding side in the 2nd over. There are no other entries to be made at this time. An award has also been made to the batting side in the 4th over. These runs would also be recorded in the batting sheet and in the cumulative run tally.

The entries required to add runs awarded while fielding at the start of the batting innings, in this case three awards making 15 runs:

Cumulative Run Tally										End of Over				Pen	
	1	2	3	4	5	6	7	8	9	Ov	Runs	W	B	B	F
10	1	2	3	4	5	6	7	8	9	0	15				
20	1	2	3	4	5	6	7	8	9	1					
30	1	2	3	4	5	6	7	8	9	2					

Fielding Extras	Byes				
	Leg Byes				
	Penalties	prev inn	15	this inn	

The entry required when runs awarded when fielding are to be added to the provisional score of a previous innings. In this example 10 runs are added into both the bowling and batting sections:

118	9		BOWLING TOTALS
20	0		Extras & other dismissals
138	9		PROVISIONAL SCORE
10			Penalties in other innings
148	9		FINAL SCORE

PROVISIONAL SCORE FOR INNINGS	138	for 9 wickets
Penalties awarded in following innings	10	
FINAL SCORE FOR INNINGS	148	for 9 wickets

Ball Not to Count as One of the Over

There are certain situations where the ball is delivered by the bowler and received by the striker, yet it still does not count as one of the over. The scorer must be aware of these scenarios, as entries need to be made to explain the action. They must also be taken into consideration when counting balls bowled as it will appear that an over of more than six balls has been bowled.

Balls do not count as one of the over when:

- a fielder who has returned without permission comes into contact with the ball while it is in play;
- a fielder illegally fields the ball;
- either batsman is wilfully distracted after a delivery has been received by the striker;
- there is deliberate distraction of the striker while he is receiving the ball.

In all cases, the striker will have received the delivery and so there will be entries in both the batting and bowling sections. A margin note should be made to explain that the ball does not count as one of the over. Sometimes, the umpires may not make it immediately clear what has happened, so it may be worth confirming it with them at the next interval.

Conclusion of match

As the match is nearing its conclusion, players and others may be tempted to interrupt scorers to request information. Provided they cause no distraction, they should be permitted to look over the scorers' shoulders to glean the information they seek. If this is not possible, or if distractions occur, they should politely be discouraged as concentration must be maintained until the scoring record is balanced and the result is confirmed to the umpires.

Other duties scorers may be asked to complete may include:

- compiling match statistics
- completing match reports.

Scorers should ensure they leave their scoring position as they would hope to find it – clean and tidy.

MAIN CAUSES OF INACCURACIES

Inaccuracies, errors or mistakes can occur because of:

- lack of regular checks within the scoring record and with the other scorer
- poor signalling by umpires
- umpire failing to wait for scorers' acknowledgement and continuing play
- failure to consult with umpires on doubtful matters
- lack of knowledge of the Laws and of scoring techniques
- personal discomfort, location etc. causing distractions

- interruptions by players, officials, etc.
- updating the scoreboard while play is in progress
- only one scorer appointed
- problems with player recognition

The importance of regular checking cannot be overstated: it ensures that mistakes are quickly identified and corrected. If a mistake is not easily identified then one scorer should continue recording the events while the other searches for the error.

OVERLEAF:

The story of the innings of Northbrook CC in the match Wellsted CC versus Northbrook CC. A 25-over, one-innings match played at Wellsted Park on 31 July 2004. Wellsted batted first and their provisional score is 136 all out.

		WELLSTED			CC versus		NORTHBROOK

In a **25 OVER, ONE INNINGS** Match   Played at   **WELLSTED PARK**

Batsman	Time In/Out	Mins Balls	Innings of	NORTH-BROOK	CC
1 T. STONES	17.00 / 17.19	19 / 18	...... + ..11 /² .. 4 .... w //		
2 W. BELL	17.00 / 17.34	34 / 33	.... 4 ..... /⁴.1 ...☺... 2 /⁷2 ...... 44./¹⁷..w //		
3 G. HARRIS	17.20 / 17.27	7 / 5	..41w //		
4 C. WELLS ✷	17.28 / 17.53	25 / 25	..... 241 .. /⁷.2 ◯... 4 ... /¹³.12.w //		
5 S. PEARCE	17.35 / 18.15	40 / 17	13△ .... /⁴143211w //		
6 T. BARTON	17.54 / 18.04	10 / 14	..1..4. ③▽2/¹⁰..w //		
7 P. MOORE †	18.05 / 18.09	4 / 4	.... ⅃ʷ //		
8 B. JARVIS	18.10 / 18.35	25 / 22	.... 4 ..... /⁴4 .... 2. /¹⁰..		
9 R. FOWLER	18.16 / 18.26	10 / 7	.1144.w //		
10 H. BROWN	18.27 / 18.32	5 / 3	21w //		
11 D. SOUTH	18.33 / 18.35	2 / 3	462		
		151	Total balls received		Total boundaries scored

Fall of wicket; score & No of Batsman out

Wicket	1	2	3	4	5	6	7	8	9	10
Score	25	34	42	72	97	101	106	125	130	
Bat out	1	3	2	4	6	7	5	9	10	
Partnership B	15	9	8	30	25	4	5	19	5	

O Underlining to show that the batsmen cross before the catch
P Batsmen run 3 but only the 2 runs needed to win are scored

Bowler	BOWLING ANALYSIS									
	1	C 2	3 D	4	E 5	6	7	8	9	10
1 J. WILLIAMS	M → 0	+ . 1 / . . / 2	. .☺ / . . / 5	2 . / 2 . / 9	w 〉/ 9-1	2 1 / 4 . / 1 . / 17-1				
2 T. JACKSON	. . / 4 / . . / 4	1 1 / . . / . . / 6	4 . / . . / w / 10-1	. 1 / 4 . / 4 . / 15-1	4 . / 4 . / w / 23-2					
3 F. BARKER F	3 .◯ / 2 . / 6	4 . / . 1 / 11	. . / . ③ / 4 ⊞ / 19	4 . / 3 . / w . / 26-1			O	P		
4 M. GREEN G	△M → 0	2 . / . 1 / w 1 / 3-1	▽⊡ / 1 . / 2 . / 6-1	2 ⅃ʷ / 1 . / . . / 10-2	w . / . . / 1 . / 11-3	4 w / 4 . / . . / 19-4	w 2 / 4 . / 6 . / 31-5			
5 W. SMITH L	1 4 / . . / 5	1 . . / 4 . / 10	2 . / 1 . / 2 / 15	J K						

J Moore stumped off a Wide. Score 1 wide extra before the fall of the wicket
K Umpire calls over after only 5 balls that count in the over
L Leg byes not awarded – no runs scored
M Deliberate short running – runs disallowed. 5 Penalty runs to the fielding side. Amend the
    Wellstead score in the cumulative run tally. An explanation side note is needed

CC	RESULT:	NORTHBROOK CC WON BY 1 WICKET

on 31st July 2004

4/6	Scoring Rate 50 / 100	How Out	Bowler	Score
1	m / m / b / b	BOWLED	T JACKSON	6
3	m / m / b / b	Ct P. COX	T JACKSON	17
1	m / m / b / b	HIT WICKET	J WILLIAMS	5
2	m / m / b / b	St E DIXON	M GREEN	16
1	m / m / b / b	LBW	M GREEN	16
1	m / m / b / b	BOWLED	F BARKER	10
	m / m / b / b	St E DIXON	M GREEN	0
2	m / m / b / b	NOT OUT		10
2	m / m / b / b	Ct N BLACK	M GREEN	10
	m / m / b / b	BOWLED	M GREEN	3
1 / 1	m / m / b / b	NOT OUT		12
14 / 1	D H	BATSMEN TOTALS		105

End of Over / Pen

Ov	Runs	W	B	B	F
0	10				B
1	10	1			
2	14	2			
3	16	1			
4	18	2			
5	21	1			
6	25	1	2		
7	29	1			
8	34	2			
9	34	2	1		
10	42	3	2		
11	50	1			
12	61		3	1	F
13	65	4			
14	70	3			
15	73	4	4		
16	81	3			
17	90		4	1	I
18	97	5	3		
19	101	6	4		
20	106	5			
21	107	7	4	1	M
22	117		5	1	N
23	125	8	4		
24	130	5			
25	142	4			
26					
27					
28					

24.4 Overs

Bowling Extras	No balls	311	5		7
	Wides	11	2		
Fielding Extras	Byes	4	4		30
	Leg Byes	1 B	1		
	Penalties	prev inn 10	this inn 555	25	

PROVISIONAL SCORE FOR INNINGS	142	for 9 wickets
Penalties awarded in following innings	-	
FINAL SCORE FOR INNINGS	142	for 9 wickets

Number of Wides	No balls	Balls bowled	Overs	Mdns	Runs	Wkts	Ave
1	1	38	6	2	17	1	17
1	1	30	5	0	23	2	11.5
	11	26	4	0	26	1	26
	2						
1		40 I	6.4	1	31	5	6.2
1		19	3	0	15	0	-
2	3	153	24.4	3	112	9	BOWLING TOTALS
less Wides	2				30	-	Fielding extras & other dismissals
		151	24.4	3	142	9	PROVISIONAL SCORE
					-		Penalties in following innings
					142	9	FINAL SCORE

Notes

A Mark the Wellstead CC provisional score in the Cumulative Tally

B Penalties awarded in the first innings

C Williams bowls a Wide – batsmen did not run

D Williams bowls a No ball that was not hit & batsmen run 2. No ball penalty plus plus 2 runs scored against the bowler and as No ball extras. Not a maiden.

E Harris out Hit wicket – the bowler is credited with the wicket

F, I & N 5 penalty runs credited to the batting side – need a side note indicating when and why the penalty was awarded

G As the only score in the over is from Byes it is a maiden over

H Clarke scores 3 off a No ball – 3 runs to Clarke and 1 to No ball extras

29	30	31	32	33	34	35	36	37	38	39	40

Over	Bowler	Delivery		Incident
0		A		Highlight the provisional score of Wellsted CC
		B		Enter 10 penalty runs awarded in the first innings
1	J Williams			T Stones facing
		1st		Batsmen do not run. No signal
		2nd		Batsmen do not run. No signal
		3rd		Batsmen do not run. No signal
		4th		Batsmen do not run. No signal
		5th		Batsmen do not run. No signal
		6th		Batsmen do not run. No signal
2	T Jackson			W Bell facing
		1st		Batsmen do not run. No signal
		2nd		Batsmen do not run. No signal
		3rd		Batsmen do not run. No signal
		4th		Batsmen do not run. No signal
		5th		Umpire signals **Boundary 4**
		6th		Batsmen do not run. No signal
3	J Williams			T Stones facing
		1st	C	Batsmen do not run. Umpire signals **Wide ball**
		2nd		Batsmen do not run. No signal
		3rd		Batsmen do not run. No signal
		4th		Batsmen run 1. No signal
		5th		Batsmen do not run. No signal
		6th		Batsmen do not run. No signal
		7th		Batsmen do not run. No signal
4	T Jackson			T Stones facing
		1st		Batsmen run 1. No signal
		2nd		Batsmen do not run. No signal
		3rd		Batsmen do not run. No signal
		4th		Batsmen run 1. No signal
		5th		Batsmen do not run. No signal
		6th		Batsmen do not run. No signal
5	J Williams			W Bell facing
		1st		Batsmen do not run. No signal
		2nd		Batsmen do not run. No signal
		3rd		Batsmen do not run. No signal
		4th	D	Batsmen run 2. The umpire signals **No ball** and then gives the **Bye** signal

Over	Bowler	Delivery	Incident
		5th	Batsmen do not run. No signal
		6th	Batsmen do not run. No signal
		7th	Batsmen do not run. No signal
6	T Jackson		T Stones facing
		1st	Batsmen run 2, stop and return to their original ends. The umpire signals **Boundary 4**
		2nd	Batsmen do not run. No signal
		3rd	Batsmen do not run. No signal
		4th	Batsmen do not run. No signal
		5th	Batsmen do not run. No signal
		6th	T Stones out – **Bowled** The new batsman is G Harris
7	J Williams		W Bell facing
		1st	Batsmen run 2. No signal
		2nd	Batsmen run 2. No signal
		3rd	Batsmen do not run. No signal
		4th	Batsmen do not run. No signal
		5th	Batsmen do not run. No signal
		6th	Batsmen do not run. No signal
8	T Jackson		G Harris facing
		1st	Batsmen do not run. No signal
		2nd	Batsmen do not run. No signal
		3rd	The umpire signals **Boundary 4**
		4th	Batsmen run 1. No signal
		5th	Batsmen do not run. No signal
		6th	Batsmen do not run. No signal
9	J Williams		G Harris facing
		1st E	As he plays a shot the bails fall from his wicket. On appeal the striker's end umpire gives him **out – Hit wicket** The new batsman is C Wells (Capt.)
		2nd	Batsmen do not run. No signal
		3rd	Batsmen do not run. No signal
		4th	Batsmen do not run. No signal
		5th	Batsmen do not run. No signal
		6th	Batsmen do not run. No signal

Over	Bowler	Delivery	Incident
10	T Jackson		W Bell facing
		1st	The umpire signals **Boundary 4**
		2nd	The umpire signals **Boundary 4**
		3rd	Batsmen do not run. No signal
		4th	Batsmen do not run. No signal
		5th	Batsmen do not run. No signal
		6th	The batsman hits the ball which is caught P Cox
			The bowler's end umpire gives Bell **out**
			The new batsman is S Pearce
11	J Williams		C Wells facing
		1st	Batsmen run 2. No signal
		2nd	The umpire signals **Boundary 4**
		3rd	Batsmen run 1. No signal
		4th	Batsmen run 1. No signal
		5th	Batsmen do not run. No signal
		6th	Batsmen do not run. No signal
12	F Barker		S Pearce facing
		1st	Batsmen run 3. No signal
		2nd	The ball runs through the legs of the wicket-keeper and strikes a helmet on the ground behind him. No runs attempted.
		F	The umpire signals **five penalty runs to the batting side**
		3rd	Batsmen run 2. No signal
		4th	Batsmen do not run. The umpire signals **No ball**
		5th	Batsmen do not run. No signal
		6th	Batsmen do not run. No signal
		7th	Batsmen do not run. No signal
13	M Green		S Pearce facing
		1st G	The umpire signals Bye and then signals **Boundary 4**
		2nd	Batsmen do not run. No signal
		3rd	Batsmen do not run. No signal
		4th	Batsmen do not run. No signal
		5th	Batsmen do not run. No signal
		6th	Batsmen do not run. No signal
14	F Barker		C Wells facing
		1st	The umpire signals **Boundary 4**
		2nd	Batsmen do not run. No signal

Over	Bowler	Delivery		Incident
		3rd		Batsmen do not run. No signal
		4th		Batsmen do not run. No signal
		5th		Batsmen do not run. No signal
		6th		Batsmen run 1. No signal
15	M Green			C Wells facing
		1st		Batsmen run 2. No signal
		2nd		Batsmen do not run. No signal
		3rd		The ball goes through to the wicket-keeper, E Dixon, who breaks the wicket. The striker's end umpire gives the batsman **out – Stumped** The new batsman is T Barton
		4th		Batsmen do not run. No signal
		5th		Batsmen do not run. No signal
		6th		Batsmen run 1. No signal
16	F Barker			T Barton facing
		1st		Batsmen do not run. No signal
		2nd		Batsmen do not run. No signal
		3rd		The umpire signals **Boundary 4**
		4th		Batsmen do not run. No signal
		5th	H	Batsmen run 3. The umpire signals **No ball**
		6th		Batsmen do not run. No signal
		7th		Batsmen do not run. No signal
17	M Green		I	Following discussion with his colleague the umpire signals five penalty runs to the batting side. (Later he informs the scorers that this was for pitch damage.) T Barton facing
		1st		Batsmen run 1. The umpire signals **Leg bye**
		2nd		Batsmen run 1. No signal
		3rd		Batsmen run 2. No signal
		4th		Batsmen do not run. No signal
		5th		Batsmen do not run. No signal
		6th		Batsmen do not run. No signal
18	F Barker			S Pearce facing
		1st		The umpire signals **Boundary 4**
		2nd		Batsmen run 3. No signal
		3rd		T Barton **out – Bowled** The new batsman is P Moore (Wicket-keeper)

Over	Bowler	Delivery		Incident
		4th		Batsmen do not run. No signal
		5th		Batsmen do not run. No signal
		6th		Batsmen do not run. No signal
19	M Green			S Pearce facing
		1st		Batsmen run 2. No signal
		2nd		Batsmen run 1. No signal
		3rd		Batsmen do not run. No signal
		4th	J	The ball goes to the wicket-keeper, E Dixon, who removes the bails.
				The bowler's end umpire signals **Wide ball**
				The striker's end umpire gives the batsman **out – Stumped**
				The incoming batsman is B Jarvis
		5th		Batsmen do not run. No signal
		6th		Batsmen do not run. No signal
			K	The umpire calls Over
20	W Smith			S Pearce facing
		1st		Batsmen run 1. No signal
		2nd		Batsmen do not run. No signal
		3rd		Batsmen do not run. No signal
		4th		The umpire signals **Boundary 4**
		5th		Batsmen do not run. No signal
		6th	L	After the ball hits the striker's pad the batsmen complete one run.
				The bowler's end umpire signals **Dead ball** and the batsmen return to their original ends
21	M Green			S Pearce facing
		1st		Pearce is hit on the pads. The bowler's end umpire gives him **out – LBW**
				The new batsman is R Fowler
		2nd	M	Batsmen run 2. Having previously warned the batting side for deliberate short running the umpire considers they have again deliberately run short and signals **five penalty runs to the fielding side**
		3rd		Batsmen run 1. No signal
		4th		Batsmen do not run. No signal
		5th		Batsmen do not run. No signal
		6th		Batsmen do not run. No signal

Over	Bowler	Delivery		Incident
22	W Smith			R Fowler facing
		1st	N	Batsmen run 1. No signal. The umpire signals **five penalty runs to the batting side** for deliberate obstruction of the batsman
		2nd		The umpire signals **Boundary 4**
		3rd		Batsmen do not run. No signal
		4th		Batsmen do not run. No signal
		5th		Batsmen do not run. No signal
		6th		Batsmen do not run. No signal
		7th		Batsmen do not run. No signal
23	M Green			R Fowler facing
		1st		The umpire signals **Boundary 4**
		2nd		The umpire signals **Boundary 4**
		3rd		Batsmen do not run. No signal
		4th		The batsman hits the ball in the air; the batsmen cross before N Black catches the ball
			O	The new batsman is H Brown. Jarvis is facing
		5th		Batsmen do not run. No signal
		6th		Batsmen do not run. No signal
24	W Smith			H Brown facing
		1st		Batsmen run 2. No signal
		2nd		Batsmen run 1. No signal
		3rd		Batsmen run 2. No signal
		4th		Batsmen do not run. No signal
		5th		Batsmen do not run. No signal
		6th		Batsmen do not run. No signal
25	M Green			H Brown facing
		1st		Brown **out – Bowled** The new batsman is D South
		2nd		The umpire signals **Boundary 4**
		3rd		The umpire signals **Boundary 6**
		4th	P	The batsmen run 3. No signal The umpire calls Time and removes the bails

PART IV

The Appendices

Appendices A, B and C illustrate the facts in the Laws about the wickets, creases and wicket-keeping gloves, laid down in Laws 8, 9 and 40 respectively.

Appendix E gives extremely detailed information about the materials, construction and measurements of the bat. It was introduced to accompany a major revision of Law 6 in 2008. Although umpires can use it as a reference, it is largely of value to the manufacturers and to the authorities who may have to decide whether a particular bat is 'legal' or not. Guidance for manufacturers, retailers, players and, most importantly in the context of this book, umpires was issued by MCC at the same time. This guidance supplements the statement in Law 3.6(b)(ii) on the responsibilities of umpires with regard to the legality of bats and gives advice on how to proceed in the case of a suspect one. By the time of the publication of this book in 2011, most questions should have been sorted out – except that, in the 2010 edition of the Laws, what had been previously Grades A, B, and C changed to Types A, B and C. This should not cause difficulty. Appendix E. and the guidance leaflet mean that umpires should at least know where to look in the unlikely situation of a problem arising. Additionally, specific questions can be directed to MCC at laws@mcc.org.uk or by telephone on +44 207 616 8500.

Appendix D is an essential and invaluable supplement to the Laws. It gives precise definitions of phrases, often used and generally but not always precisely understood by all those involved in cricket. One example is the difference between a fielder and a member of the fielding side. Sometimes such distinctions can be very important. Another example is a definition of the full extent of a batsman's ground. Umpires should read Appendix D carefully, not necessarily to absorb all its detail but to be aware of what it contains, so that they know where to turn for help if needed.

APPENDIX A
Law 8 (The wickets)

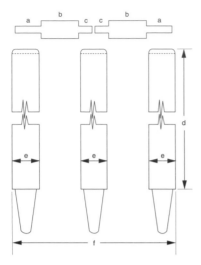

Bails

	Senior	Junior
Overall	4 ⁵⁄₁₆ in / 10.95 cm	3 ¹³⁄₁₆ in / 9.68 cm
a =	1 ⅜ in / 3.49 cm	1 ¼ in / 3.18 cm
b =	2 ⅛ in / 5.40 cm	1 ¹³⁄₁₆ in / 4.60 cm
c =	¹³⁄₁₆ in / 2.06 cm	¾ in / 1.91 cm

Stumps

	Senior	Junior
Height (d)	28 in / 71.1 cm	27 in / 68.58 cm
Diameter (e)		
max.	1 ½ in / 3.81 cm	1 ⅜ in / 3.49 cm
min.	1 ⅜ in / 3.49 cm	1 ¼ in / 3.18 cm
Overall		
Width (f)	9 in / 22.86 cm	8 in / 20.32 cm
of Wicket		

APPENDIX B
Laws 7 (The pitch) and 9 (The bowling, popping and return creases)

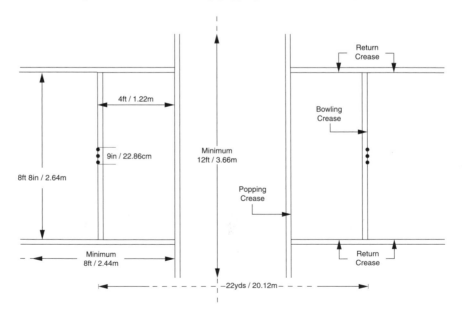

APPENDIX C

These diagrams show what is meant by:

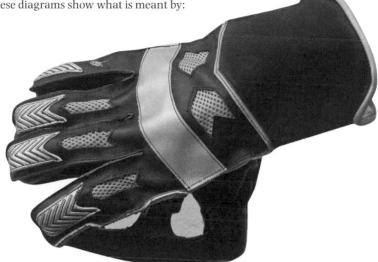

- no webbing between the fingers
- single piece of non-stretch material between finger and thumb as a means of support
- and, when a hand wearing the glove has the thumb fully extended, the top edge being taut and not protuding beyond the straight line joining the top of the index finger to the top of the thumb.

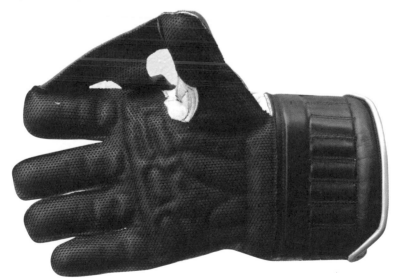

APPENDIX D
Definitions and explanations of words or phrases not defined in the text

The Toss is the toss for choice of innings.

Before the toss is at any time before the toss on the day the match is expected to start or, in the case of a one-day match, on the day the match is due to take place.

Before the match is at any time before the toss, not restricted to the day on which the toss is to take place.

During the match is at any time after the toss until the conclusion of the match, whether play is in progress or not.

Conduct of the game includes any action relevant to the match at any time on any day of the match.

Implements of the game are the bat, the ball, the stumps and bails.

The field of play is the area contained within the boundary edge.

The square is a specially prepared area of the field of play within which the match pitch is situated.

The outfield is that part of the field of play between the square and the boundary edge.

Inside edge is the edge on the same side as the nearer wicket.

Behind in relation to stumps and creases is on the side further away from the stumps and creases at the other end of the pitch. Conversely, 'in front of' is on the side nearer to the stumps and creases at the other end of the pitch.

The place where the striker stands to receive a delivery from the bowler is **the striker's end** only insofar as it identifies, independently of where the striker may subsequently move, one half of the field of play; the other half being **the bowler's end**. The striker's end is also referred to as the **wicket-keeper's end**, in situations where the position of a batsman in relation to the wicket at that end is involved.

In front of the line of the striker's wicket is in the area of the field of play in front of the imaginary line joining the fronts of the stumps at the striker's end; this line to be considered extended in both directions to the boundary.

Behind the wicket is in the area of the field of play behind the imaginary line joining the backs of the stumps at the appropriate end; this line to be considered extended in both directions to the boundary.

Behind the wicket-keeper is behind the wicket at the striker's end, as defined above, but in line with both sets of stumps and further from the stumps than the wicket-keeper.

A batsman's ground – at each end of the pitch, the whole area of the field of play behind the popping crease is the ground at that end for a batsman.

Original end is the end where a batsman was when the ball came into play for that delivery.

Wicket he has left is the wicket at the end where a batsman was at the start of the run in progress.

Off side/on side – see diagram below

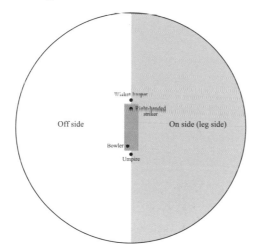

Over the wicket / round the wicket – If, as the bowler runs up between the wicket and the return crease, the wicket is on the same side as his bowling arm, he is bowling over the wicket. If the return crease is on the same side as his bowling arm, he is bowling round the wicket.

Umpire – where the description **the umpire** is used on its own, it always means 'the bowler's end umpire' though this full description is sometimes used for emphasis or clarity. Similarly **the umpires** always means both umpires. **An umpire** and **umpires**

are generalised terms. Otherwise, a fuller description indicates which one of the umpires is specifically intended.

Umpires together agree applies to decisions which the umpires are to make jointly, independently of the players.

Fielding side is the side currently fielding, whether or not play is in progress.

Member of the fielding side is one of the players nominated by the captain of the fielding side, or any authorised replacement for such nominated player.

Fielder is one of the 11 or fewer players who together compose the fielding side. This definition includes not only both the bowler and the wicket-keeper but also nominated players who are legitimately on the field of play, together with players legitimately acting as substitutes for absent nominated players. It excludes any nominated player who is absent from the field of play, or who has been absent from the field of play and who has not yet obtained the umpire's permission to return.

A player going briefly outside the boundary in the course of discharging his duties as a fielder is not absent from the field of play nor, for the purposes of Law 2.5 (Fielder absent or leaving the field), is he to be regarded as having left the field of play.

Delivery swing is the motion of the bowler's arm during which he normally releases the ball for a delivery.

Delivery stride is the stride during which the delivery swing is made, whether the ball is released or not. It starts when the bowler's back foot lands for that stride and ends when the front foot lands in the same stride.

The ball is struck/strikes the ball unless specifically defined otherwise, mean 'the ball is struck by the bat'/'strikes the ball with the bat'.

Rebounds directly/strikes directly and similar phrases mean 'without contact with any fielder' but do not exclude contact with the ground.

External protective equipment is any visible item of apparel worn for protection against external blows.

For a batsman, items permitted are a protective helmet, external leg guards (batting pads), batting gloves and, if visible, forearm guards.

For a fielder, only a protective helmet is permitted, except in the case of a wicket-keeper, for whom wicket-keeping pads and gloves are also permitted.

A protective helmet is headwear made of hard material and designed to protect the head or the face or both.

Clothing – anything that a player is wearing, including such items as spectacles or jewellery, that is not classed as external protective equipment is classed as clothing, even though he may be wearing some items of apparel, which are not visible, for protection. A bat being carried by a batsman does not come within this definition of clothing.

The bat – the following are to be considered as part of the bat.
– the whole of the bat itself.
– the whole of a glove (or gloves) worn on the hand (or hands) holding the bat.
– the hand (or hands) holding the bat, if the batsman is not wearing a glove on that hand or on those hands.

Hand for batsman or wicket-keeper shall include both the hand itself and the whole of a glove worn on the hand.

Held in batsman's hand – contact between a batsman's hand, or glove worn on his hand, and any part of the bat shall constitute the bat being held in that hand.

Equipment – a batsman's equipment is his bat as defined above, together with any external protective equipment he is wearing.
A fielder's equipment is any external protective equipment that he is wearing.

Person – a player's person is his physical person (flesh and blood) together with any clothing or legitimate external protective equipment that he is wearing except, in the case of a batsman, his bat.
A hand, whether gloved or not, that is not holding the bat is part of the batsman's person.
No item of clothing or equipment is part of the player's person unless it is attached to him.
For a batsman, a glove being held but not worn is part of his person.
For a fielder, an item of clothing or equipment he is holding in his hand or hands is not part of his person.

APPENDIX E – THE BAT: LAW 6
All Law references are to sections of Law 6

Categories of bat – Types A, B and C are bats conforming to Law 6, sections 1 to 8 inclusive. Bats which do not qualify for any of the three categories are not recognised in the Laws. Type A bats may be used at any level. Bats of Type B or Type C and any other bats may be used only at or below levels determined by the Governing Body for cricket in the country concerned.

The blade – The face of the blade is its main striking surface. The back is the opposite surface.

The shoulders, sides and toe are the remaining surfaces, separating the face and the back. The shoulders, one on each side of the handle, are along that portion of the blade between the first entry point of the handle and the point at which the blade first reaches its full width.

The toe is the surface opposite to the shoulders taken as a pair.

The sides, one each side of the blade, are along the rest of the blade, between the toe and the shoulders.

Adhesives – Throughout, adhesives are permitted only where essential and only in minimal quantity.

Materials in handle – As a proportion of the total volume of the handle, materials other than cane, wood or twine are restricted to one-tenth for Types A and B and one-fifth for Type C. Such materials must not project more than 3.25 in/8.26 cm into the lower portion of the handle.

Binding and covering of handle – The permitted continuation beyond the junction of the upper and lower portions of the handle is restricted to a maximum, measured along the length of the handle, of

2.5 in/6.35 cm for the twine binding
2.75 in/6.99 cm for the covering grip.

Length and width
(a) The overall length of the bat, when the lower portion of the handle is inserted, shall not be more than 38 in/96.5 cm.
(b) The width of the bat shall not exceed 4.25 in/10.8 cm at its widest part.
(c) Permitted coverings, repair material and toe guards, not exceeding their specified thicknesses, may be additional to the dimensions above.

Length of handle – Except for bats of size 6 and less, the handle shall not exceed 52% of the overall length of the bat.

Covering of blade – The cloth covering permitted for Type C bats shall be of thickness not exceeding 0.012 in/0.3 mm before treatment as in 6.6(d).

Protection and repair of blade – The material permitted in 6.6(a) shall not exceed 0.04 in/1 mm in thickness. In 6.6(a)(ii), the repair material shall not extend along the length of the blade more than 0.79 in/2 cm in each direction beyond the limits of the damaged area. Where used as a continuous binding, any overlapping shall not breach the maximum of 0.04 in/1 mm in total thickness.

In 6.6(d), the use of non-solid material which when dry forms a hard layer more than 0.004 in/0.1 mm in thickness is not permitted.

Toe and side inserts – The wood used must not be more than 0.3 in/0.89 cm in thickness.

The toe insert shall not extend from the toe more than 2.5 in/6.35 cm up the blade at any point.

Neither side insert may extend from the edge more than 1 in/2.54 cm across the blade at any point.

Toe protection – The maximum permitted thickness of protective material placed on the toe of the blade is 0.12 in/3 mm.

Commercial identifications – These identifications may not exceed 0.008 in/0.2 mm in thickness. On the back of the blade they must occupy no more than 50% of the surface. On the face of the blade, they must be confined within the top 9 in/22.86 cm, measured from the bottom of the grip.

Index

Appeals 153 et seq
  Answering 152, 154
  Batsman leaving wicket under
    misapprehension 153, 155
  Consultation by umpires 153, 155
  'How's That?' 152, 153
  Jurisdiction of each umpire 152, 154
  Timing of 152, 153
  Umpire may change his decision 7, 153,
    155
  Withdrawal of 153, 155
Awarding a match 118, 122

Bails 57
  Dispensing with 58, 160
  Size 57, 278
  Spare 11
Ball, the 49 et seq
  Approval and control 10, 40, 50, 51
  Becoming unfit for play 50, 51
  Changing condition of 216, 229
  Drying 10, 11, 216, 229
  Frequent and irregular inspections 51,
    216, 229
  Junior 50
  New 10, 50, 52
  Polishing 216, 229
  Replacing 50, 51, 216
  Spare 10, 52
  Valid – definition 124
    when penalties awarded 228
  Weight and size 49
  Women's 50
Bat, the 52 et seq, 284
  Blade and covering 53, 254
  Breaking 156, 184
  Contact with 54, 283
  Definition of 53, 284
  Holding 54, 163, 283
  Specifications 52, 284
  Width and length 52, 54–5, 284
Batting practice 92–96
Batsman
  Batsman's end *see batsman's ground*
  Batsman's ground 164, 281
  Commencement of innings 29, 34

Continuing to run after grounding foot
  162, 199
Damaging pitch 221–223, 234
Dismissed 152, 154
Leaving his wicket 153, 154, 155
Out 154
Out of his ground 162, 163
Permitted protective equipment 282–3
Person of 283
Resuming innings 29, 34
Retiring/leaving field 29, 34
Returning to original end 99, 103
Returning to wicket he has left 100,
  103
Stealing a run 223, 237
Who has a runner 28, 35, 201
  see also Striker who has a runner
Out of game when not striker 28, 35
Boundaries 105 et seq
  Agreeing 36
  Allowances 36, 40
  Fielding near 112 et seq, 168, 172–174
  How marked – rope, line, fence, other 105,
    106
  Local customs 41, 110
  Obstacles 36, 41, 110
  Overthrows 108, 115
  Runs scored 107, 114
  Sight-screens 109
  When scored 106, 110–114
  Wilful act of fielder 108, 115
Bowled 165
  To take precedence 165, 168
Bowler (absence) 30, 282
  Bowling after return from absence 31
    Calculation examples 31–33
  Changing ends 125, 127
  Completion of over 86, 125, 127
  Not to bowl consecutive overs 125, 127
  Not to get credit 169, 175, 178, 196, 198
  Running on protected area 221, 229, 234
  Unable to complete over 83, 125
Bowler taken off
  Changing condition of ball 216
  Dangerous and unfair bowling 219
  Deliberate high full pitches 219

Running on protected area 221
Shown in scoring record *see part III*
Throwing 133
Time wasting by fielding side 220
Bowling crease 59, 278
Byes 147 et seq
How entered in scoring record *see part III*

Captain 24, 25
Authorising change of nominated player 25
Deputy 24, 25
Nomination of teams 24, 25
Pre-match conference with umpires 36, 40
Responsible for playing within the Spirit of Cricket 24, 215
Caught 168 et seq
See also Obstructing the field
Caught to take precedence 168, 175
Completion of catch 168, 172
Fair catch 165
Fielder within the field of play 169, 172–174
No runs scored 169, 174
Cessation of play 80 et seq
Calculation of minimum number of overs 82
Examples 92
Call of Time 81
significance 83, 93
technique 85
Completing over in progress 86
Conclusion of match 83
Last hour of match 81–82, 88 et seq
Removal of bails 14, 81
Umpires' interval duties 14
Checking with scorers 9, 39, 123
Clearing debris from pitch 61, 65
Clock or watch 10, 36, 40
Consultation 7, 38, 44, 155, 282
Covering the pitch 66 et seq
Agreement for full covering 67
Before the match 67
Bowler's run up 67
During the match 67
Removal of covers 67, 68
Creases 12, 15, 41 et seq, 59, 278
Bowling 59, 278
Creases and crease markings 59, 278
Popping 59, 60
Re-marking 60, 62
Return 59

Crossing in running 18, 43, 102, 223, 227

Damage to pitch 64, 221–223, 234
Batsmen 223, 235
Bowler running on protected area 221, 234
Fielders 222, 235
Dangerous and unfair bowling 218–221, 230 et seq
Action by umpire 218
Fast short pitched balls 218, 231
High full pitches 218, 232
deliberate 219, 233
Over head height 218, 231
Dead ball 127 et seq
Ball automatically dead 127, 129
Ball ceases to be dead 128
Ball to be called dead by umpire 128
Ball to count in over 128, 130
Finally settled 127, 129
Laws requiring Dead ball call 131
Time when striker vulnerable 128
Declaration 72
Insufficient time to complete rolling 72
Notification of 72
Time of 72
Deputy captain 24, 25
Appointment 24, 70
Batsmen at wicket 76, 80
Who can be deputy 24, 25
Dismissed, definition of 152, 154
Distraction of
batsman, deliberate 128, 217, 230
striker 128, 131, 217, 230
Draw 119, 121
Dress, umpires' 8
Drinks intervals 76
Agreeing daily 80
Agreement to forgo 76, 78, 86
Duration 76
Rearranging 76, 80
Drying the ball 11, 216, 229
Duties of umpires - summarised 11
Before the match 12
During the match 13
Interval duties 14

Encroachment
By fielders on the pitch 211, 213
By on-side fielders 211, 214
By wicket-keeper 206, 208–209
End of match
Agreement with scorers 39, 49

Confirming result 49
Reporting 13, 14, 31, 98, 208, 211, 213,
    216–225, 230, 237
Equipment 283
    Batsman's 283
    Fielder's 283
    Permitted protective 282
    Scorers' *see part III*
    Umpires' 4 et seq
Exceptional circumstances 37, 43
    As reason to suspend play 37, 43

Fair and unfair play 22, 37, 215 et seq
    See also Penalty runs
    Breaches of Spirit of Cricket 224
    Not covered within the Laws 215, 224,
        237
    Responsibility of captains 215
    Responsibility of umpires 215
    Spirit of Cricket 22, 225
    Umpires sole judges of 37, 215
Fast short pitched balls
    See Dangerous and unfair bowling
Fielder 210
    Absent or leaving the field 27, 287
    Damaging the pitch 222
    Definition of 282
    Fielding beyond the boundary 210, 212
    Fielding the ball legally/illegally 112–114
    Limitation of on-side fielders 211, 213
    Member of fielding side 282
    Not to be on or over pitch 211, 214
    Obstructing batsman in running 217, 280
    Protective equipment 210, 282
        external, permitted 212, 282
        helmet – *see separate heading*
    Returning without permission 27, 31, 225
    Significant movement 212, 215
    Waiting/penance time 31–33
    Within field of play 169, 172–174
Fitness of
    Ground, weather and light 37, 42
    Pitch 55, 56
Follow-on, the 71
    Insufficient time to complete rolling 71
    Lead on first innings 71
Footholds 63
    Batsmen, bowlers, securing 63, 64
Foot holes, maintenance of 67
Forfeiture 72
    Either innings 72, 73
    Insufficient time to complete rolling 72, 73
    Notification 72

Full pitched balls – high 218, 232
    See also Dangerous and unfair bowling
    Deliberate 219, 233

Glove
    Hand or glove as part of bat 54, 55, 283
    When part of person 283
    Wicket-keeper's 206, 207, 208, 279
        Specifications 206, 279
Ground
    Batsman's ground 162–164, 281
    Fitness of 37, 42

Handled the ball 175 et seq
    See also Obstructing the field
    Runs scored 99, 175, 176
Helmets 285
    Batsman's 200
        not to be Caught 168, 171
        not to be Run out 198, 200
        not to be Stumped 203, 204
    Fielder's 200
        lodging in 127, 171
        on the ground 127, 171, 200
        striking 127, 171
        umpires not to carry 9
    Wicket-keeper's
        rebounding from 203, 204
High full pitches 218, 232
    See also Dangerous and unfair bowling
    Deliberate 219, 233
Hit the ball twice 177 et seq
    See also Obstructing the field
    Action by umpire 178
    Ball lawfully hit more than once
        overthrow going to boundary 178
        runs permitted/not permitted 177, 181
        runs scored 177, 180
    Caught 168, 175, 182
    No ball called 180
    Obstructing the field 177, 195
    Returning ball to fielder 196
    Runs from ball lawfully struck more than
        once 177, 180–182
Hit wicket 183 et seq
    Broken bat 156, 184
    Items no longer part of person 156, 184
    Not out Hit wicket 183
    Striker's end umpire's jurisdiction 183
    Time when striker vulnerable 184–185

Illegal fielding 210
    Ball hitting helmet on ground 211, 213

Fielding other than with person 210, 212
  items falling off 213
  items taken off 213
Innings 68 et seq
  Alternate 68, 70
  Choice of (the toss) 69, 70
  Commencement of batsman's 29, 34
  Completed 70, 71
  Following 71
  Forfeiting 72, 73
  Limited by time or overs 68
  Number of 68, 69
Intervals 73 et seq
  Agreement of 74
  Agreement to forgo 76, 78
  Between innings: no allowance for 74, 77
  Changing agreed times 75, 78–79
  Drinks 76, 80
    agreement to forgo 78
    arranging times 80
    rearranging times 76, 80
  Scorers to be informed 80
  Tea – 9 wickets down 76
  Technique when interval due 85
  Umpires' interval duties 14, 80

Junior cricket
  Balls – weight and size 50
  Wickets 57
    bails 58
    pitched – for each age group 57
    stumps 68

Last hour of match 82
  Bowler unable to complete over 83
  Calculation of overs 81–82
    examples 89–92
  Interruption in play 81
  Interval between innings 82
  Minimum number of overs 81
  When to commence 81, 88
Leg before wicket 185 et seq
  Being ready for appeal 186
  Criteria 185–186, 187–192
  Distance between pitching and impact 189
  Interception of ball 187
  Striker not attempting to play ball 193–194
Leg byes 147 et seq
  Action by umpire 148, 151
  After second strike 177, 178
  How recorded see part III
  Not affecting dismissal 151

Not allowed 147, 150
  Umpire's signal 15, 48, 152
Light, fitness of 37, 42
Lost ball 116 et seq
  See also Ball – becoming lost or unfit
  Ends at which batsmen should resume 118
  Intervention by umpire 117
  Runs scored 117
Lunch interval 73
  Agreeing time and duration 73
  Changing time 75, 78–79
  To be agreed length 77

Methods of dismissal 165 et seq
  End to which not out batsman to go 99–100, 104
  Runs scored 98–99
Mistakes
  General 6, 7
  In counting 125, 126
  In scoring 120, 123
    action by umpires 120, 123
  Minimising 121, 123
Movement by
  fielders 212, 215
  wicket-keeper 207, 209
Mowing 62
  Not possible 62, 66
  Outfield 62
  Pitch 62
  Responsibility for 62, 63
  Timing 62

No ball 132 et seq
  Ball bouncing more than twice or rolling along the ground 134, 138
  Ball coming to rest in front of striker's wicket 134, 138
  Ball thrown towards striker's end 138
  Fair delivery
    the arm 133–137
    the feet – illustrations 133, 136–137
  Fielder encroaching on pitch 211, 214
  How recorded see part III
  List of Laws involving No ball 134
  Mode of delivery 132, 135
  Not to count as ball in over 134, 138
  Out from a No ball 135
  Penalty for a No ball 134, 139
  Revoking a call 134
  Runs from a No ball 135
  Throw, definition of 133

To over-ride Wide 134
Wicket-keeper encroaching 206, 208
Nominated players 24, 25
Changing 24, 25
List given to umpire 24, 25
Non-striker, position of 163, 164
Non-turf pitches 56, 63, 66
Normal guard position 141, 145

Obstructing the field 195 et seq
Accidental obstruction 177
Obstructing ball from being caught 177, 197
Returning ball to fielding side 176, 196
Runs scored 98–99, 196, 197
Wilful obstruction 196
Obstruction of batsman in running 217, 230
Off side of wicket 186, 195, 281
On-side fielders, limitation of 211, 213
Out of his ground 162
Outfield, mowing of 62, 65
Over, the 124 et seq
Ball not to count in over 124, 126
Bowler changing ends 125
Bowler finishing over 125, 127
Bowler unable to complete over 15, 83, 125, 127
Call of Over 125, 126, 128
Completing over in progress 81, 86–87, 127
Starting over 81, 87, 124, 126
Valid balls 124
Overthrows 108, 115, 177, 178, 180

Penalties, runs awarded for 98
Penalty runs 224
Ball hitting helmet 210
Basic pattern for action 225–227
Batsmen stealing a run 223, 237
Changing condition of ball 216, 229
Damaging pitch 221
batsman 223, 235
fielder 222, 235
Deliberate attempt to
distract striker 217, 230
obstruct batsman 217, 230
How recorded *see part III*
Illegally fielding ball 210, 212
Signal to scorers 47
Time wasting by
batsman 220, 234
fielder 220, 233

Person, definition of 283
Pitch 55 et seq
Changing 56
Clearing of debris/sweeping 61, 65
Covering 66–68
Damage by players 64, 221–223, 234–236
Definition 65
Fitness for play 37, 42, 55
Maintenance 61, 63, 65
Measurements 55, 278
Mowing 62, 65, 66
Non-turf 56, 66
Rolling 61, 64, 65, 66
Selection and preparation 55
Sweeping 62, 65
Watering 62, 65
Play
See also Start of play
has taken place 71, 72
Players 24
Changing shirt or boots 26
Conduct of 22, 224–225, 229, 237
Nomination 24, 25
Number of 24, 25
Polishing the ball 216, 229
Popping crease 59, 278
Positioning of
non-striker 163, 164
striker who has a runner 35
umpires 15, 43, 104, 161, 202
Practice on field of play 93 et seq
Fielding practice 95
who can take part 94
Penalty for contravention 94, 95
Trial run up 95, 96
When permitted 94
Where permitted
outfield 94
pitch 93
square 93
Protected area 221, 234
Diagram 234

Qualifications – scorers', umpires' *see part III*
Personal 5
Physical 4
Technical 5–6

Refusal to play 118, 122, 166
Action by umpires 118, 122, 167
Reporting instances of unfair play Laws 2, 18, 24, 41, 42 all sections except 1, 2, 15, 17

Result, the 118 et seq
  Correctness of scores/result 39, 44, 49, 120, 121
  Draw 119
  Match awarded 118, 120, 122
  Match conceded 118, 120, 123
  Mistakes in scoring 120, 123
  Not to be changed 121, 124
  Statement of 120
  Tie 119
  Umpires awarding match 118, 122
  Under agreement to limit by overs or time 119
  Win 118
  Win by penalty runs 122
  Winning hit or extras 119, 122
Return crease 59, 278
Rolling the pitch 61, 64, 65
  After delayed start 61, 63, 65
  Choice of rollers 61
  Frequency and duration 61
  Insufficient time to complete 61, 64, 71, 72
  Timing 61, 65
Run out 197 et seq
  Avoiding injury 198, 199
  Ball rebounding from fielder's helmet 198
  Batsman continuing to run in same direction 162, 199
  Before ball is delivered 223, 236
  Not touched by fielder 198, 200
  Striker who has a runner 28, 35
  Which batsman is out 198, 199, 201, 202
Runners 28, 34
  Entitlement 26, 30
  Equipment 28
  Position of 35
  To be nominated player 28, 34
  To have batted 28
  Transgression of Laws 28, 35
Runs, scoring of 97 et seq
  See also Short runs
  After lawful second strike 177–178, 180–182
  Batsmen returning to ends 99, 100
  Definition of run 97
  Occasions when scored 97, 98, 102
  Scored when batsman dismissed 98–99
  When disallowed or not allowed 97, 100

Sample scoresheets see part III
Scorebook, the see part III
Scorers, the 49, 80

  see also part III
Acknowledgement of signals 49
  see also part III
Appointment 49
  see also part III
Checking 49
  see also part III
  own book 49
    see also part III
  with each other 49
    see also part III
  with umpires 49
    see also part III
Consultation with umpires 49
Duties before match see part III
Equipment see part III
Qualifications see separate heading
Recording runs see part III
Scorers and umpires as a team 8, 11
  see also part III
Scoring 240 et seq
  see also part III
  Ball not to count as one of the over 266
  Batting section 251–255
  Bowling section 251–255
  Box scoring method 247–265
  Checking with umpires 258
  Completing Analysis see part III
  Cumulative run tally 249
  Entries in scoring record see part III
    Byes see part III
    Inaccuracies, causes of see part III
    General see part III
    Leg byes see part III
    No balls see part III
    Penalty runs see part III
    Runs see part III
    Wides see part III
  Entry at fall of a wicket 255
  Entry at injury or illness to bowler 254
  Entry at interruptions in play 258
  Entry at last hour 257
  Entry at retirement of batsman 256
  Laws affecting – listed
    See part III
  Recording penalty extras 262
  Scorer's duties 241–243
    Pre-match 266
    After Time called 259
    Post-match 266
  Scorer's equipment 243
  Scoring symbols 246
Seam, lifting of 216, 229

Short pitched balls, fast 231–232, 233
Short runs 97, 101
   Accidental 97, 101
   Deliberate 97, 102
   Umpire's signal 47
Sight-screens 105, 109–110
Signals by umpires 19, 38–39, 44, 45–48
   Acknowledgement by scorers 39, 46, 49
   During play 19, 38, 48
   Illustrated 45–48
   Order of 17, 18
   When ball is dead 19, 38, 44
   With calls 18
Special conditions affecting play 36, 40
Spirit of Cricket/Spirit of the game 7, 22, 24,
   42, 155, 224, 225, 228, 237
Start of Play 71, 72
   Call of Play 80, 83
      significance 83
      when 80
   Umpires' duties 12, 84
   Umpires' field technique 84
Starting an over
   See under Over
Stealing a run 223, 237
Story of innings
   See part III
Striker who has a runner 28, 35, 201, 202
   Always has wicket-keeper's end 35, 201
   Himself Run out 28, 201
   Stumped 28, 201
Stumped 203 et seq
   Ball rebounding from wicket-keeper 203
   No ball 204
   Not out Stumped 204
   Striker who has a runner 20, 28, 205
Stumps, specifications 55, 278
Substitutes 26, 30
   Entitlement 26, 30
   Not to act as captain, bat, bowl or keep
      wicket 26
   Objection to 26
   Umpires; discretion to allow 26, 30
Sweeping the pitch 62, 64

Tea interval
   Agreement to forgo 76, 78
   Between innings 74
   Changing time of 75
   Continuation of play 78–79
   Nine wickets down 76
   To be agreed length 74, 77
Teams 24

Nomination 24, 25
Not eleven players 24, 25
Throw 132, 133
   Definition of 133
   Umpires' action 132, 133
   Umpires' responsibility for judging
      137–138
Tie 119
Time
   See Cessation of play
Time wasting 220
   by batsman 220, 234
   by fielders 220, 233
Timed out 166
   Action by umpires 167
      as for Match Awarded 167
   Protracted delay 167
   Which batsman 168
Toss, the 69
   Deputy to act for captain 24, 25, 26
   In presence of umpire 12, 69
   Notification of decision to bat or bowl 69
   When and where 69
Trial run up 95, 96

Umpires 36 et seq
   And scorers as a team 8, 11
   Appeals 153–156
   Appointment and attendance 36
   Balls, umpires to
      approve (with captains) 10, 36, 50,
         51
      choose replacement if lost or unfit
         50–51
      keep control of 50, 51
      make frequent and irregular inspections
         51, 216, 229
      take possession of, when 50, 51, 229
   Change of 36, 42
   Changing ends 38, 43
   Conduct of game 37, 280
   Consulting 7, 8, 38, 44, 101, 118, 153,
      155, 195, 216, 230
   Decision is final 153, 156
   Dress and equipment 8
   Duties
      at end of match 49
      at intervals 14, 85–86
      before match 12
      during match 13
   Jurisdiction of 154
   Miscounting over 123, 126
   Pre-match conference 36, 40

Qualifications
  See separate heading
Role of 6
Special conditions affecting play 36, 40
Suspension of play in
  dangerous conditions 42
  unreasonable circumstances 43
To intervene for unfair action 22, 215, 225
To keep control of match balls
To take possession of ball, when 50, 51,
  229
Wickets, creases and boundaries 36, 41,
  57, 59, 60, 68, 105, 106, 110
Unacceptable behaviour 215, 224, 237
Unfair play 215 et seq
  See also Dangerous and unfair bowling
Batsmen stealing a run 223, 237
  Changing condition of ball 216, 229
  Reporting instances of unfair play
    See separate heading
  Responsibility of captains 24, 215
    before toss 40
  Time wasting 220, 233
  Umpires are sole judges 215
  Unfair actions not covered by the Laws
    215, 226, 237

Valid balls, definition 124

Watering the pitch 62, 65
Weather, fitness of 37, 42
Wicket 37, 57
  Definition and dimensions 57, 58
  Is down 156 et seq
    all stumps out of the ground 158
    dispensing with bails 58, 157, 160
    one bail off 157, 158
    remaking the wicket 157, 157
    putting down the wicket 156 et seq
Wicket-keeper 206, 207
  Gloves 206, 209
  Encroaching 206, 208–209
  Interference by striker 207, 209
  Interference with striker 206, 209
  Movement 207, 209
  Position of 206, 208
  Protective equipment 206
  Putting down wicket 203
  Restrictions on actions of 207, 209
  Stumping 200, 201
Wickets, the 57–58
  Dimensions 57, 58

Junior cricket 57
Pitching 57
Pre-match inspection 12, 37
Remaking 157, 158
Size of stumps and bails 57, 278
Width 57
Wide ball 141 et seq
  Ball not dead 142, 146
  Ball not to be judged wide 142, 145
  Call of Wide ball 142, 146
  Judging 141, 143–145
  No ball to over-ride Wide 142, 146
  Not to count as one of over 142, 147
  Out from a Wide 142, 147
  Penalty for a Wide 142, 146
  Revoking a call of Wide ball 142, 146
  Runs from a Wide 142, 146
    how scored 142
    method of entry in scoring record
      See part III
Win 118
  By penalty runs 122
  Definition of 118
  How stated 120
Winning hit or extras 119, 122
Women's cricket, weight and size of
  ball 50